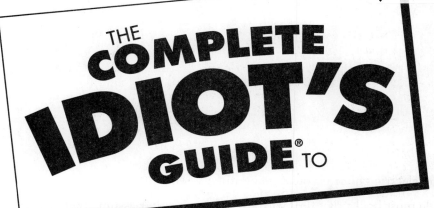

THE COMPLETE IDIOT'S GUIDE® TO

Playing Rock Guitar

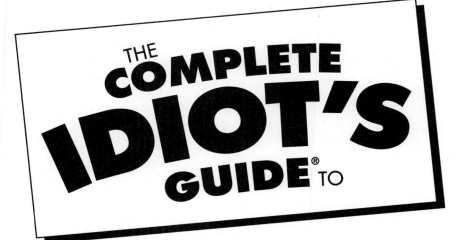

THE COMPLETE IDIOT'S GUIDE® TO

Playing Rock Guitar

by David Hodge

ALPHA

A member of Penguin Group (USA) Inc.

This book is dedicated to Paul Hackett, creator of Guitar Noise (www.guitarnoise.com), who personifies all the inclusive qualities of rock and roll and who inspires people from all over the world to take up the guitar and to bring music into their lives.

ALPHA BOOKS

Published by the Penguin Group

Penguin Group (USA) Inc., 375 Hudson Street, New York, New York 10014, USA

Penguin Group (Canada), 90 Eglinton Avenue East, Suite 700, Toronto, Ontario M4P 2Y3, Canada (a division of Pearson Penguin Canada Inc.)

Penguin Books Ltd., 80 Strand, London WC2R 0RL, England

Penguin Ireland, 25 St. Stephen's Green, Dublin 2, Ireland (a division of Penguin Books Ltd.)

Penguin Group (Australia), 250 Camberwell Road, Camberwell, Victoria 3124, Australia (a division of Pearson Australia Group Pty. Ltd.)

Penguin Books India Pvt. Ltd., 11 Community Centre, Panchsheel Park, New Delhi—110 017, India

Penguin Group (NZ), 67 Apollo Drive, Rosedale, North Shore, Auckland 1311, New Zealand (a division of Pearson New Zealand Ltd.)

Penguin Books (South Africa) (Pty.) Ltd., 24 Sturdee Avenue, Rosebank, Johannesburg 2196, South Africa

Penguin Books Ltd., Registered Offices: 80 Strand, London WC2R 0RL, England

Publisher: *Marie Butler-Knight*
Editorial Director: *Mike Sanders*
Senior Managing Editor: *Billy Fields*
Acquisitions Editor: *Tom Stevens*
Development Editor: *Jennifer Moore*
Senior Production Editor: *Megan Douglass*
Copy Editor: *Cate Schwenk*

Cartoonist: *Steve Barr*
Cover Designer: *Rebecca Batchelor*
Book Designer: *Trina Wurst*
Indexer: *Heather McNeill*
Layout: *Brian Massey*
Proofreader: *Laura Caddell*

Contents at a Glance

Contents

Introduction

Few instruments create whole genres of music. You can play classical music without a violin, you can even play polkas without an accordion or bluegrass without a mandolin, but it's close to impossible to think of rock music without the guitar. The rock guitarist carries the history of all rock music with him each time he plays a note or a chord.

Few instruments inspire people to play as the rock guitar does. It's the stuff of modern legend to be standing in an arena, belting out a loud, powerful solo to tens of thousands of rapt, attentive fans. Sometimes the solo is flashy, fast and furious, and sometimes it is a piercing melancholy wail. But whatever its volume, tempo, or tone, it is always powerful. It always seems to be the audio equivalent of emotion.

Playing rock guitar is within almost anyone's abilities. It only requires a guitar (and, usually, an amplifier), a desire to make music, and willingness to learn and to practice.

Why This Book Is for You

The Complete Idiot's Guide to Playing Rock Guitar is a step-by-step guide designed to get you started playing rock guitar. It is a book for a total beginner; even if you've never held a guitar before in your life, you will be able to read this book and jump right into playing rock music. From "Part 1" onward, you learn and develop the basic techniques needed to play rock guitar.

In order to accomplish this goal, this book starts you out working on what I call "developing finesse." An amplified electric guitar is not kind to beginners—every missed and slightly out of tune note is presented to you (and the world!) and that can make matters more than slightly frustrating. A great deal of time is spent on helping you learn to not overplay, to finger notes correctly, and to pick just the strings you want in order to get a clean, rock sound.

If you've read my *Complete Idiot's Guide to Playing Bass Guitar* or any of my Internet or magazine lessons, you know I abide by the "teach a man to fish" philosophy when it comes to learning and playing music. In other words, it's my job to explain the "whys" and "hows" of playing rock guitar and provide you with a logical process for learning to play. But it's up to you to be part of that process, through both practicing and listening.

The Many Faces of Rock Guitar

And listening, as you'll read over and over again in these pages, is one of the most important skills a guitarist (or musician or even just a human being) can have. It's easy to think that metal players have no use for open chords, or that lead players don't need to know how to read or understand rhythms (or to even play in rhythm) or that speed, volume, and distortion will make you a great guitar player, but nothing could be further from the truth.

Rock music, like all great music, has deep roots that grow out of almost every type of musical style you can think of. The more music you listen to, the more you learn. As you read through this book, be certain to listen for the various techniques that you are working on and playing in the music that you listen to on a daily basis, whatever type it may be. Doing so can't help but make you a better guitarist.

What You'll Find in This Book

The Complete Idiot's Guide to Learning Rock Guitar is arranged in five general parts.

Part 1, "Let There Be Rock," starts you off with an introduction to the electric guitar, its basic parts and components, and how to go about shopping for your first one. You also learn how to tune your new instrument and get started on making music right away as well as get a quick (and painless!) lesson on reading musical directions like guitar tablature.

Part 2, "Pick Up My Guitar and Play," covers all the fundamental techniques you need to play rock guitar. More important, it does so in a systematic manner, designed to get you playing power chords, vibrato, and other vital "touch" techniques right from the start. You also jump right in on rhythm, learning how to read rhythms and how to play them steady and true.

Part 3, "Rocking the House," takes the basic skills from Part 2 and carries them further, teaching you to play full barre chords as well as partial chords and arpeggios. You discover that it's easy to play very complicated rhythms by keeping the simple skills you've already learned at the front of your mind. Plus, you get a start on tackling riffs, even putting one together step by step.

Part 4, "From Scales to Solos," guides you step by step through the process of building scales and chords to creating your own riffs, fills, and solos. You get the "gift" of the pentatonic scale as well as an understanding of other scales and modes.

Part 5, "The Quest for Tone," examines the personal touch that defines "tone." As you develop your unique style, you can use different guitars, strings, pickups, amplifiers, and effects to pursue the guitar tone you are looking for. Even tuning your guitar differently or using a slide can alter your tone, so you get a brief lesson on those topics as well.

At the end of the book you find helpful appendixes, containing a glossary and a list of the exercises on the CD accompanying this book, as well as a list of books to help you continue your learning as a rock guitarist.

Using the CD

Throughout this book you find an icon that looks like this: **Track 0**

This indicates that the example in question is on the audio CD included in this book. The very first track is a tuning track, and you find audio examples for most of the exercises in this book. Your CD also contains several "practice songs," specifically written to work on the various techniques that you learn in this book, as well as a number of "jam along" tracks to serve as backup when you want to work on soloing.

In keeping with the "beginner philosophy" of this book, we've gone out of our way to keep these tracks simple and clean. The guitar (Ibanez Artist) is recorded straight out of a Carvin tube amplifier using a slight bit of distortion. Matt Sermini (whom I cannot thank enough) provides the exceptionally cool rocking drumming on the "practice song tracks."

Speaking of which, to best utilize these "practice songs," simply cue up the track you want and then hit the "repeat track" function on your CD player (or your computer's CD player). This way, you can work on a specific song to your heart's content.

Many thanks go to Todd Mack and Will Curtiss of Off the Beat-n-Track Studio in Sheffield, Massachusetts, for their invaluable assistance in putting together, mixing, and mastering the CD. Both Will and Todd are great to work with and it's an honor to have their talents and assistance in creating the music for this book.

Other Icons

In addition to the text, music examples, and audio examples, you will also find numerous sidebars, each offering definitions or containing tips or other information that you will find useful in your studies. These are the four types of sidebars that occur in this book:

def•i•ni•tion

These sidebars provide definitions and details about specific musical terms and playing techniques.

Getting Better

Here you find tips and advice on practicing as well as on the various rock guitar techniques themselves.

Note Worthy

These sidebars contain little bits and pieces of information that can help you to understand more about music and your guitar, as well as the occasional tidbit of inside information you might find interesting, useful, or amusing.

Hear How

Turn to these sidebars for specific songs and/or artists to listen to in order to better hear or understand a particular guitar technique or style.

Acknowledgments

I'd like to thank my agent, Marilyn Allen, and Tom Stevens at Alpha Books for making this book possible, not to mention all the rest of the wonderful people at Alpha who worked on turning this project into a reality, including Marie Butler-Knight, Mike Sanders, Billy Fields, Jennifer Moore, Megan Douglass, Cate Schwenk, Trina Wurst, Steve Barr, Rebecca Batchelor, Heather McNeill, Brian Massey, and Laura Caddell.

Thanks also go out to all my students for continually challenging me to become a better teacher, and to the Guitar Noise (www.guitarnoise.com) website readers, all 2 million of them, who also have helped me grow as both a player and a tutor. Speaking of students and teachers, I don't think I could possibly list all the wonderful rock guitarists I've had the pleasure of playing with and learning from, such as Bill Supplitt, Jeff Brownstein, Paul McKenna, Tony Nuccio, Kathy Reichert, Michael Roberto, Rich Schroeder, Wes Inman, and Jim Martin.

Finally, I'd like to thank Karen Berger, a wonderful piano teacher, whose patience, assistance, and experience (both in music and writing) continues to be priceless.

Let Me Know What You Think

As a teacher, and as a writer, your thoughts and opinions are not only appreciated, but usually quite helpful. Please feel free to write me anytime at dhodgeguitar@aol.com. I do try to answer every e-mail but sometimes with my teaching schedule it's very difficult and I fall a bit behind in my correspondence. Rest assured that every e-mail gets read and each one is appreciated, and I will do my best to reply to you as soon as possible. I look forward to hearing from you and to hearing how things are going with your guitar playing!

Special Thanks to the Technical Reviewer

I want to especially thank Greg Nease for serving as technical editor on *The Complete Idiot's Guide to Playing Rock Guitar*. I could write a volume of books on what Greg knows, not to mention about his playing and how much I've learned from him as a guitarist. I am indebted to him for his participation in this project, for taking the time to answer my questions, to discuss many things that are still way over my head, and for making certain that this book gives you the best possible instruction.

Trademarks

All terms mentioned in this book that are known to be or are suspected of being trademarks or service marks have been appropriately capitalized. Alpha Books and Penguin Group (USA) Inc. cannot attest to the accuracy of this information. Use of a term in this book should not be regarded as affecting the validity of any trademark or service mark.

Part 1

Let There Be Rock

If you're going to be a rock guitarist, you're going to need a guitar. To help you get started, we take a quick look at what makes an electric guitar tick, and also discuss how to find the best possible guitar for you. We also discuss amplifiers and other equipment you probably need.

After you have your guitar, you learn how to tune it and get started on playing it. You read about how to best position your hands to produce good clean notes, how to use the pick, and how to coordinate both hands to accurately play single notes and double stops. You also get to sit in and play along with some cool sounding beginner rock practice songs.

In addition, you get a quick lesson on reading both guitar tablature and standard notation, both of which you find incredibly useful as you learn how to play rock guitar.

Chapter 1

Start Me Up

In This Chapter

- ◆ A little guitar history
- ◆ The basic parts of your guitar
- ◆ Things about strings
- ◆ Shopping for your guitar
- ◆ Other items you'll need or want

Power.

If you had to describe rock guitar with one word, *power* certainly fits the bill, both literally and figuratively. First, and most obvious, whenever we think of rock guitar, an electric guitar immediately comes to mind. When powered through an amplifier, the electric guitar delivers a much more potent punch than its acoustic and classical counterparts.

Far more powerful than volume, and far more important, is the power of the *voice* of the rock guitar. Few other instruments are capable of the electric guitar's range, not only in terms of notes, but in terms of the emotion and soul those notes can convey. All you have to do is think of the rock guitarists you know and the emotions they create in their music, from the urgent rock anthems of Pete Townsend and the melancholy loneliness of David Gilmour to the dark and driven growls of Metallica's James Hetfield and Kirk Hammett to the dizzy shredding of Joe Satriani or Steve Vai.

Power is the word you want to keep in mind for another reason, too, especially as you start learning the electric guitar. It's so easy to be misled into thinking that rock guitar is all about attitude or volume or speed. Or to think that it's the equipment, the right guitar, the right gauge of strings, and the right amplifier and effects chain that create tone. Yes, all this is certainly part of rock guitar, but it doesn't define it. Rock guitar is all about developing the power to say what you want to say with your instrument and to know how all these parts (along with numerous playing techniques) work together under *your* power to create rock music.

In order to do any of this, though, you first need an electric guitar, plus an amplifier. So let's get started!

Get Plugged In!

There are all sorts of guitars out there. Classical guitars with nylon strings that make Spanish and flamenco music sound so enticing. Acoustic, steel-stringed guitars recall evenings spent around a campfire singing folk songs. But if you really want to rock, you want to have an electric guitar, which also means that you're going to need an amplifier in order to hear your electric guitar.

Right now, you probably don't know all that much about guitars, let alone electric guitars, and you've probably got a lot of questions. But I'm going to ask you to take a leap of faith with me. Like it or not, a lot of your learning is going to come from handling the guitar. Not from reading about it or analyzing the (many) choices you're going to face, but by digging in and getting your hands dirty right from the start.

In other words, we're not going to spend a lot of time discussing the merits of this sort of guitar compared to that one. Once you're learning and can understand what you want to do with the guitar, then you'll be in a much better position to make those sorts of decisions.

So please don't worry so much about your first guitar, as in all likelihood it's going to be just that: your *first* guitar. This doesn't mean that it's not important to choose well. It simply means that you're very probably going to develop your own personal style and tastes for what you want in an instrument, and there's no way you're going to know what any of that is right now.

Your immediate concern is to get a guitar that's comfortable for you and to start learning how to play it.

The Old School Philosophy

It wasn't all that long ago that if you wanted to learn to play guitar, everyone told you to start out on an acoustic. This wasn't an effort to discourage would-be rockers as much as it was a way to save money. Fact was that even the cheapest serviceable electric guitars were way out of the price range of most aspiring musicians.

And many teachers (and guitarists) will still tell you today that starting out on an acoustic is a better way to go, as playing on an acoustic helps develop finger strength a bit faster. And it's also a plus to not have your every mistake and slip of the finger amplified for the world to hear!

Nowadays, decent, economically priced electric guitars can be found almost anywhere in the world, so price isn't the factor it once was. And when it comes down to it, there are pros and cons for whichever type of guitar you pick up first. While it's true that the electric guitar will broadcast all your mistakes at whatever volume you're playing, very essential elements of rock guitar, such as power chords and barre chords, come a lot easier on an electric guitar than they do on an acoustic.

The bottom line is this: if rock guitar is your driving motivation, then you might as well go out and get an electric guitar, if for no other reason than you're much more likely to practice a lot (and hopefully harder) on a guitar that you're happy playing.

A (Very) Short History of the Guitar

You can spend a lifetime tracking down the family tree of the electric guitar. There are distant ancestors like the sitar and tanbur of India and Asia and more recent cousins like the Roman cithara, the Arabic oud, and various lutes of European lineage. Like our modern day marvel, these ancient instruments had long necks, and sounds were produced by plucking strings (made of whatever material happened to be available) with one hand and changing the tone of the note with the other.

Evolution doesn't take place overnight. Through endless variations of body styles and shapes, neck lengths, and number of strings, people tinkered on, making adjustments and improvements that eventually, in the late 1700s, became the standard (for as much as anything could be called standard!) six-string design that we all know and love.

Like almost everything else in history, guitars (and guitarists) experienced periods of both great popularity and indifference. And also like almost everything else in history, they readily made use of the latest developments in technology in order to improve themselves. Guitar bodies and necks were reinforced, giving birth to acoustic guitars that could bear steel strings, rather than the gut strings of the classical instruments. Body shapes were tinkered with, all for the sake of getting more and more sound.

One could argue that a lot of the guitar's history, at least in the 1900s, was all about making the instrument louder. Even in smaller bands, an acoustic guitar was easily drowned out by its bandmates' instruments. The traditional solution to making something louder was simply to make it bigger (think about the acoustic bass), but there was only so far one could go with the guitar. Even the creation of the all-steel resonator guitars, fitted with cones much like banjos, was a temporary answer at best.

The Sonic Boom

Fortunately, folks were also harnessing the power of electricity and putting it to all sorts of wonderful uses. As early as the 1930s, people were experimenting, using electromagnetic devices to pick up the vibrations of the strings of acoustic guitars, which would then be sent to an amplifier. There were, of course, hits and misses, but progress was being made. Jazz legend Charlie Christian was one of the earliest proponents of the newfound electric guitar, and his playing was so influential that he was inducted into the Rock and Roll Hall of Fame in 1990.

Hear How

Charlie Christian, who played guitar in Benny Goodman's band, was the hot topic among guitar lovers—electric, acoustic, jazz, or otherwise—in the early 1940s. He is universally accredited with bringing the guitar out of the rhythm section and into its rightful place as a soloing instrument in a band.

His influence can be heard in the solos from great jazz guitarists like Wes Montgomery, Barney Kessell, and Herb Ellis to blues giant, B. B. King, to the early rock guitar wizards like Eddie Cochran, Scotty Moore, and Chuck Berry. Factor in the "guitar gods" Les Paul, Carlos Santana, and Jimi Hendrix, all of whom built on Charlie's pioneering work on the electric guitar, and you can understand why rock guitarists everywhere owe this jazz master a big tip of the hat.

The companies manufacturing these electrically enhanced acoustic guitars then began experimenting with solid body, all electric guitars. Guitar legend Les Paul is credited with creating one of the earliest models built with a body of a solid piece of wood (it's worth noting that the Rickenbacker International Corporation had built a cast-aluminum model that was much like a lap-steel guitar) in the early 1940s.

But it was Leo Fender and his solid-body Esquire that ushered in the age of the electric guitar in 1950. The Esquire had a single pickup (a device used to convert the guitar's string vibrations into electric signals), was reasonably priced and reliable, and proved to be a big hit with country/western musicians. A two-pickup model went into production and the guitar went through a few name changes—the Esquire becoming the Broadcaster, which in turn became the Telecaster that we all recognize more than 50 years later. He then topped himself by designing the three-pickup Stratocaster in 1954.

The Accidental Rocker

Unbeknownst to anyone at the time (but not for long!), these creators of the electric guitar were actually giving guitarists a much more powerful instrument than they knew. In fact, they were changing the way the guitar would sound. Instead of merely getting an amplified acoustic guitar, the new electric had a voice that easily held its own with other soloing instruments, such as the saxophone and trumpet. Distortion and sustain, two by-products of amplifying a guitar, gave the instrument a new and powerful voice, one capable of breathtaking beauty as well as primal urgency.

And the musicians of the time not only learned this, they also worked with the various manufacturers of both guitars and amplifiers in order to further explore the miraculous musical mutant they had in their hands. When Link Wray poked holes in the speakers of his amplifier to create distortion on an even more powerful scale, rock guitar would jump ahead of its acoustic ancestors as if it were leaping on the moon.

Electric Guitar Anatomy 101

Even though electric guitars come in all shapes and sizes, at heart they are pretty much made up of the same elements, as shown in the following illustration.

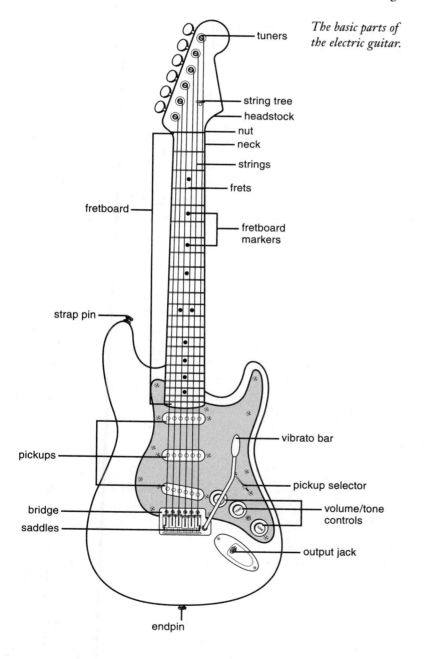

The basic parts of the electric guitar.

It's easiest to think of your guitar in three main parts: the head, which is where the tuning machines for the strings usually are found, the body, which is the area you'll normally be doing your strumming and picking, and the neck, which is where you'll be fretting the notes. Let's start at the top and work down.

Headstock

Unless you have a headless guitar, the headstock is located at the end of the neck farthest from the body. This is where the tuning machines for the strings are found.

Most guitars have either all six tuning machines on one side of the headstock or three tuning machines on each side, but some guitars have different configurations (four on one side, two on the other, for example).

The tuners anchor one end of each string and also are used to tighten or loosen the string's tension so that you can set each string to the proper pitch before playing. You'll learn more about them in the following chapter.

On most electric guitars you access the guitar's truss rod adjustment at the base of the headstock (near the nut). The truss rod is an adjustable rod of steel that helps reinforce the neck against the tension of the strings. The truss rod tension is adjustable to set the neck geometry for optimal playing.

Nut

The nut is a slotted strip of hard plastic or bone that sits where the neck and headstock meet. Each string has an individual slot to pass through as it moves from the neck to its allotted tuning post.

Along the face of the neck is the fingerboard or fretboard, which is where you find the frets, thin strips of metal. When you place your finger on a string anywhere on the neck, the fret closest to the finger (on the body side) stops the string, shortening it, if you will, creating the note you hear when you pick the string.

Body Parts

Think of the guitar body as the control center of your instrument. Because the body of the guitar is the biggest part, most of the controls and electrical parts are found here.

Depending on how many pickups your guitar has, there is usually a pickup selector, a switching device that allows you to choose which of the guitar's pickups (or combination of pickups) are active when you play. We discuss pickups a great deal in Chapter 18.

Almost every guitar has at least two control knobs, one for volume and one for tone. The tone knob adjusts the balance between the higher and lower frequencies produced when you pick the strings. Again, depending on the type of

---

Note Worthy

Double-necked guitars have two necks projecting out from the guitar body. Usually one neck has the normal six strings while the second neck either has four strings like a bass guitar or twelve strings like a twelve-string guitar. This allows the guitarist to switch from one neck to the other midsong.

guitar you have and the number of pickups it has, you may have additional volume and tone controls to compensate.

For most guitars, the bridge is where the strings are anchored to the body by means of an assembly of metal parts. Often the saddle, an individual device where each string (although sometimes a pair of strings) sits before passing over the pickups, is part of the bridge assembly.

On some guitars, the strings do not pass through the body of the guitar but are simply attached to a tailpiece.

The end button and strap button are short metal posts at the rear and front edge of the body, respectively. This is where you attach a strap. Usually the strap pin is on the top of the front edge or horn of the guitar, but some guitars have the strap pin on the back of the body, close to where the body joins the neck.

And finally, there's the output jack, which is where you plug in the guitar cable (also called a lead) that carries your guitar's signal to the amplifier. On most guitars, you'll find the output jack on the lower edge of the body, toward the endpin. Some types of guitars have the output jack on the face of the body, usually down past the volume and tone controls.

Vibrato Bars

Some guitars have a small metal bar, called a vibrato bar, that is attached to (or gets screwed into) the bridge or tailpiece. Pushing and pulling on the vibrato bar causes the strings to dramatically change pitch. The vibrato bar is also known as a tremolo or whammy bar.

The Beauty Within

Most electric guitars have one or two access panels in the back of the body that allow you to get at the electronic systems of the pickups and volume and tone controls.

If your guitar has a whammy bar, then there may also be a large access panel for the tremolo system that, more often than not, includes a number of heavy duty springs that anchor part of the bridge to the body.

Strings

You may come to think of the six strings of your guitar as a small, six-member choir. They are your voices as you play, and you will be guiding them to sing the notes you want to hear. So it goes without saying that your strings are a vital part of your instrument.

Whatever guitar you buy will have a set of strings on it. Don't assume that because you're buying a new guitar the strings are brand new. You have no idea how long the guitar has been sitting in the shop (the strings being used every day by prospective buyers) or stored at the factory before being shipped out. The strings of your "new" guitar could be months old and already oxidized and well-worn.

If you purchase a guitar from a store, it never hurts to ask if they'll throw in a new set of strings for you. You could also ask for them as part of the setup, which we discuss at the end of this chapter.

Can You Spare a Nickel?

Most guitar strings are made of either a plain steel filament or, for the thicker strings, by using a steel filament as a core and then wrapping that core with another round wire, usually of the same material, which for the electric guitar is steel. This design makes perfect sense because you want a highly magnetic material whose vibrations will be easily sensed by the guitar's electromagnetic pickups. Steel strings have great volume and sustain qualities and usually hold these qualities for a long time.

Some players, though, find all-steel guitar strings a little rough and noisy. They produce a good deal of string noise as you slide your fingers up and down along the fretboard. These guitarists tend to prefer to play strings with either stainless steel wrap windings or wrap wound strings that are nickel-plated. Adding nickel to the string's surface gives the string a very smooth finish that one's fingers simply glide over. Nickel players feel that their string of choice is faster and a little easier on the fingers. Nickel-plated strings are also less vulnerable to rust and corrosion than plain steel strings.

Gauging Your Needs

Guitar strings come in different gauges, or string diameters. Generally, the lighter the gauge of string, the easier it is to perform techniques like bending (covered in Chapter 4), while medium and heavy gauge strings provide more volume and sustain.

For a beginner, instructors may recommend light gauge strings, primarily to ease the new player into the rigors of fretting, bending, and sliding while developing the finger strength needed for these (and other) rock guitar techniques. Once some skill and confidence are acquired, the guitarist may then try out heavier strings.

Note Worthy

Even smoother than common nickel-plated steel-wound strings are flatwound strings, which are made by wrapping the round core string with a flat, ribbon-like string instead of a round one (hence the term *round wound* for normal electric guitar strings). While this cuts down string noise to almost nothing, it also cuts down on sustain and brilliance in tone. This makes flatwound strings a big favorite among jazz players, who don't want a lot of extraneous ringing; but it's truly rare to find a rock guitarist who swears by flatwound strings.

As you learn more and more about playing rock guitar, you will have many opportunities to try out different types of strings. You owe it to yourself in this beginner's period to experiment and to see what gauges you like, as well as which of the several available string compositions best suit you.

Buying Your First Guitar

It's hard to shop for something when you're not sure what you want or need. Add to this fact that most music stores seem a bit daunting to the new player. There are all these people who seem to be able to play impressively and effort-lessly and they also seem to be speaking a foreign language at times, talking about vibrato and active pickups and impedance and looping. But if you keep a few tips in mind, buying a guitar doesn't have to be some mystical experience.

First off, talk with the staff. Most people who work in music stores are incred-ibly friendly, and they remember what it's like to be totally overwhelmed by the zillions of choices facing a new guitarist. That's what they deal with every day, in fact!

Be sure to take a small notebook along with you so you can write down your observations. And don't overdo it. When you feel that every instrument is start-ing to feel and sound the same, then call it a day. Don't be in a hurry to buy your first guitar, unless one happens to totally knock your socks off.

The saying goes that you should buy the most guitar you can within your bud-get. This, of course, implies that you've been smart enough to set a budget in the first place. But also remember that your budget is probably going to include an amplifier and accessories in addition to your guitar.

A Little Research Goes a Long Way

Talk with your friends and other people who own electric guitars about their experiences buying their instruments as well as about what went into the partic-ular choices they made. Most guitarists are more than willing to talk shop and to help someone take his or her first steps into the world of music.

You can also read reviews in guitar magazines as well as find numerous customer reviews on the Internet. One thing to keep in mind, though, is that these reviews are not always about the instrument as much as they can be about the reviewer. Don't worry about 1 negative review out of 10, but if a small problem seems to come up in numerous reviews, you definitely want to pay attention to it.

Taking Things into Hand

You may not play guitar just yet, but you still have the ability to feel whether or not an instrument is comfortable in your hands. Is it too heavy? Can you reach the frets closest to the headstock with ease? Do you feel any rough edges of frets as you slide your hand along the neck? How is the guitar's *action*, that is, the height of the strings from the frets, all up and down the neck?

def•i•ni•tion

The **action** of a guitar is the height of the strings above the frets along the neck. If the guitar's action is too high, the strings may be hard (and painful!) to fret; too low, you end up getting a lot of fret buzz (undesirable buzzing noises that occur while playing a fretted note).

If you can, take a friend who plays guitar along with you when you shop. Have him or her play so you can listen to how the guitar sounds. Or have someone from the staff play for you. One big word of advice on this, though: make sure whoever's playing plays something *simple*, the same sort of things that you'll be playing as you start out on guitar, like basic chords or single note riffs. In fact, have him or her play the same exact thing on each guitar you test out just so you can compare how the instruments sound. When someone plays something that's obviously beyond your capabilities, whatever guitar it's played on is going to sound like it's priceless, so concentrate on the sound and not the complexity. You can always give your demonstrator a few moments to shred to his or her contentment after you've gotten a good feel for what the guitar is going to sound like for you.

Can't Get to a Store?

Many people buy guitars via the Internet, either through online music stores or auction sites such as eBay or electronic advertisers like Craigslist. Online sites often offer an unlimited selection of guitars to choose from. You can occasionally find a real bargain, although more often than not there won't be all that much difference between the prices online and at a music store.

Note Worthy

Nowadays you can find guitars everywhere, especially around the holidays, even in grocery stores. But be careful! Although a very cheap guitar may seem like a dream come true, quite often these holiday deals are very hard to play because of very high action, tuners that can't hold a string in tune for very long, and a lot of other shortfalls. If you're serious about the guitar, be serious about your shopping, too. Don't become someone who tried to play and then gave it up without knowing the guitar was at fault and not the player.

The very real downside is that you won't know exactly what you've bought until you've already paid for it and it's been shipped to you. This is one reason why visiting a music store first, if only to test out the type of guitar you'd like to get, can be very helpful.

Before ever buying online, make certain you know what, exactly, the return policies are concerning the guitar you want to buy. Try to buy from people or stores that have a good reputation and positive feedback from numerous other buyers. Double check on who's taking care of the shipping insurance and what, exactly, that coverage covers. And make certain that you give good feedback if your buying experience is positive.

Other Avenues

Sometimes it's worth looking at pawn shops or the "for sale" advertisements in your local papers. Posters with gear for sale may occasionally grace your community bulletin boards, such as those found in grocery stores, schools and colleges, coffeehouses, and, naturally, music stores. That's one way to come full circle back to where you started!

Amplifiers

Compared to the guitar, the amplifier seems fairly mundane. It's a box with knobs that might look as though it came from a set of a cheap science fiction television show from the 1970s. Here is a clear case where form is not as important as function, because one's amplifier is an integral part of one's rock sound.

In simplest terms, an amplifier consists of two parts: the actual amplifier, which accepts the signal from the guitar and increases its power, and the speaker (or speakers, as the case may be with some amplifiers), which broadcasts the sound.

Often the amp and speakers are encased together in the same unit. This is called a *combo amp*, and for small to moderate sized amplification needs (playing at a friend's home or at a small club) it's certainly easier to lug around than a separate amplifier and speaker cabinet.

These days, thanks to digital technology, even small powered amps in the low-budget range often have on-board effects, such as reverb and chorus, not to mention a second channel that boosts the signal in order to create the much desired distortion that rock guitarists love.

Unless you're planning on doing a gig at a stadium later this week, a small practice amp (around 15 watts) should meet your needs at this stage. However, if you know you're going to be playing with other people in a band setting before too long, then you might want to start at 30 watts or so for your first amplifier.

Other Options

Even a small amp can make a lot of noise, so some people use amp headphones to practice with. And while this is certainly a workable solution, you run a great risk of causing serious ear damage by having the headphone volume or guitar volume set too loud. Should you decide to use headphones, please take care and remember to save your volume for when you're on stage.

People sometimes try to make do using their stereo speaker system or a bass amp as a substitute for a guitar amplifier. Stereo speakers are not meant to take the high volume, sharp attacks, and distortion of the electric guitar, and you could very easily, and permanently, damage your speakers. You can use a bass amp, but being made for the low tones of the bass, it will not give you the tones you're used to hearing from a guitar amplifier.

Ultimately you're going to need to get a guitar amp, so it's usually a good idea to include it in your budget and get the right tool for the job from the start.

Getting Better

Remember that your amplifier is just as much a part of your equipment as your guitar. Get to know it inside and out. Experiment with various settings and write down and keep track of the ones you like and want to use a lot. Quite a number of guitarists never get as good as they'd like to be because they ignore their amplifiers and don't know how to get the sounds they want to from them.

Note Worthy

Used guitar amplifiers are often a good deal. Usually they are being sold because a guitar player wants to move up to a bigger, more powerful amp and not because of any damage to the unit. And buying a used amp means you can put more of your overall budget toward the guitar.

Necessities and Accessories

Besides a guitar and an amplifier, you need a few other things before your guitar shopping adventure is over. You're going to want guitar picks, a guitar case, and a cable at the very least. Other items, such as a tuner, might seem like accessories at the present, but could easily become necessities for you in a very short time, so take a moment and think about not only what you need in order to play your guitar immediately but also what will be helpful to you in the long haul.

Cases and Cables

You have to have a guitar case, especially if you plan on playing your guitar somewhere besides in your house or apartment. Usually, you'll have two types to choose from—a hard shell case and a gig bag. The hard shell case is exactly what you'd expect it to be, fairly heavy and protective and, if you plan on both carrying your guitar and placing it in gear-filled vans, you usually can't go wrong with one.

If, on the other hand, you plan to hand carry your instrument everywhere and never let it out of your grasp, the lighter gig bag might be a better match for you.

Either way, make absolutely certain that the case fits your guitar. Not all cases are made for the various shapes and sizes that electric guitars can come in, so double-check before buying one.

Sometimes a music store (in the real world as well as online) includes a case as part of the purchase package. It never hurts to ask beforehand. With a little luck, they might also throw in a guitar cable for good measure.

The guitar cable is your lifeline, carrying the signal produced by the pickups in response to the vibrations of the strings to your guitar amp, where they are turned into glorious sound. One end of the guitar cable attaches to the guitar's output jack and the other is plugged into your amplifier.

Cables come in varying lengths, so think about how far from your amplifier you like to be or about how much you think you're going to be moving around while playing! But don't go for too long a cable! Longer cables mean your signal has to travel farther to the amp, and that can affect your tone.

Straps

A guitar strap is essential if you plan on playing guitar standing up. Many people, myself included, encourage you to have one on even when you're playing sitting down.

Straps come in various lengths (most are adjustable), shapes, colors, and materials. If you have a heavy guitar, a strap with a padded or very wide shoulder area is a good idea.

Strap locks are also something to think about. They are little devices that ensure your guitar strap doesn't accidentally slip off the guitar.

You'll Thank Yourself One Day

Without a doubt, the smartest long-term investment you can make at the start of your guitar adventure is to buy an electronic guitar tuner. You can pick up a good one, usually for less than $25, that will last you for as long as you play guitar. You'll need batteries, of course, but if you're careful about turning the tuner off when not in use, you won't need to replace them all that often.

Having a guitar stand is also a smart idea. When you're just starting out on guitar, you want to play it as often as possible, so putting your pride and joy out where you can see it will make you want to play it more than if it were hidden away in its case somewhere. Be smart and put it right in front of the television so that you *have* to pick it up a lot!

Among the other guitar and music items that many people find helpful are a metronome (a device that keeps the beat for you while you practice), a string winder (which helps you wind the strings faster when you're putting new strings on your guitar), a cleaning or polishing cloth, and possibly a capo. We discuss all these items later on in this book.

Spares

It never hurts to have extras of things, especially when it comes to the items you use a lot, such as strings and guitar cables. An extra full set of strings is smart, and if you discover you have a tendency to break certain strings, such as the high E string, on a regular basis, then also having some single spare strings on hand is even smarter.

And picks! Be sure to have more spare picks than you will ever need.

Being Prepared

Once you have your gear, think about getting a small carry-case that holds all the equipment that doesn't fit into your guitar case. This "gig bag" should be able to hold, at minimum, your tuner, spare strings, cables, batteries, possibly an extension cord with multiple outlets, plus a few tools (screw driver, wire clippers) that you might find yourself needing.

Some folks go all out and get bags big enough to hold a guitar stand, music stand, microphone stand (always carry the microphone separately or encase it in something *very* sturdy and protective), as well as extra fuses for the amp, duct tape, and so on.

It doesn't hurt to have a checklist as part of your gig bag as well. That way you always know what's supposed to be in your carry-case.

Setting Off with a Setup

One final bit of advice: if you've purchased a guitar at a music store, ask the folks there if they will give your guitar a setup before you take it home. For the guitar, getting a setup is like getting a tune up for a car before you drive it off the lot. It's just a good way of making certain everything is in its place and running smoothly.

If you have bought a guitar from an online source or from a friend, you still should take it to your local music store to give it a good looking over. Doing so may solve a number of problems beginners may experience, from buzzing notes to chords that sound slightly out of tune, before they even occur.

The Least You Need to Know

- ◆ Before buying an electric guitar, do your best to test out as many guitars as possible!

- ◆ A guitar amplifier is a must-have with electric guitars.

- ◆ Do yourself a favor and buy a case, cable, and strap to use with your new guitar.

- ◆ However you buy a guitar, take it to a music store for a setup as soon as you can.

Chapter 2

Come On Feel the Noise

In This Chapter

- ◆ Getting your guitar in tune
- ◆ Optimal playing postures
- ◆ How to hold and use a pick
- ◆ Fretting your strings
- ◆ Getting warmed up
- ◆ Your first rock songs

Okay, you've got your guitar and amp, so it's time to start playing some rock and roll! In order to make it sound more like music and less like random noise, you need to get your guitar in tune. After getting the strings of your guitar tuned to the correct notes, you'll learn how to fret the strings in order to produce the notes that you want to play.

You also want to learn how to read a few basic symbols that can show you exactly where to put your fingers on the frets. Once you've gotten the hang of this (and it will take less time than you've already spent reading this paragraph), you'll be ready to start rocking!

Getting in Tune

When you strike a string of your guitar, the sound that the string makes is a *note*. In order to play the music you like and enjoy, you need to have your guitar in tune, meaning that the strings each play a specific note when struck.

There are, as you learn later in Chapter 19, many ways of tuning your guitar. To make things simple, let's start by having your guitar in what's called *standard tuning*.

Learning the Ropes, er, Strings

Working our way from the thickest string (the one that is farthest from the floor when holding the guitar) on down to the thinnest string (the string closest to the floor), in standard tuning the notes of the guitar are tuned as follows: E, A, D, G, B, and E again. These two Es sound similar but not exactly the same. More on that in a moment! The following illustration shows you the strings and note names:

These are the notes your guitar strings are tuned to in standard tuning.

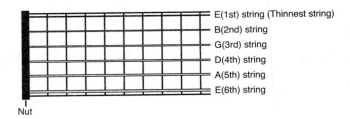

- E(1st) string (Thinnest string)
- B(2nd) string
- G(3rd) string
- D(4th) string
- A(5th) string
- E(6th) string

Nut

def•i•ni•tion

A **note** of music is often referred to as a tone. In many books the words are interchangeable.

In **standard tuning** on a guitar, the strings are tuned, low to high, E, A, D, G, B, and E. Many people come up with mnemonic sayings, such as "Elephants And Donkeys Got Big Ears" or (my favorite) "Eddie Ate Dynamite Good Bye Eddie!"

Notice that in the accompanying illustration the thickest string is in the lowest position while the thinnest one is the highest string. This may seem counter-intuitive—most people think that the thickest string should be on top since it's the one closest to them when they play. Also notice the string numbers, as they can be important when tuning, too.

It's very important to know the names of your strings. The string names serve as a reference point as to where you put your fingers in order to make other notes or to play chords or fancy riffs.

Okay, knowing the names of the strings, or rather the name of the notes to which they are tuned is one thing. But how do you get your strings tuned to these specific notes? Glad you asked!

Tuning with a Tuner

The easiest way to get in tune is to use a tuner. And if you were paying attention last chapter, you picked yourself up one at the guitar store!

If you bought a tuner specifically for an electric guitar, it has a place where you can plug directly into it, just as you would plug your guitar into an amplifier. While there are many different makes of tuners, most of them function the same way. Pluck a string (best to start off on the thickest one) and the name of a note, as well as the string number, should appear somewhere on the tuner's screen. So for example, when you hit the thickest string, you should see the letter *E* and the number *6* appear.

The tuner should also indicate if you are higher or lower than the desired pitch, usually by means of an arrow or colored lights (or both). Adjust the tuning head of the guitar so you've got the correct pitch and then move on to the next string.

If you see a letter higher than *E* (*F* or *G*), then you are too high and want to lower the pitch. Similarly, if you see a letter lower than *E* (*C* and *D*, for example), then you are too low and you want to raise the pitch until you get an *E* on your screen.

And if you didn't buy a tuner, don't worry because we're looking out for you! The very first track of the CD that comes with this book is a tuning track.

All you need to do is put the CD in your computer or the CD player of your choice, punch up the first track, and then tune up by matching your pitch to the one on the recording.

Track 1

Relative Tuning

With the exception of the notes found on the first four frets of your low E string and the very highest notes of the high E string, every other note on your guitar can be played at various places on the fingerboard. After you've gotten your low E string in tune, place your finger at the fifth fret of the low E string and play only that string. Then immediately strike the open A string. They should sound exactly the same because, when your guitar is correctly tuned, they are the same note.

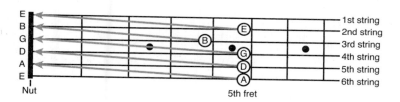

Where to find the correct notes to tune the guitar to itself.

With your A string now in tune, you repeat this process, using the fifth fret of the A string to match against the open D string and then matching the fifth fret of the D to the open G string.

Then there's a slight glitch in the system. The open B string should be tuned to the fourth fret of the G string and not the fifth as you've done on the previous strings. Once the B is in tune, then you use the fifth fret of the B to get the open high E string in tune. Well done!

Posture and Position

Now that you're in tune, it's time to get playing. You might not think so from watching guitarists perform, but having good posture and positioning can make a huge difference to you when starting out as a beginner.

Playing guitar is about creating notes by fretting the strings of your guitar, either individual notes, as in most leads or riffs, or groups of notes as chords. So you would think it goes without saying that being able to fret notes cleanly, clearly, and quickly is important, right?

But many people just taking up the guitar often hinder their own ability to play notes well by not paying attention to their posture and their playing position. It doesn't matter if you're performing on stage in front of a huge crowd or simply sitting on a couch at home, you want to be able to play your notes well.

(Don't) Get a Grip

A couple of pointers: first and foremost, relax! Get loose by shaking out your hands, wrists, and arms. Roll your shoulders and try to get all the tension out of your system.

Second, remember that your fretting hand needs to be able to move freely and smoothly and that you need to be able to position your fingers so that the tips can fret the notes. Don't grab the neck of the guitar like a baseball bat! We discuss this more in a minute.

Ideally, whether sitting or standing, your fretting hand should be about chest high, where it will have optimal movement along all of the neck of the guitar.

Taking a Seat

If your mother was always telling you "Don't slouch!" she probably knew you planned to play rock guitar one day! Try to use a chair with a good back, one that encourages you to sit straight and still be comfortable. Obviously you don't want to use one with arms, as that will certainly make it difficult to get your arms in a good position for playing guitar.

The guitar should sit comfortably on your right leg. Some people find it easier to play with the right leg slightly raised in order to lift the body of the guitar into a better playing position. Others use their right forearm to steady the guitar, and still others sit slightly forward. However it works for you, if you can sit with the guitar in place and then take your left hand entirely off the guitar (maybe to wave at someone in the audience) and not have the guitar move a whit out of position, then you're doing fine.

And speaking of your arms, don't use your left leg as an armrest. Remember that you want to be able to get the tips of your fingers on the fretboard, and if your wrist is lying atop your leg, you're going to find it difficult to play your notes cleanly. More important, forcing your hand to play the neck at that kind of angle may lead to a lot of discomfort.

Also remember that when you're sitting, your natural tendency is going to be to tilt the guitar so that you can see the frets better. This is normal, but it also can hamper your fingers from getting up on their tips to fret a note. Try to keep the tilting to a minimum or, better yet, once you've seen where you want to place your fingers, shift the guitar so its face is straight forward.

Taking a Stand

You might notice, especially in videos, a lot of guitarists play with their guitars slung fairly low on their bodies when standing. But if you pay close attention to the guitarists you think play very well, you'll also notice that these particular players hold the guitar slightly higher or angle the neck so that their fretting hands are not locked down around their waist.

Getting Better

It's a good idea to wear your guitar strap whether sitting or standing while playing. Wearing the strap while sitting can help you to keep your guitar's neck at a good angle that allows your fretting hand easy movement in reaching the notes, especially if the guitar is "neck heavy" and tends to nose dive toward the floor.

If you end up performing a lot, chances are likely you'll be spending most of your playing time in a standing position. So it pays not only to be comfortable but to find a stance that allows you to play the best you can. Obviously you want to look cool, too, but you also have to take into account what position allows you the best mobility to play. If you're only pouring out power chords close to the headstock, then you certainly can get away with strapping your guitar on fairly low. But if you're also going to be playing leads and complicated riffs and fills, then you want to give your hands their best chance—and that means getting at least the neck of your guitar up a little higher.

Ready on the Right?

We discuss this topic a lot more in Chapter 4, but it's good to talk a little right now about finesse. I know that most beginners would like nothing more than to be able to do some flashy moves right from the get-go.

But remember that you're playing rock guitar, so you're playing through an amplifier, right? Well, it's not only your notes that are going to be amplified, but every single sound you make on the strings with either hand—whether you meant to do so or not.

So before you play some huge chord and also accidentally add in two or three strings you didn't mean to hit, you've got to develop some control and touch. And that starts here at the beginning, especially with your right hand, which will be doing the picking and strumming for you.

Your right hand, all relaxed and ready to play, should be crossing the strings at anywhere from a forty-five to sixty degree angle. And again, even though we won't be discussing palm muting for a while yet (see Chapter 5), try to get used to having the far edge of your palm very close to the strings, right around the saddle area to start. Getting comfortable with staying close and using minimal movement for strumming and picking right from the start will make learning more complicated techniques much easier down the road.

Picking a Pick

The vast majority of rock guitarists use a pick (also called a plectrum) for strumming chords, playing single notes, and just about everything in between.

Most picks are made of plastic, but you can also find picks made from all sorts of materials from stone to metal. And everyone has a story about having to come up with a "pick in a pinch" by using a coin or a cut up plastic bottle top or even a very thick bit of cardboard (though not for long!).

While the size and shape of a pick can make a difference in how you hold it and how it strikes the strings, it's the various thicknesses of a pick that tend to be the major determining factor in choosing which pick is for you. Many beginners like thin picks because they seem easier to use at first, but then move on to thicker ones.

Just like with your guitar, pick choices tend to be highly personal. As you're learning, try out different types and thicknesses and see how they feel to play with and what they make you sound like. You may become a guitarist who only uses one brand and thickness or you may become one who uses a different pick depending on what he's playing in a particular song.

Guitarists not only like to compare and talk about picks, they also talk a lot about how best to hold them. More often than not, you see a guitarist hold a pick like this:

Holding a pick.

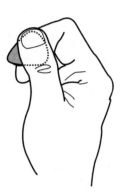

First hold your hand, thumb up, and fingers out, and then point at something. Now curl your index finger back under your thumb, set the pick on it and hold it in place with your thumb, leaving the tip of the pick sticking out perpendicular from the thumb. You don't want to have a lot of the tip exposed as doing so makes the pick harder to control as you strum.

There are, of course, many, many ways of holding a pick and at least half of those have been labeled as "the correct way." Watch other guitarists and check out what they are doing. Different pick holds create different attacks on the strings, and you may find yourself changing styles depending on the kind of sound you want to get out of your guitar.

Proper Picking

However you decide to hold your pick, it's important to get into some good picking habits right away. First, try to pick across the strings and not down into the guitar. You also want to avoid getting under the strings and pulling the pick up and away from the strings. There is certainly a time and a place for using both of these types of attacks, but when you're just starting out, either one can make sounding a clean note a bit of a nightmare.

Also, think economy of movement. It's easy to let the pick fly all over the place, but try to keep the movement to a minimum. Use just enough motion and movement to strike just the string or number of strings that you want to pick and then be ready for the next strike.

In the same vein, get used to using both downward and upward motion when picking. The temptation at the start is to only use downstrokes, but in order to play the guitar with any speed you're going to have to be adept at upstrokes. Keeping this in mind gives you a leg up when you learn alternate picking in Chapter 4.

When strumming or picking, most of the movement should be generated by the wrist and forearm. There will be times when more of your arm will get involved, but for right now try to concentrate on not having your whole arm moving up and down.

Look Ma, No Plectrum!

A surprising number of rock guitarists don't use picks. Two that you're probably very familiar with are Mark Knopfler of Dire Straits and Lindsey Buckingham of Fleetwood Mac. And it's been more than 20 years since guitar great Jeff Beck played with a pick. So playing with just one's fingers is certainly possible. Not surprisingly, using just one's fingers to play an electric guitar can lead to all sorts of interesting attacks and tonal qualities.

For a beginning guitarist, going without a pick can be strange, to say the least, not to mention challenging in many ways. For starters, just how do you want to strike the strings? If playing full chords, it's easy enough to strum down with the thumb and up with a finger, but more often than not the rock guitarist is busy playing a varying number of strings at any given time.

Probably the simplest approach is to hold the fingers of the right hand, when striking the strings, as if holding a pick. With the "economy of motion" mind-set mentioned earlier, combined with a bit of practice, you can find yourself attacking the string with either the fingernail of the index finger, the pad of the index finger, the pad of the thumb, or the nail of the thumb. With more practice, you can combine parts of both finger and thumb. You definitely will find a world of tone there.

A different approach for single-note playing would be to strike a string downward with the thumb while simultaneously pinching upward with a finger. Essentially, it's the same motion as snapping your fingers, but you use the index finger instead of the middle or ring finger most people use when snapping their fingers. As you might imagine, this also involves a fair amount of practice to get comfortable with, but it helps to provide a bit of punch in your lead guitar playing.

Hear How
To check out more "fingers only" guitar wizardry, definitely give any Lindsey Buckingham solo CD a listen. For many guitarists, not to mention many of his fans, the song "Big Love" is a benchmark of how electrifying finger playing can be. His most recent release, "Under the Skin," shows that he hasn't lost a step in his fingers!

The Left Hand

Let's leave the right hand be for a moment and concentrate on the left one. First, get yourself an empty glass, preferably a medium sized one and one that you can see through. Set it in front of you and pick it up. Did you grab it like a baseball bat? Not very likely!

Now look at your fingers. Chances are that your fingers are evenly spread across one side of the glass and that the pressure you're exerting to hold it up is also evenly spread among all four fingers. Your thumb is probably nicely aligned between your index and middle finger and you're certainly not squeezing like crazy with your thumb because you think the glass is going to fall out of your hand.

Okay, you can put the glass down now and pick up your guitar. Only this time talk yourself into thinking that the neck of the guitar is made of glass, like the one you just held, and not made of wood. Don't think about things of wood that you've held before, like baseball bats or hammers or guitar necks.

As I've already mentioned, and will be repeating a lot throughout this book, the guitar is an instrument you need to finesse. Yes, there will be times to grab it and choke every last note out of it. But you have to start by knowing how to best get your notes, and you will find that the more heavy-handed you are at this stage, the longer it will take you to play well.

Fretting the Frets

Let's make some music, shall we? Okay, maybe more notes than music, but it will become music before you know it.

Pick up your guitar and then relax. Shake out both hands. Now place your left hand on the neck of your guitar as shown in the following illustration:

Fretting a note.

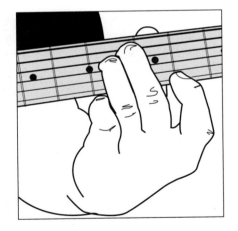

Getting Better

Be certain to use all your fingers when working out the "one finger one fret" warm up exercises. Beginners have a habit of diligently using all four fingers for about two days and then suddenly forget that they have a pinky. You're going to need all your fingers as things get more complicated so get them into the mix early!

Remember—don't grab the neck with your thumb! Doing so pulls your fingers down toward the floor and limits their reach and flexibility. You want to get the very tips of your fingers on the strings.

With your right hand, pick the open high E string. Then place your index finger of your left hand in the space between the nut and the first fret, about three quarters of the way, and pick the string again with the right hand. Congratulations! You've played your first fretted note.

Take the time to listen to the note as you play it. Is it clean and clear? Do you hear any buzzing? If so, you may want to slide your finger a little closer to the metal fret. If you're right on top of the metal fret and not getting a clear note, then you should slide back a bit toward the midpoint between the fret and the nut.

Okay, now take your middle finger and do the same thing, only this time placing in between the first and second frets. Again, listen to the note and adjust yourself accordingly. Then repeat the process with the ring finger (in the third fret) and the pinky (in the fourth fret).

The object here is not speed, but tone. You'll learn later on that "tone starts with the fingers," and you want to train your fingers to get the best tone—or note—possible.

"One Finger One Fret" Warm Up Exercise

Repeat this "one finger one fret" exercise until you are comfortable making notes on the high E string. Then move on to the B string and go through it all again. When you get to the point where you can do this on all six strings, it should sound like the second track of the CD that comes with this book.

Track 2

It's also important to note here that you should not worry about keeping your first finger in place while you get the other notes. Your hand is probably not used to making stretches like that and you might not be able to get good clean notes with your ring finger and pinky. So don't be afraid to kind of throw your fingers at the frets! The more you do this warm up exercise, the more your fingers acclimate themselves to the stretching and, before you know it, you'll probably be able to keep all your fingers in place on each string.

Getting Better _____

Don't limit your "one finger one fret" warm up exercises to the first four frets of the fingerboard. Playing up higher on the neck is an excellent way to prepare yourself for being able to use all your fingers for more complicated leads that you'll attempt one day!

And don't be afraid to play around with this exercise, either! When you finish doing it as we've done, try it again only going in both directions on each string. Go one way on one string and then the other way on the next. Mix up the order in which you use your fingers. There are so many possibilities that you should never get bored.

Whenever you sit down (or stand up) to practice, start out with a few of these to loosen up your fingers and to get your hands relaxed and ready to play some serious rock guitar.

Two Strings at a Time

First off, listen to the song, "Two String Rock," on the CD.

The song starts with four clicks, which sets the beat. We're going to take this deliberately slow. After all, it's your first song!

Track 3

You're going to play two strings at once, those two strings being the open low E string and the A string. But of course, there's a catch. You need to have your index finger on the second fret of the A string.

Play both strings, striking them together with the right hand. (In the recording I'm using a pick, but you can use your fingers if you've decided to do so.) Do this twice and then place your ring finger on the fourth fret of the A string and strike both strings together again twice.

Hear How

While our first two songs may seem simplistic, these "rock shuffles" are the building blocks of many songs. Just listen to "Do It Again" by the Beach Boys, "Get Back" by the Beatles, Bruce Springsteen's "Pink Cadillac," or Led Zeppelin's "Rock and Roll," and you hear different variations on this theme. It's definitely a classic!

You've just completed a set of four strikes. You're going to do a total of four sets of four.

When you've finished the four sets of four, shift strings, so that you're now striking the A and D strings—the A string is now open while your left hand fingers are now shifting between the second fret and the fourth fret of the D string. Again, do four sets of four.

Now repeat both sets of four (one set on the low E and A strings and one on the A and D strings) one more time and end with one final set of four on the low E and A strings. Not too bad!

This may seem a little simple to start, but you're working on developing touch and finesse, and you already know this is important.

Don't worry about making mistakes. You're going to! Everyone does, so don't be left out. What's important is to keep a steady rhythm and to try not to lose your place. If you do stumble, just wait for next "change of string." That is your cue to come in again.

A Little Rock 'n' Roll

Track 4

Because you're probably flushed with success, let's try one more. "Nine Note Rock" is slightly faster in pace and also requires a little more work, but it should still be a lot of fun. First, have a listen.

You're still playing two strings at once, but this time you're starting with the A and D strings. We've also added another note to our pattern. Here you start with your index finger on the second fret of the D string and then go to the fourth fret as before. This time, though, add your pinky to the fifth fret of the D string and play that twice before going back to the fourth fret.

Let me repeat that: second fret, fourth fret, fifth fret, fourth fret. And then repeat. That is our new series.

You start with four series on the A and D strings and then play two series using the D and G strings. Remember that the D string is open and you do all your fretting on the G string. Follow this with two series again using the A and D strings and then two series using the low E and A strings. Finally, play one series on the A and D strings again and end with one hit of both the A and D strings.

Congratulations! You are now a fledgling rock guitarist!

The Least You Need to Know

- The guitar strings are tuned (low to high) E, A, D, G, B, and E.
- Good posture and positioning help to make playing easier.
- You can strum with either a pick or your fingers.
- Hold the guitar lightly and fret the strings with the very tips of your fingers.

Chapter 3

I Read the News Today Oh Boy

In This Chapter

◆ Reading chord charts

◆ Understanding guitar tablature

◆ A painless introduction to note reading

◆ Combining tablature with rhythm notation

◆ Using double stops

So now that you've played your first bit of rock 'n' roll, what should we do next?

That's actually an interesting question. I'm sure you're very anxious to play and to learn some more cool rock guitar, and I'm more than ready to teach you. The real question isn't "what should we do next?" It's "how do I tell you what to do?"

Music is all about communicating. Rock guitarists use their instrument to paint musical pictures full of wonder and emotion. So how do they communicate with each other about specific musical ideas? How do you know which fret (or frets) on which string (or strings) to press down if I say, "Play B5."

Clearly we have to be able to talk with each other in a common language. And fortunately, we have a number of ways to do this when it comes to the guitar.

A Few Things to Read

One of the reasons the guitar is so popular is because you don't need to be able to read music in order to play. That is absolutely and undeniably true.

But it's not the whole story. Guitarists have to have some grounding in music—musical terms at the least—in order to give and receive directions from their fellow band mates and musicians. If you and I are unable to communicate when we sit down to play a song together, chances are that what you play and what I play, when played together, might sound more like gears grinding than like music.

However, if I were to tell you, "play an E minor chord while I play a short solo" and you knew what an E minor chord was and how to play it, then we'd be in business.

Chord Charts

As you probably have figured out, the guitar is a polyphonic instrument, meaning it is capable of playing several notes at the same time. Up to six notes, actually, because there are six strings.

When you play a single string, you are playing one note. When you play two or more strings at a time, that combination of notes is called a *chord*. Chords are at the heart of learning guitar. The more you learn about how chords are formed and the various *chord shapes* that you use to fret the strings, the easier playing guitar gets. Even if all you want to do is play solos, knowing chord positions helps you find the right notes to play whenever you're soloing.

The easiest way to learn how to play chords is to learn how to read a chord chart. Because I brought up the E minor chord a moment ago, let's start there. By the way, musicians usually write out E minor with the symbol Em as the little *m* stands for minor. See? You're communicating in musical terms already!

E minor (Em) chord chart.

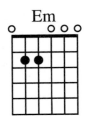

Chord charts (also called chord boxes or chord diagrams) are simple grid maps. Take your guitar and hold it directly in front of you so that you can see the fretboard. The chord chart is aligned in the same way. The heavy dark line at the top of the chord chart represents the nut of your guitar.

> **def•i•ni•tion**
>
> **Chords** are created when you play a combination of two or three different notes. **Chord shapes** are the positions of the fingers on the fretboard when playing a chord. This distinction is important because many different chords can be made by moving the same chord shape from one part of the fretboard to another.

> **Getting Better**
>
> It may seem like a huge task right now, but try to memorize chords as soon as you can. The sooner you don't need to rely on a chord chart to remember how to play a chord, the sooner you can play a song much smoother and with few, if any, noticeable gaps in your timing.
>
> As you get more comfortable forming chords and changing between various chords, you'll surprise yourself at how easy it is to remember them all, even when you start knowing more than two dozen!

Each of the vertical lines represents a string. From left to right, they are the E, A, D, G, B, and E strings. In other words, the thickest string, the one that's furthest away from the floor when you hold it, is the string on the far left of the chord chart.

The horizontal lines in the chord chart are your frets. Chord charts can vary in the number of frets shown on a chart. Usually there are three or four.

For some chords, such as Em in our example, there will be an O above the nut directly over a string. Or over several strings, as the case may be. This O indicates that you should play this string open, meaning that you don't put a finger on that string at all.

On other chords (and you learn a good many of them in Part 2), there may be an X over a string (or strings). This tells you to *not* play that string when playing the chord. X is a big part of rock guitar in many techniques, so don't be thinking that you want to hit all six strings of your guitar every time you strum.

A dark circle in the grid of the chord chart shows you on which string or strings, and which fret or frets to place your fingers. Many chord charts also have numbers within the grid circles; these are suggestions for which fingers to use to fret the notes of the chord. A *1* denotes your index finger, *2* is your middle finger, *3* is your ring finger, and *4* is your pinky.

To form this Em chord, you want to place a finger on the second fret of the A string (the suggestion is to use the middle finger) and another finger on the second fret of the D string (the ring finger is suggested). Once you have them set in place, strum across all six strings, from the thickest one to the thinnest. And congratulations, again! You've just played your first chord!

> **Note Worthy**
>
> As you learn more complicated chords, you often see a number listed to the right of the chord chart, just to the side of the first grid. This number indicates the fret along the neck that is represented on the chart. A 6, for instance, means any fingers in the first set of boxes are on the sixth fret. The second set is now the seventh fret, and so on.

Cheat Sheets

You probably noticed that playing an Em chord wasn't all that hard. Playing it cleanly is important, and we'll get back to this chord in just a brief moment.

First, though, I have to tell you that while reading a chord chart is an important skill to have, many times you're not going to be lucky enough to have a chord chart as a reference while playing a song.

Most times when people get together to play music, they use what I call "*cheat sheets*," which are usually just the lyrics of a song printed (or written) on a piece of paper with the occasional chord name written above the lyric to indicate when to change from one chord to another. An example of a cheat sheet is on the next page.

This is what you might get if someone wanted to play "House of the Rising Sun." You would play an Em chord when the singer sings the second word, *is*, and then switch to a G chord at the word *house*. When the word *New* comes around, you change to an A chord and then play C when the second syllable of *Orleans* is sung.

HOUSE OF THE RISING SUN

Em   G   A   C   Em   G   B7
There is a house in New Orleans they call the rising sun
           Em   G   A   C   Em   B7   Em   B7
And it's been the ruin of many a poor boy and God I know I'm one

      Em   G   A   C   Em   G   B7
My mother was a tailor   sewed my new blue jeans
      Em   G   A   C   Em   B7   Em   B7
My father was a gambling man   down in New Orleans

A typical "cheat sheet."

If you've ever gone online looking for chords to songs on the Internet, this type of cheat sheet is pretty much what you find. An important point to notice: unless you know the song fairly well, you have no indication of the amount of time to hold onto a particular chord. After all, different singers might hold the notes of the melody for different lengths. Does that mean you need to change your chords at different times depending on who is singing this tune?

Clearly there must be a better way to determine how to go about playing a song, one that gives a guitarist a better grasp of when, exactly, the chords might change.

Fake Books and Piano/Vocal Books

Cheat sheets are poor descendents of what used to be called "fake books." The first line of our "House of the Rising Sun" example, would look like this when written out as a song page in a fake book:

House of the Rising Sun

Traditional

First line of "House of the Rising Sun" as you'd find it in a fake book.

This may not seem like much of difference to you, or much of an improvement for that matter, but to someone who knows a bit of music—even just the very rudiments—it's a huge step up from the cheat sheet.

First off, the lyrics are presented with the melody of the song. The melody is the series of notes that are sung, the *do, re, mi* of "do, re, mi," if you will.

Because the melody is written in standard music notation, which means that there is a time signature indicating the beat and pulse of the song, it's a lot easier to figure out where the chords are going to change.

You may find this all a little confusing right now, but stick with it. We have to learn two more things and you'll be all set to get playing! We're also going to go over all this fairly quickly right now, but rest assured that we'll take the time to go over it again later as it will be very helpful to you.

Picking Up the Tab

Many guitarists learn to read music by way of *guitar tablature.* Tablature, or tab for short, uses a staff of six lines to represent the six strings of the guitar. The lowest line is your low E string, the thickest one, and the top line is the thinnest string, the high E.

Numbers, anywhere from 0 to 21 or 22 are placed on these lines to indicate which fret to play on which particular string in order to get the desired note. The *0* would indicate playing that particular string open, that is, without any fingers on the frets of that string.

Let's see what the melody of the first line of "House of the Rising Sun" would be like in guitar tablature:

First line of "House of the Rising Sun" in guitar tablature.

Play this by starting with a finger on the second fret of the A string. After you play that note (which corresponds to the first word of the lyric), then play the note at the second fret of the D string. The note for *a* is at the fourth fret of the D string while the note played for *house* is the open G string (remember that *0* means open string).

Track 5

You then play the open B string, followed by the note at the second fret of the G string, followed by the note at the second fret of the D string again, but this time you play that note twice because there are two *2*s in a row.

For the second half of the line, beginning with the word *they*, hit the second fret of the D string one more time and then jump to the open high E (thinnest) string and play that note twice. Finally play the note at the third fret of the B string and then finish by playing the open B string twice.

Once you get used to it, reading guitar tablature isn't all that hard, but it puts you back at square one in that if you didn't know this song and were just handed a sheet with lines and numbers on it, how would you know how long to hold each note?

Things of Note

Cast your mind back to your school days. They may not have been all that long ago (they may still be going on!) or they might have been last century. At some point you probably had a music class, and the only thing you can remember from it is "Every good boy deserves favor." Some people prefer *fudge* to *favor.* That's okay.

Getting Better

Reading music is a skill that anyone can develop. The key, as with most things about playing guitar, is practice, and it's easy to practice music reading. Even when you don't have a guitar with you, it's easy enough to have a music book or some sheet music so you can familiarize yourself with reading. Just 10 minutes a day means more than an hour of reading practice each week.

You might even remember that notes have names. Okay, maybe "names" is a little generous as they are simply called by the first seven letters of the alphabet. Musically, notes go A, B, C, D, E, F, and G and then start all over again. There are other notes as well, called *accidentals*, which share the letter name but add the word flat or sharp to it. A flat is indicated by a symbol (♭) that looks like a small *b* that someone heavy sat on while a sharp is represented by the "pound" or "number" sign (♯).

One thing that might help here is to picture a piano or another type of keyboard instrument. The regular notes are the white keys while the accidentals, the notes that are flat or sharp, are the black keys. We go over all this in greater detail in Chapter 12, so don't worry too much about it at the moment. If it's not sinking in right now, trust me, it will later.

Standard music notation involves writing notes on a staff of five lines. For guitar music, we're only concerned with what's called the G clef or treble clef staff, which is shown at the far left of the following illustration:

Where to find the notes on a treble clef.

E F G A B C D E F

Exactly where a note appears is important. The notes on the lines, from bottom to top, are E, G, B, D, and F, which is where the "every good boy" line comes from. The notes occupying the spaces, from bottom to top, are F, A, C, and E.

Lines, Spaces, and Ledger Lines

So far, so good, except that the guitar covers a lot more than the nine notes we just listed. If you think about it logically, you'll notice that each note occupies a line or a space and that each note occurs sequentially, one after the other. So since E is the note at the lowest line of the staff, it makes perfect sense that D would be the note in the space immediately below that line. That specific D note, by the way, corresponds to the note of the open D string on the guitar.

If you want notes lower than this D, then additional lines, called ledger lines, are drawn in below the staff so that it's easier to keep track of the notes.

This same logic works for notes higher than the F located on the top line of the staff, as shown in the following illustration:

Notes on ledger lines.

Converting Notes to Numbers

All that remains now is to figure out how the notes of standard notation correspond to the numbers of guitar tablature. Allow me to do that for you:

The notes on a treble clef and their guitar tablature counterparts.

It might interest you to know that you've just done a good bit of standard music reading, and you seem to have survived it. Knowing how to read the notes, in terms of the note names doesn't take all that long to learn. Here we're dealing with 18 different notes. That means if you learn one note position each day, you'll have them all memorized in less than three weeks! That's certainly worth thinking about …

Rhythm Notation

The true advantage that standard musical notation has over guitar tablature is that the notes in musical notation are able to do two things at once. They not only tell you what note to play, which, as you've just learned, is determined by the note's placement on the staff, but they also tell you just how long to hold that particular note.

Look closely at the earlier example of the fake book version of "House of the Rising Sun." You see that some of the notes vary in appearance as well as in position on the musical staff. The way a note looks tells you how many beats, or even fractions of a beat, to play it.

Being able to keep a steady solid rhythm is important for all musicians, and the guitarist is no exception. A lead guitarist who cannot find the beat is going to sound lost. And let's not even talk about how bad a band can sound if the rhythm guitarist doesn't know how to play in time with his band mates.

Time Signatures

Songs, like people, have pulses, a steady rhythm that pushes the music along from start to finish. The tempo, or pace, of the pulse can be fast or slow.

For most songs, these pulses are counted in sets of four. You've undoubtedly been to a concert or show and heard one of the musicians of the band count off four beats before the band starts in on a song. If you ever saw the Ramones, you probably were amazed that they could turn "one, two, three, four" into a single syllable!

In printed sheet music, every song starts with a *time signature*, which is usually two numbers that look like a fraction, such as these:

Various time signatures.

The top number of the time signature, for now at least, is the number you want to pay the most attention to. It tells you how many beats are in a measure, which is indicated by a single vertical line that crosses through the horizontal lines of either music notation or guitar tablature, as shown here:

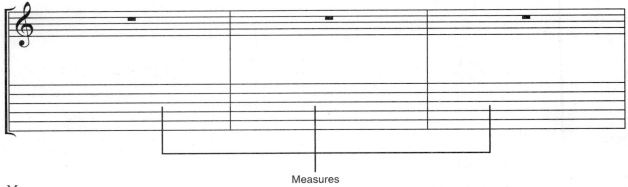

Measures

Measures.

Most rock songs are in 4/4 timing, that is, each measure contains four beats. Remember, though, that beats aren't the same as notes. A single note can last for several beats or it can be as short as a fraction of a beat.

Breaking songs, or guitar solos you might want to learn, into measures makes learning them a little more manageable. No matter how many notes are in the measure, they still add up to four beats in total.

Quarter Notes and Eighth Notes

To get a better grip on all this, let's take a look at two types of notes guitarists use a lot, quarter notes and eighth notes.

Quarter notes look like little black dots on a musical staff. They have a single stem attached to the dot and that stem can either be upturned or downturned, like this:

Examples of quarter notes.

A quarter note lasts a single beat. So when you are counting, "one, two, three, four," you are counting off in quarter notes.

Listen to the CD as you read this example. You hear me begin by counting off four beats to set the tempo and then you hear the guitar playing each note (either the open G string or the A note at the second fret of the G string) right on the appropriate beat.

Track 6

Eighth notes are a half beat in length. In music notation, they look a lot like quarter notes, except they have a single flag attached to their stems. When eighth notes are grouped together in music notation, those flags become a solid bar. Here is an example of eighth notes:

Examples of eighth notes.

To make this easier to understand, I change how I'm counting out the measures. Instead of "one, two, three, four," I'm counting "one *and* two *and* three *and* four *and* …" steadily and evenly. And I'm playing the appropriate note at the appropriate time, on both the numbers and the "ands."

Track 7

And now let's try mixing quarter notes and eighth notes together, like so:

An exercise with both quarter and eighth notes.

Track 8

Because we're using both quarter and eighth notes in this exercise, I'm going with the "one and two and three and four and" style of counting. You can hear that the first quarter note lasts through both the count of *one* and the *and* that immediately follows it, while the next two eighth notes are played on both the *two* and the *and* count.

This may seem like a very simple concept, but it is also very important as you are learning the difference between *beats* (the numbers, when counting out loud) and *offbeats* (the *and*s when counting out loud). A lot of rock rhythms fall on the offbeats, so it's vital to start hearing the time value of notes early on.

Remember Our First Two Songs?

To practice our reading a little more, let's go back to the rock song examples we used at the end of Chapter 2. "Two String Rock" is shown on the next page.

Notice the solid line with the two dots at the end of the last measure? This is a repeat sign, and it tells you to go back to the beginning of the song and play the whole thing all over again.

"Two String Rock"

"Nine Note Rock," written out, is shown on the next page.

I've written out both of these songs in straight quarter notes, but you should try them out as all eighth notes or even a combination of the two, just to get used to the idea of keeping a steady beat.

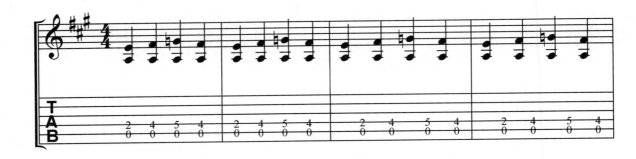

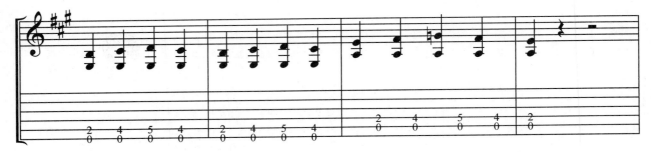

"Nine Note Rock"

Double Stops

Now let's go back to that Em chord you learned earlier in this chapter. We're going to use it to help you learn one more important rock technique.

First, play your Em chord by strumming across all six strings. Then much like you did in the first two rock songs, pick *only* the A and D strings. In other words, play just the two strings your fingers are fretting.

Two notes on adjacent strings are called *double stops* when played at the same time. All guitarists use this technique, whether chugging out chords for rhythm or playing leads. For the rhythm player, double stops plus a bit of distortion gives you a thick rhythm riff without playing entire chords, which can sound muddy when there's either a lot of volume, a lot of distortion, or a lot of musical movement among the other members of the band.

Double stops also help the lead player in much the same way, as you hear in a moment, adding some depth to what otherwise might just be a single note lead line.

It's also important to note here that double stops, while always on adjacent strings, will *not* always be on the same fret. Other common double stops can be one or two frets apart. For instance, a particular rock riff might call for a double stop involving the note at the first fret of the B string played with the note at the second fret of the G string.

Getting Around

Here's a good example of double stops that might sound familiar:

Double stops in the style of "Revolution."

Track 9

The use of double stops in this example is reminiscent of the opening of "Revolution" by the Beatles, although the timing of the notes in this example is different.

This example also introduces the use of *sliding*, a guitar technique that is covered in more detail in Chapter 8. To play this, place your index finger so that it covers *both* the high E and B strings (the two thinnest ones) at the third fret. On the first beat, strike both strings with the pick at the same time, wait half a beat and then slide your index finger up to the fifth fret *without picking the strings again*. The next time you pick the strings will be at the start of the second beat.

One Finger or Two?

When playing double stops, you have to make the decision whether to use two fingers for the notes, as you did with the Em chord, or a single finger covering two strings, as in the "Revolution" example you just played.

There's no right or wrong answer to this. Throughout this book I give you fingering suggestions, but it's important to understand that they are just that—suggestions. Everyone's hands and fingers are different, and what is easily done one way by one guitarist may not be as easy for another.

Just as important, the music itself often dictates what happens. Here's an example of that.

Using both one and two fingers.

Track 10

Personally, I find the easiest way to play this example is to use two fingers (specifically the middle and ring fingers as in the Em chord) for the four notes in the first measure and then, in the second measure, get my index finger to cover the double stops on the fifth fret while my ring finger handles the double stops on the seventh.

At this point in your musical development, it's good to experiment and take note of what works and doesn't work for you. Also, be sure to watch other guitarists as they play and try to pick out what they do when performing this sort of riff. Many do it the same way I described, but definitely not everyone does.

A Rest in Development

You might think, especially if you listen to a lot of fast punk rock, guitarists get paid by the note. The more notes they play the faster the dollars pour in. Nothing could be further from the truth. Music is organic and needs to breathe. And in order to breathe, one must occasionally stop to take a breath, right?

Another advantage to music notation is that in addition to the notes, which tell you when to play, you also have symbols for *rests*, which indicate when to *not* play.

A Short Break

Just as there are different types of notes depending on the length you want the note to be, there are different symbols for rests, and the shape of the symbol tells you how long to rest for.

Here are the symbols for quarter rests, which last for one beat, and eighth rests, which are a half beat long:

Quarter note rests and eighth note rests.

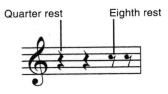

Quarter rest   Eighth rest

def•i•ni•tion

A **rest** is a symbol of music notation that tells you to *not* play on a specific beat, fraction of a beat, or even multiple beats.

When playing a phrase with rests, simply not playing doesn't always work. Your strings will ring a long time after you strike them, so you often will have to assist in making a rest a true moment of silence.

Muting strings, which we discuss a lot in later chapters, can be done in many ways. With the left hand, you can mute a note simply by easing the pressure just enough to stay in contact with the string. Stopping the string vibration deadens the note. To mute the strings with the right hand, you bring the pick to rest against the string just after striking it. You can also stop the string's vibration by resting the heel of your right hand atop the string. Controlling your strings is important. Try to position your right hand so it stays very close to the strings when you're picking, as shown in the following illustration:

Getting Better

Counting the rhythm out loud helps you grasp the rhythm of a song. This is particularly true as you get into trickier rhythms and riffs. Developing an internal metronome takes practice, so whatever you can do to get yourself consistently and steadily locked onto the beat is a good thing.

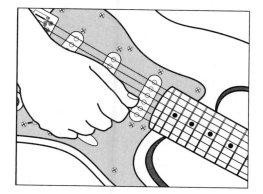

Keeping the right hand close.

Now let's put the rests to practical use with this exercise:

Track 11

A simple exercise involving rests.

Tying Things Together

Obviously, notes don't have to be only one beat or a half beat long. Some are shorter and some are longer. One way of indicating longer notes is the *tie*, which is a short line (looking much like half a parenthesis lying on one side) connecting two notes.

When you see two notes tied together in notation, you play *only* the first note and hold that note for its normal duration *as well as for the duration of the second note.*

Listen to the counting as well as the playing in the following example to make certain you grasp this concept. It's going to be *very* important in upcoming chapters.

Counting with ties.

Track 12

You see in the music notation, as well as hear on the CD, that the third note of this example (an eighth note) is tied to the fourth (a quarter note). This means that the total duration of these tied notes is a beat and a half. So when I play the note at the second half of the second beat, the next note played occurs at the first half of the fourth beat.

Similarly, the last note of the second measure (an eighth note) is tied to the first note of the next measure (a quarter note) so the total length of these tied notes is one-and-a-half beats even though they are spread over two measures. This is a very typical rhythm for a guitarist in rock music.

"Double Stop Rock"

So let's take everything we learned in this chapter and put it to good use. Here is a very cool exercise that I call "Double Stop Rock."

Track 13

Remember to take this very slowly at first, even though it's not a fast song to begin with. Once you have the timing correct, you should feel free to play this song even faster than how it's done on the CD. Just be sure you're playing cleanly and that the rests are still as distinct as they were at slower speed.

"Double Stop Rock"

The Least You Need to Know

◆ Chord charts show you where to put your fingers on the strings in order to play chords.

◆ Guitar tablature tells you what frets to play to produce a note (or notes).

◆ Double stops can be used for both lead and rhythm playing.

◆ Using rests and ties can make guitar rhythms and leads much more interesting.

Part 2

Pick Up My Guitar and Play

Despite what you see, playing rock guitar is a matter of touch and finesse. Learning how to pick just the strings you want, how to get the right sound out of a single note, how to play clean and crisp power chords—these are the building blocks of solid rock guitar. And none of these techniques mean anything if you cannot keep a steady rhythm.

In this part, you find all the basic techniques you will ever need as a rock guitarist, laid out in a step-by-step manner to help you master them quickly. Plus you get some great practice songs to help you work on these fundamentals.

Chapter 4

Finding Finesse

In This Chapter

- There's more to playing than meets the eye
- The importance of listening
- Getting a voice with vibrato
- A new chord—Am
- String bending as an expressive technique

Playing guitar, especially rock music on an electric guitar, is a matter of finesse. You hear seasoned pros say over and over again that making your guitar sound its rocking best starts "with the fingers."

Getting your fingers to make beautiful music when you're just starting to struggle with placing them on the fretboard probably sounds a little daunting. But this is precisely the best time to start thinking about what you want your fingers to do for you.

Developing finesse with your fingers at this early stage also helps you to develop a musician's most important skill—listening.

Even though music is an audio medium, it's amazing how many would-be guitarists want to learn with their eyes instead of their ears. Granted, many people are more visual learners than aural learners, but when it comes to learning to play guitar, it's very easy to be misled by the visual component of playing and, again, this is especially true with rock music.

Don't Be Fooled by What You See

When you watch someone playing guitar at a concert or on a video, can you tell how hard he is strumming or picking the notes? Can you see if he is strumming all six strings of his guitar or just hitting two or three of them?

Try this experiment with your own guitar: First, set the volume of your amplifier at a reasonably low setting (the *2* or *3* on the volume control of the amp) and then set the volume control of your guitar as high as it goes. Needless to say, if it's too loud at these settings, then turn down the volume of your amplifier until the sound is at a reasonable level.

When you're set with the volume, finger your Em chord and strum, with a pick, across all six strings of the guitar. Play with some confidence, but don't overdo it. Listen to how loud you are.

Now strum harder. Really give your guitar a good solid hard strum. Listen to what happens. You'll get a strong initial attack on the strings, yet the volume won't be noticeably louder. But it will be noticeably different in terms of both the sound and the overall tone, or timbre.

Now try playing softer. Again, the initial attack certainly changes, but listen to the change of mood you've created simply by varying the strength of your strum across the strings.

There's More Than Meets the Ear

Now strike just the open A string of your guitar and listen. You hear the A note ringing clean and clear, right? Well, that's really only part of what you're hearing. When you strike a string (regardless of whether you've fretted a note or you're playing the open string) you've generated a lot of tones. The strongest tone that you hear is the actual note that you've played, in this case the A note of the open string. This strongest tone is called the *fundamental*. In addition to the fundamental, you've also caused the string to create a number of *harmonics*, or overtones, that are ringing out at the very same time as the fundamental.

The slightest variations in your picking, whether with the picking hand or the strumming hand, can cause all sorts of changes to the *timbre* or tone of the notes you produce. If you use your fingers instead of a pick to strum, you get a wider range of results because your fingers are capable of hitting the strings much differently and in more varied ways than a pick. Your flesh has more give and take than the consistent surface of the pick.

This is why finesse is one of the two most important aspects to playing rock guitar. There will be times to really belt away at a power chord and times to apply a delicate touch to playing an arpeggio. You wring out notes through bending the strings and you gently coax out harmonics. Simply banging away at your guitar severely limits your ability to produce music that's limited only by your imagination.

Playing vs. Performing

When you watch a band or artist in concert you are seeing both *playing* and *performing*. And there often is a big difference between the two.

def•i•ni•tion

When you pick a string of your guitar, the predominant sound of the note you hear is called the **fundamental**. In addition to the fundamental, the string is also simultaneously generating **harmonics**, overtones that occur naturally from the vibration of the string. Different instruments, even two different guitars, create different sets of harmonics when played, giving them their individual **timbre** or tonal qualities.

Performing is putting on your rock persona and putting on a show. This isn't to say that you're not playing guitar. Quite the contrary! You usually have to be pretty good at playing in order to make it look like you're wildly flailing away at your instrument while still getting exactly the notes and sounds you intend to play.

Many beginners, though, start out trying to learn to play by copying the performances of their guitar idols. They are using the "finished" product as a reference and don't realize that there was a point in time (the "point" probably being many months if not years) that their idol had to work on playing well. In other words, he had to sound like a rock guitarist before he could perform like one.

You Have Six Strings, But ...

When it comes to playing rock, you won't usually find yourself beating away at all six strings of your guitar. More often than not, even when playing rhythm, you probably just use two, three, or four strings at a time.

Playing power chords, which you learn about in the next chapter, generally involves playing two or three strings. And power chords make up a lot of the rhythm guitar work in a lot of rock songs.

Even when you are strumming full chords, you're more likely to find yourself playing *partial chords*, just two or three strings at a time, rather than the full chord. Or perhaps an *arpeggio*, which is playing the full chord one string at a time. Both of these techniques are covered in Chapter 8.

Playing full chords across all six strings of your guitar can sound very muddy when done at high volume levels. You get a lot more clarity, not to mention a better overall sound, when you just play pieces of the chord. Remember that you'll also be playing with a bassist and probably a second guitarist (not to mention possibly a keyboard player or an additional instrumentalist), so all that sound is going to be fighting to be heard.

Likewise soloing, as a rule, tends to involve single notes, and that means playing one string at a time.

Developing the Touch

You may have noticed that so far in this book, with the exception of learning the Em chord, all of the exercises have dealt with playing one or two strings at a time. Partly, this is to help you simply get used to your guitar—to getting your fingers used to making clean notes that sound clear and ring true.

But it is also to help you start to develop some sense of touch, and this finesse will help you become a better rock guitarist right from the start.

One thing you can do to help yourself, particularly at this stage of your learning, is to listen very closely to the notes you're making. When you play one

Getting Better

One of the best ways to develop your ears is to listen to other musicians, whether live or on recordings. Start by listening to songs you know fairly well and see if you can pick out the guitar parts. Then try to determine how many different guitars (if more than one) are playing. Finally, try to listen closely enough to determine whether the guitarist is playing single notes (one string at a time) or strumming two or more strings at once. This may seem a bit simplistic, but if you've not tried listening this way before, it will pose a bit of a challenge.

string or two, do you hear extraneous notes or noise? If so, work on shortening your picking stroke. Keep it compact and economical. Get used to picking only as far as you need to in order to play the notes you want to play.

In time, and with practice, you'll be able to combine your ability to play with performing. Right now, though, it's up to you to work on playing so that you'll sound your best instead of relying totally on show.

Giving Your Guitar a Voice

Fingerprints notwithstanding, everyone's fingers are different. Would-be guitarists who obsess about tone, trying their best to copy the sound of their idols by buying the same make and model guitar (and amplifier, effects, picks, and on and on), never seem to want to consider that their most basic equipment is right at the tips of their hands. One of the biggest reasons guitarists develop highly individual styles and tones is simply because no one else has their hands and fingers.

Take a moment and go back to the "one finger one fret" exercise you did back in Chapter 2. Pick any string, place any finger on any fret, and then play that note. Now experiment a bit and listen to how many subtle differences in that one note you can get by shifting your finger around a bit on that fret.

You often hear people talk about making a guitar "sing." One might consider this a bit of a backhanded compliment as human voices rarely hit a note square on or hold it steady. Vocal notes bend and quiver, and emotion plays as much a role as technique when it comes to singing.

It's the same with you and your guitar. As a beginner you might hit some notes well and with confidence while others may sound a bit tentative and shy. Believe it or not, being able to harness the ability to do both at will is simply a matter of practice and listening. This is how you start to develop both touch and ear skills. And it's the first step toward two very important rock techniques, vibrato and string bending.

Vibrato and Classical Vibrato

An intentional quavering of a note is called *vibrato*. This quavering is a fluctuation of pitch, the fundamental note becomes slightly higher (sharp) or lower (flat) and then returns to its original pitch. The change in pitch is usually quite minute, yet it manages to give the note a more voicelike quality. As you'll see, it's all in the touch.

Vibrato is a technique used by both vocalists and instrumentalists across all genres of music. For stringed instruments, such as the guitar or nonfretted ones such as the violin, vibrato is also a technique used to increase a note's sustain or duration.

Classical-style vibrato is done by playing a fretted note and then rapidly rolling your finger *along* the string in the same direction of the neck (parallel to the other strings) within the fretted area of that note. This style of vibrato is easier to perform on fretless instruments but rock guitarists do employ it on occasion. Because of the frets on the guitar, it requires a bit more finger strength than one might think.

Rock Vibrato

Rock vibrato can be a lot less subtle than classical vibrato. Instead of rolling the finger along the string after playing a note, rock vibrato is achieved by gently pushing and pulling the string *up and down*, perpendicular to the neck, as shown in the following illustration:

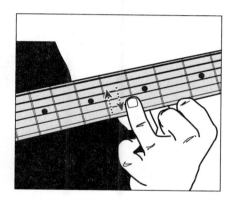

Adding vibrato to a note.

def•i•ni•tion

Vibrato involves a change of pitch, which produces a quavering effect on a note as it momentarily becomes higher (or lower), then returns to the original pitch, becomes higher (or lower) again then returns again to the original pitch, and so on. This quavering occurs very quickly and you may not even hear it as a change of pitch, but it's a vital part of vibrato.

By continually pushing and pulling the string, you give the note a quavering pitch, much like a human voice. You can use your fingers to control how big a range of tones that wavering occurs over. You also control when the vibrato starts or stops.

Note Worthy

Both vibrato and bending (discussed later in this chapter) require you to push the strings of your guitar in order to change the pitch of the original note. As a rule, most guitarists tend to push or pull in a direction toward the center of the neck. In other words, you initially push the three thinnest strings away from the floor and pull the three thickest ones toward the floor.

The initial direction of a vibrato or a bend is often an individual preference, like many aspects of playing the guitar. So experiment with both directions in the early stages of your playing and see, feel, and hear which you way you feel most comfortable with.

Vibrato might look like it's all in the fingers, but just as with bending strings (as you soon learn), the power and control of the vibrato actually comes from the fingers working together with the wrist and forearm.

How Much and When?

Vibrato is an ideal technique to use when playing a single note for more than two or three beats. Not only does the vibrato help you sustain the note in the first place, but it also gives the note a dynamic quality that keeps it interesting to listen to.

As you're learning this technique, try to use it as often as possible, not only so that you can get comfortable with it, but also so you can begin to hear and judge the qualities that you want in your vibrato. Some solos and notes call for an energetic fast quaver while others might seem right for a long and slow-paced vibrato. Ultimately you want to be able to have any style right in your hands when you decide to use it, so don't be afraid of a bit of overkill in these early stages while you get a handle on exactly how to do what you want and when you want to.

By the way, in written music, whether standard notation or guitar tablature, vibrato is indicated by a heavy, wavy line drawn above the note to which the vibrato is applied:

Track 14

Vibrato in music notation.

A Minor

Let's take a break from all this single string work and learn a new chord. This is the open-position A minor or Am chord:

A minor chord.

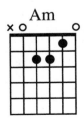

The conventional way to finger this chord is to use your index finger on the first fret of the B string, your ring finger on the second fret of the G string, and your middle finger on the second fret of the D string.

This chord is a good example of the finesse we discussed earlier. Even though the open E note on the sixth string is part of an Am chord, strumming this chord across all six strings sounds a bit muddy (and we get into the reason for that in the next chapter). Try to start your strum of the Am with the A (fifth) string. This takes a little getting used to, but with repetition you will find yourself doing it without thinking twice about it.

A great exercise at this point is to work on changing chords. First, strum your Em chord (from Chapter 3) eight times and then switch to Am and play that eight times as well. For the time being, use only downstrokes and keep the pace relatively slow.

Changing the chords doesn't involve a lot of work. You simply shift your fingers of the Em chord (ring finger on the second fret of the D string and middle finger on the second fret of the A string) one string closer to the floor and then add your index finger to the first fret of the B string to complete the Am.

The goal is to be able to make the switch between the two chords without breaking the pace of the tempo. This is why it's important to start at a speed that allows you to consistently (and cleanly) move from one chord to the next. Once you can perform this change every eight beats, then try it every four beats, then every two, and finally make the change on every beat.

When you have mastered this, gradually start to pick up the tempo. Be sure to go back to changing the chords every eight beats when you do so, as this helps give you the confidence to make the first change at the new tempo.

"Good Vibrato-ations"

Here is a rock song/exercise designed to help you work on your vibrato technique.

This song starts out with a full strum of the Em chord, which you can play either as a downstroke or an upstroke. On the CD, I'm playing an upstroke and also using the pick fairly close to the bridge of the guitar, which is another finesse technique that creates a different timbre than one might otherwise get from strumming the chord with the pick at the center of the guitar body.

> ### Hear How
>
> "Good Vibrato-ations" is inspired by surf music of the 1960s. You can't get better examples of this rock genre than listening to Dick Dale or the Ventures, led by Bob Bogle on guitar. Surf rock, typically instrumental songs usually played on Fender guitars combined the basic rock guitar sound with some jazz-style drumming and a touch of the Latin influences of Southern California's Mexican population.

As with the other songs in this book, I've deliberately taken this at a slow tempo so that you can hear and work through the song with few problems.

When you are comfortable with the piece, feel free to jump the tempo of the song up a few notches and have even more fun with it.

Track 15

"Good Vibrato-ations"

Around the Bends

Perhaps nothing better demonstrates the need for finesse in playing rock guitar than the technique of string bending. Bending is one of the four major ways of slurring notes on a guitar (the other three—hammer-ons, pull-offs, and slides—will be covered later on in Chapter 8). A slur is when you start with a note you play normally (meaning you fret the note with one hand and pick the string you're fretting) and then create a new note just with the fretting hand (as opposed to picking the string a second time).

In essence, bending a note involves the same technique as the vibrato, only a lot more so! Instead of trying to get a slight quaver or modest change in the overall texture of the initial note, you are often trying to get another note altogether. And instead of moving the string in two directions (back and forth to raise *and* lower the pitch), you're only going in a single direction.

To perform a bend, start by fretting a note and then picking that string. After you strike the string, use the finger fretting the note to push the string out of its normal position and toward the center of the neck (width wise). The motion will be very much like turning a door knob or turning the key in a car's ignition. Your finger should push the string *along* the neck and not down into it.

Getting good at bending requires developing the right touch in manipulating the strings, but you're also going to need your ears to help you navigate your way from your starting note to the desired target.

Tracking Your Target

Before getting you started on bending, I'd like to take a moment to help you and your ears understand the task at hand. Listen to the following CD track:

I first play the note at the ninth fret of the B string and then you hear me play the note at the eleventh fret of the B string. The third time I play, I fret the note at the ninth fret of the B string again but, after I do, I bend that note until I reach the note I would normally get by fretting the eleventh fret. This is a bend of a full step (two frets), which (rather appropriately) is often called a *full bend*.

Track 16

After this demonstration, I repeat the exercise, only this time the second note is at the tenth fret of the B string. So the next bend you hear will be a *half bend*, meaning that I bent the note a half step (one fret) higher.

When you are just starting out, make it a point to play the target note, getting it into your head so that you can practice hearing that you've gotten to your desired note. Listening is three quarters of the work in making successful bends.

Bending Tips

The actual mechanics of bending a note are a lot like vibrato. Most of the power of the bend comes from the motion of the wrist and forearm working together.

To give yourself a **good** chance of early success with this technique, start with the thinner strings (E, B, and G), preferably on the higher frets (between the ninth and fifteenth should be good).

Use your ring finger to fret the starting note and also place your middle finger and index finger on the same string, as shown in the following illustration:

Getting Better

Use at least two, if not three, fingers when you're starting out learning how to bend strings. As you get more comfortable with the technique, you'll soon find yourself able to perform most bends using only one finger.

Performing a string bend.

Use your wrist motion to push the fingers, which then push the string. It's important to note here that you don't want to push the string down into the fretboard as much as along it. They should actually be pushing more from the side of the strings than from the top of it. And yes, you will undoubtedly hit the next string when you do this. Don't worry about that yet! As you develop more confidence in your ability, you'll be able to use, surprisingly, a lot less force to get the desired bend.

Timing Counts

Just as performing bends is an art, getting the timing of a bend is also a matter of finesse. Sometimes you want to jump on a note and bend it immediately, but there will also be occasions where you'll want to take your leisure in getting to the target.

When you're playing on your own, the choice is obviously yours, but when you're going off of notation, you need to be able to follow the timing directions concerning the bend.

Take a look at, and listen to, the following examples:

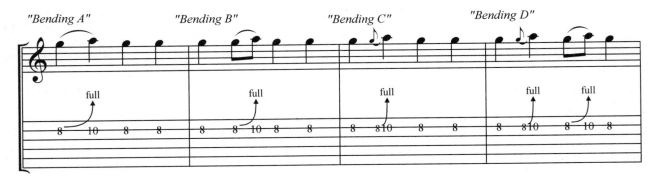

Straight-time bends and grace-note bends.

Track 17

The first two examples are straightforward in terms of timing, the first ("Bending A") using all quarter notes and the second ("Bending B") a combination of quarter notes and eighth notes.

The third example, "Bending C," starts with a *grace note*. That's the very tiny note in the notation (and the tablature number is also smaller). Think of a grace note as an "oops!" You hit the initial note but you have to get to the target note as soon as humanly possible. Ideally, they'd have no timing but that is, of course, impossible. So the idea is to just move as quickly as you can to the next note.

"Bending D," the final of these four examples, combines both grace-note and straight-time bends.

Types of Bends

I cannot stress enough at this point that you are attempting the most difficult task you've faced so far in your learning. Try to relax and don't grind the string into the neck and you'll be fine! The biggest task at hand is to *hear* the target note. Your fingers may take a while to develop, but you have to be able to hear where you want to go.

Full Bends

Start with a full bend, as shown in the following illustration:

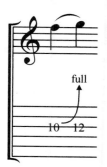

Example of a full bend.

Track 18

Note Worthy
If you find string bending difficult, you might find it helpful either to switch to lighter gauge strings (use extra lights if you're already using lights) or to tune each of your guitar strings down a half step in pitch (more on that in Chapter 19). Each of these suggestions results in less initial string tension, which should make bending the strings a little easier.

Half Bends

It only gets easier from here! Next up is the half bend:

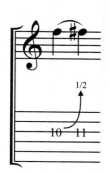

Example of a half bend.

Track 19

Quarter Bends

So far, so good!

Finally, there is what's called the quarter or incidental bend. In spirit, this bend is very close to the idea of vibrato—you're actually targeting a note that technically doesn't exist by name! Use the same targeting technique that you do for the half-step bend, but this time when you bend don't quite get there. You're aiming for a kind of grey area somewhere between the original starting note and the note one fret away.

Track 20

Example of a quarter bend.

These quarter bends truly give your guitar the quality of a human voice, not quite on target, but close enough to give the melody or lead a bit of a melancholy feel.

More Tips

As with vibrato, you want to practice bending with *all* your fingers, including the pinky, which often gets the call for bends on the lowest (thickest) string while playing rhythm.

Also like vibrato, the general rule is to push or pull the bend toward the center of the fretboard. Again, you may find you are very comfortable pulling or pushing in a single direction.

Backward and Forward

Track 21

Of course, what goes up must come down. As you're practicing your bends, you also want to pay attention to releasing your bends. This is where reading the timing of the notes can be very important, so read carefully before you play the following example:

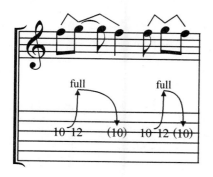

Playing a bend and release.

Unison Bends

Bends are often played in conjunction with other notes, often as double stops (from Chapter 3). In a *unison bend*, you are trying to bend a note on one string to match a note being played at the same time on another string, as in the first of these two examples:

Track 22

Unison bends.

The tricky part of playing a unison bend is in holding one finger steady while performing the bend with a different finger.

Unison bends can be played quickly, as in "Unison A." You're probably thinking that sounds a little like the end of the guitar solo on "Stairway to Heaven," right? A grace-note style unison bend can instantly add a bit of dynamic punch to a single note solo.

And as demonstrated in "Unison B," bends can also be dramatic and slow, especially in bluesy songs, or, at moderate paces, downright rocking in the style of Chuck Berry.

"Bending Matter"

Let's wrap up this chapter with a song designed to give you more than enough practice with the various bends and vibratos you've learned about.

Track 23

"Bending Matter"

The Least You Need to Know

◆ Finesse is vital to playing rock guitar.

◆ Vibrato adds a voicelike quality to notes played on the guitar.

◆ Changing chords takes practice. Changing chords in proper timing takes more practice.

◆ Bending notes is another way of giving your guitar voicelike expression and carries a lot of musical emotion.

◆ Your ears are the most important tool to use when bending notes.

Chapter **5**

Power Chords to the People

In This Chapter

- The E and A Major chords
- Creating power chords
- How to find any possible power chord
- Playing three- and four-string power chords
- How to play octaves

You may not realize it just yet, but you have already put together enough skills to play hundreds, if not thousands, of rock songs. You're probably thinking that I'm just setting you up, but it's no exaggeration.

First off, a great many rock songs contain only three or four chords. You already know two of those chords—Em and Am—and after you're done with this chapter those two will have multiplied into two dozen!

The second reason you'll be good to go is that you won't have to play full chords, not just yet anyway. Yes, that's a bit cryptic but, as you've learned already, you don't have to hit all six strings of your guitar to play a chord. Sometimes two is not only more than enough, for some songs it's all you'll ever need.

E Chord Shapes

Let's start out by reviewing the Em chord you learned back in Chapter 3. You might remember my suggestion at the time was to use your ring finger on the second fret of the D string and your middle finger on the second fret of the A string. There was a reason for that! Right now you want to take that free index finger and place it on the first fret of the G string, which changes your Em chord into an E (also called E Major) chord, as shown in the following illustration:

Track 24

Changing the Em chord into E Major.

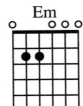

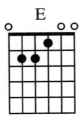

Major and Minor

Listen to these two chords being played on the CD. Do you hear a distinct difference between the Em you learned earlier and the new chord, E? Some people think that major chords sound cheerful and happy while minor chords sound a little sad and melancholy.

What you think of the difference between these chords in terms of musical emotions isn't as important as the fact that you *can* hear a difference. Play both chords and listen closely and make certain you do hear this tonal change.

Being able to distinguish between major and minor chords is a big step toward developing your ear training. When you can hear whether a chord on a recording (or at a concert) is either a major chord or a minor one, you can use that knowledge to help you figure out songs just by listening to them. Developing a sense of major and minor tonalities also helps you immensely when you're improvising a solo or trying to write a riff for a song.

Eliminating the "Tunks"

There's another good reason to ask if you can hear the difference when you play these two chords—it's very possible that you might not hear the difference. If so, then there's a chance that you might need to readjust your finger placement.

Up until this point, you've only fretted two strings at a time. Adding one more string to the mix can complicate matters. If you can't hear a difference, set your fingers in place for the E chord one more time and this time when you strum, strike each string slowly, starting with the thickest one and picking until you reach the thinnest one. Listen as you pluck each string, making certain that the notes of each ring out clean and true.

One or more of the notes might sound a bit off; in fact, you might hear a distinct unk or clunk instead of a clean note. This usually indicates that you're inadvertently muting one or more of the strings as you're trying to fret the chord.

Typically, the ring finger is the culprit in this case. Make certain that your ring finger is on its tip and that your knuckle hasn't collapsed inward. If it has, your ring finger may be brushing against the G string, and that's why you're getting a tunk there.

Another typical beginner scenario involves the high E (thinnest) string not ringing cleanly. If this is the case, you've probably forgotten the lesson of the glass from Chapter 2 and are holding the neck of the guitar too tightly. If you can feel the lower edge of the neck of your guitar against the palm of your fretting hand, loosen up! When you grab hold of the neck your fingers almost automatically slant and mute strings, and instead of six clean notes produced by proud fingertips, you end up with a handful of tunks.

Take the time here and now to get a good, clear sounding E chord. Then practice switching between the Em and E chords for a while to make certain you're comfortable with them.

E7 and Em7

Once you have your E and Em chord down, it's time to learn two new, and very easy, chords. All you have to do is to form either the E or Em chord and then lift your ring finger off the D string like so:

Track 25

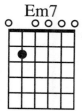 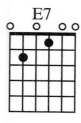

Em7 and E7.

These chords are E7 and Em7. They are called seventh chords because the flatted seventh note of the major scale has been added to them. And you can hear on the CD that the difference between E and E7 is markedly more subtle than the difference between E and Em. And Em7 might just become your all-time favorite chord because it involves using just one finger on one string!

Again, take your time here to get accustomed to these new chords and to changing between them. You don't need a set routine to do this, just play any of the four chords—Em, E, Em7, and E7—for a number of beats and then switch to another. You will probably find these chord changes fairly routine after some concentrated practice.

Taking Root

Chords, as you learned in Chapter 3, are made by combining certain notes together. Later you learn that each note of the chord serves a particular function. One such note is the *root note* of a chord. Figuring out the root note of a chord is easy, although the explanation may at first seem a bit circular. The root note of any chord is the note that shares the note name of the chord.

def•i•ni•tion

The **root note** of any chord shares the same note name of the chord. It's that easy. Remember that sharps and flats are part of note names while major, minor, diminished, and augmented, as well as various numbers you'll be learning later, are part of chord names. Even though you've never played one (or probably have never even heard of it), you can say with total confidence that the root note of the Cm13 chord, just to pick a random chord, is C. The root note of F#7 is F#.

For instance, the root note of the E chord (remember that this is also called E Major) is E. To make matters more interesting, the root note of the E minor chord (or Em, as we're used to reading it) is also E. This is because major and minor are names of chords. Our note names are A, B, C, D, E, F, and G, and each of those notes can also be either sharp or flat.

Five or Six Strings?

In learning the Am chord in Chapter 4, we briefly discussed how that particular chord sounded better when played from the A string down, instead of strumming all six strings. Generally speaking, most chords tend to sound cleaner and less muddied when the root note is the lowest note played as you strum any specific chord. Because the root note of the Am chord is A, and the lowest A note on your guitar is the note of the open A string, strumming an Am chord from the open A string down, as opposed to strumming all six strings, will give you a clearer sounding chord.

If you play an Am chord with all six strings, the harmonic overtones generated by the low E string tend to overwhelm the low end of the chord and you lose definition of the tonal center, the A in this case, which also happens to be the root note of the chord! I told you it was a circular explanation.

Knowing the root note becomes important for other reasons later on, and so does determining on which string to play that root note. When a chord has its root note on the low E (thickest) string, it is called a Root 6 chord because the low E is the sixth string (the first string being the thinnest one). Both E and Em are Root 6 chords.

Am, on the other hand, is a Root 5 chord because its root note (A) is found at the open A string. Of course, this will get slightly more complicated later on because you can find any note on any string. For the moment, just keep the idea of Root 6 and Root 5 chords in your head so we can move along to another new chord.

A Chord Shapes

The A Major chord is not all that different from Am, but it can pose some interesting questions:

Track 26

Am and A Major.

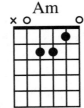

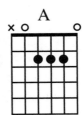

The Many Fingerings of A Major

Most people first fret the A chord by using their ring finger on the second fret of the B string, their middle finger on the second fret of the G string, and their index finger on the second fret of the D string. And usually they find this a bit awkward or uncomfortable, so they then discover that having the index and middle fingers change strings (index on the second fret of the G string and middle finger on the second fret of the D string) is not only easier to fret, but usually results in a cleaner sounding chord.

Some folks, especially those with larger fingers, have a hard time getting three fingers to fit side by side by side on any given fret. One solution is to lay one finger (usually the index) slightly flatter so that it can cover both the G and D strings while the middle finger stands at the second fret of the B string. This fingering is used quite often in classical guitar.

Another option is to lay one finger across all three strings at the second fret. This is not usually recommended as most people's fingers will also cover the high E (first) string as well, which creates a very different sounding chord. But if you have very flexible finger joints or if you can strum accurately enough to never hit that first string, this might work for you.

Getting Better

There is usually no single correct way to form any chord. Your primary concern should be to get from one chord to the next with the smoothest movements possible. Minimal movement usually translates into smooth and easy chord changes, but there will be many times when a total change of fingering will be required to fret a chord.

A7 and Am7

Making seventh chords for both A and Am is very similar to what you did with the E7 and Em7 chords. Instead of lifting a finger off the D string, it's the G string that you want to ring out as an open note:

Track 27

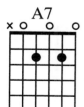 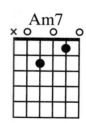

A7 and Am7.

At this point it would be good to review the new chords you've learned so far in this chapter, as well as to take time to practice switching between any and all possible combinations of these chords. You're just about ready to start playing some very serious rock and roll!

Is It Major, Minor, or Something Else?

All right, then, so far you can play E and Em, and A and Am, not to mention E7, Em7, A7, and Am7. For the time being, we're going to put the seventh chords aside (they'll come back in Chapter 9) and just concentrate on the major and minor chords.

First, play the E chord and listen to it. Then play the Em chord and listen again carefully. Hopefully by this time you're hearing the difference between the major and minor chords fairly clearly.

Now play either the E or Em chord one more time, only this time play *only the three thickest strings*, the ones closest to you. Do this again and listen closely. Is this a major or a minor chord?

Track 28

Repeat this same procedure using A and Am. For our new "mystery chord" strike only the A, D, and G strings. Both these new chords are shown (and played) in the next illustration:

E and A power chords (E5 and A5).

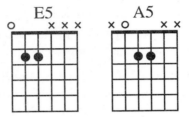

Some people hear these new chords as being major and some will hear them as being minor. How about you?

The 5th Power

Technically speaking, these new chords are neither major nor minor. You learn in Chapter 13 that major and minor chords are made up of three different notes, specifically the first (which is, by the way, the root note), third, and fifth notes taken from the major scale.

For our latest chords, you are playing only two of those three notes—the first and the fifth. These are called power chords. They are often referred to as 5 chords because they are made of the root note and the fifth note from the major scale. So for example, the E5 chord from our last example contains the E note (the root) and B note (second fret of the A string), which is the fifth note of the E Major scale. The third note, the one at the second fret of the D string, is another E. It is an *octave* higher (eight notes) than the open low E string.

The Heart of Rock

Power chords are the foundation of most rock music, the solid ground that the rock guitarist starts on. Once you can handle forming and fretting power chords, and once you get a grasp on rhythm, you can play the rhythm parts of hundreds, if not thousands, of songs.

As easy as they seem, it does take some beginners a short while to get comfortable playing power chords. You've just played the two easier ones, and we can make those two even easier by making them two-string chords instead of three-stringed ones, like this:

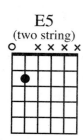

E5
(two string)

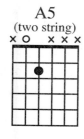

A5
(two string)

E5 and A5 using just two strings.

This is a good place to use all that picking accuracy you've developed these first four chapters. It's important to strike only the strings you want to so that your power chords sound true.

Where's the Root?

Let's examine the two-string E5 chord a little closer. The root note, E, is the open E string. The *5* note (B in this case) is on the second fret of the A string.

Looking at the two-string A5 power chord, you can see the same pattern. The root, A, is the open A string and the *5* is the second fret of the D. You also know from our earlier discussion of three-string E5 chord that this note at the second fret of the D string is E. So E is the fifth of A5. That information will be handy later.

Did you notice a pattern to these chords? The *5* note for both is on the next higher string, two frets up the neck. If you remember from our earlier discussion that the E is a Root 6 chord (the root note being on the sixth string) and the A is a Root 5 chord, you might assume that this "root/5 note" relationship could apply to any note along the fifth and sixth strings. Taking a fingering pattern of one chord and moving it someplace else on the neck of the guitar to create another is an example of a moveable chord.

Why not test this out? Pick any note you want on the low E (sixth) string. How about the one at the fifth fret? You already know from Chapter 2 (the tuning section) that this note is A. Place your index finger on that note. Now place your ring finger on the seventh fret of the A string. The ring finger is one string higher and two frets up the neck, so this should be the *5* note. Strum those two strings and see if they don't sound just like the A5.

You're probably thinking, "I know that the *5* note of A5 is E because I just read it three paragraphs ago. So if I place my index finger on the seventh fret of the A string and then put my ring finger on the ninth fret of the D string, I should have a new version of the E5 chord." And you'd be absolutely right, as you can see in the following illustration.

When you play the same chord at a different spot along the neck of the guitar, you are giving that chord a new voicing. Every chord you learn can be played in multiple places on the fretboard, and this choice of voicing can be very important, especially if you're playing with other musicians.

Different locations of E5 and A5.

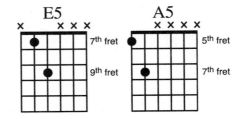

Stretching Out

Track 29

Even though these power chords are simple, beginners can find this two-fret stretch a bit much to handle at first. You'll probably find it easier to start practicing this power chord shape higher up the neck where the frets are spaced closer together. Begin with your index finger at the tenth fret (which means your ring finger will be at the twelfth fret), as shown in the following exercise:

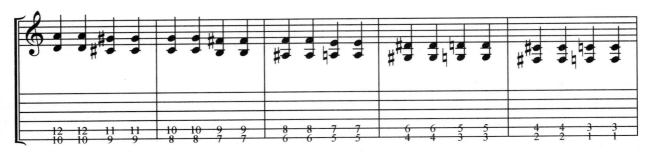

Power chord stretching exercise.

Gradually work your way down one fret at a time. When the stretch becomes too wide for you and your fingers start to hurt, stop. Relax and shake out your hand and go back to the tenth and twelfth frets and start again. Today you may only be able to get down to the fifth and seventh frets. But if you try this out every day, edging yourself a little further along as you get more and more comfortable, you should be able to make the biggest stretch (the first and third frets) within a week.

Filling Out the Power

As you are working on the previous exercise, you can also start giving your power chords a little more oomph by turning your two-string power chords into three-string versions.

You've already had a taste of three-string power chords. If there's a trick to them it's in deciding how to go about fingering the chord further up the neck. Look at the following two three-string versions of the E5 and A5 voicings you played earlier.

The typical way to play these involves your pinky. First, as shown on the A5 (Root 6) example above, you start out just as you did with the two-string version, using your index finger on the root note (fifth fret of the low E string in this case) and your ring finger on the 5 note (seventh fret of the A string). Then simply drop your pinky onto the seventh fret of the D string.

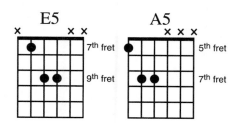

Three-string power chords.

If using your pinky feels awkward, don't give up! Chances are you've not been using it all that much (unless you've been diligent about the "one finger one fret" warm up exercises) and you are going to want that finger available for duty.

Another way many guitarists play three-string power chords is to lay the ring finger a little flatter so that it covers both notes on the A and D strings. Then use the tip of the index finger to fret the root note on the low E string.

Some players lay the ring finger totally flat because they know they don't want to hit the higher strings anyway. All that practice hitting just the strings they want to must be paying off!

Ideally, you want to be able to use either of these methods to play three-string power chords. Use the "stretching exercise" from earlier this chapter in order to get yourself used to making the stretch of three-string power chords.

But why stop at three strings when you can have four? Any Root 5 power chord can be changed into a four-string power chord by adding the note on the sixth string that's on the same fret as the root note on the fifth string, like this:

E5
(four string)

Four-string power chords.

To play a four-string power chord, you want to lay out your index finger so it covers both the fifth and sixth strings. For the D and G strings, you can use either two fingers (I suggest the ring and pinky, respectively) or use the ring finger to get the notes on both those strings.

Again, you want to use the "stretching exercise" from before to help you get acclimated to these power chords. The idea is to feel that you can make any power chord—whether two-, three-, or four-string—at any point along the neck.

Hear How

You probably won't have to dig too far into your CD collection or your MP3 player to find songs that are pretty much all power chords. From old metal bands like Black Sabbath to punk rockers like the Ramones, from AC/DC to Nirvana, you find power chords wherever you turn.

Moving About

When you think about it, learning chords is just a small part of making music. It's very important, but it's easy for beginners to get the wrong impression because the only way to learn chords is statically. You see a chord chart, you figure out where your fingers are supposed to go and which strings you're supposed to pick, and there you are.

The trouble with static learning is that, when you are playing, you have to change from one chord to the next (and to the next) until the song is done. As you're figuring out, it's one thing to play a chord and it's an entirely different matter to move smoothly from one chord to the next. That's why we spend so much time discussing changing chords in Chapter 4.

With power chords, and especially with fast-driving rock songs, you have to be able to find the place for the chord on the neck, get your fingers into the right shape, and also be sure to hit just the right number of strings, often in less time than it takes to blink.

Start Out Slow and Easy

You want to remember that getting fast is often just a matter of simple repetition. But the repetition has to be clean, so you shouldn't start out at a pace that's so quick you can't make the changes in the first place.

It also helps to begin with simple changes. Here are some common power chord shifts:

Track 30

Power chord changing exercises.

Notice that the first few changes involve simply changing strings. Get that small step under your belt first and you gain the confidence to make the moves up and down the neck in no time.

Fretboard Map

Of course, it certainly helps when you know where you want to go. Remember back at the beginning of this chapter when I told you that you'd be able to play two dozen chords? Well, you're actually going to be able to play one dozen chords in two different places!

Here is a chart of the A and low E strings of your guitar, complete with the note names on each fret:

fret	1	2	3	4	5	6	7	8	9	10	11	12
open												
A 0	A♯/B♭	B	C	C♯/D♭	D	D♯/E♭	E	F	F♯/G♭	G	G♯/A♭	A
E 0	F	F♯/G♭	G	G♯/A♭	A	A♯/B♭	B	C	C♯/D♭	D	D♯/E♭	E

Notes on the fifth and sixth strings.

Because you now know how to make power chords (both two- and three-string versions) for any note on the fifth and sixth strings, you can use this chart to help you learn what the power chord you're playing is! Remember that the root note has the same note name of the chord. So for instance, if you need to play a G♯5 chord for any reason, you will be able to figure out that you want to place your index finger on the fourth fret of the low E string (for a Root 6 power chord) or on the eleventh fret of the A string (for a Root 5 power chord) and then position your ring finger (and pinky if you're using it) on the appropriate fret to complete the chord.

Octaves

You can also use the basic three-string power chord shape to play *octaves*. Do you remember the song "Do, Re, Mi" from *The Sound of Music*? The scale is sung, "do, re, mi, fa, so, la, ti, do." Notice that the note on both ends of the scale is "do." It has the same note name but sounds higher. It is eight notes higher, if you count the note you start on as *one*, and so it's called an octave.

Using octaves can make a rhythm part more interesting than just strumming power chords all the time. And playing octaves is a good way to give a single note solo both depth and dynamics.

Mute Point

To play an octave, start with a three-string power chord. The first one in the following exercise is our old friend, the Root 5 E5 from earlier in this chapter:

Track 31

Octaves changing exercises.

Hear How

Mastering octaves requires both time and patience, not to mention careful listening (for unwanted noise) on your part. But the technique itself can be quite stunning when used well. You can find octaves used across almost all genres from jazz (Charlie Christian, Django Reinhardt, and Wes Montgomery) to recent rockers like Blink-182 and Fallout Boy.

So you've got your index finger on the seventh fret of the A string and either your ring finger or pinky on the ninth fret of the G string. Now comes the tricky part. If you try to strum across all three strings, you're going to play an extra note (the one on the D string), which isn't one of the octave notes. So you have to somehow mute this extra note. Slightly flatten your index finger so that it partially catches the D string, just enough so that you get a good tunk on that one string when you strum across all three.

Another option is to lightly touch the D string with a free finger (probably the middle or ring finger). Once again, the objective here is to get a good tunk on purpose! Just when you thought you'd never have a need for a bad habit, right?

Playing octaves is another technique that seems quite simple but usually takes a while to develop the touch and finesse required to perform accurately and at will. You can use the exercise you've just seen, but you can also use the "stretching exercise" from earlier in this chapter to help you get a good feel for what you want to do.

You Don't Have to Use a Pick

Some people really don't like the sound of the tunks, even though it's usually drowned out by the octaves as they are played. You can totally avoid the muted string by picking octaves with your fingers. Typically, you would pick the lower of the two notes with your thumb and the higher one with a finger.

Using your fingers can give both notes a sharper attack and you can also better control the volume of each note with your fingers than you can with a pick.

Another option is to use a technique called *hybrid picking*. In hybrid picking, the thumb and index fingers hold the pick (generally playing it on only the fourth, fifth, and sixth strings) while the middle, ring, and pinky fingers are used to pluck notes on the three higher strings. This technique takes a *lot* of practice, so don't expect it to come to you overnight.

"Power Point"

So how about a song to reinforce what you've learned about power chords and octaves?

This song uses some notation you haven't seen yet. The entire third line is under a bracket that starts with the number *1*. At the end of the third line notice the repeat signs. Also notice that the entire fourth line is under a bracket labeled *2*. These are called *first and second endings*. You start at the beginning of the song and play the first three lines. When you get to the repeat sign at the end of the third line, you go back to the beginning of the song and start again.

This time, though, when you get to the end of the second line, you skip the entire third line and go directly to the fourth line to finish the song.

Track 32

continues

continued

"Power Point"

The Least You Need to Know

◆ There is a big difference in sound between a major and a minor chord.

◆ Power chords are neither major nor minor and are used in thousands of rock songs.

◆ Power chords can be played on two, three, or four strings.

◆ If you can find the correct root note on either the A or low E string, then you can play any of the 12 possible power chords.

◆ Playing octaves gives both rhythm and lead parts an interesting new dimension.

Chapter 6

Some Rhythm (and a Bit of Blues)

In This Chapter

- ◆ Rhythm is king
- ◆ How to read rhythm notation
- ◆ The downs and ups of strumming
- ◆ Triplets and swing eighths
- ◆ Alternate picking

Without rhythm, music might as well be noise. It's the beat—the pulse of a song—that gets you tapping your foot or clapping or dancing. Any musician, any guitar player, whether he or she plays rock or jazz or blues or country or reggae or folk music from Bolivia, has to be able to keep a steady beat.

Not surprisingly, rhythm tends to be a major concern with beginning guitarists. Compounding the trouble is that many people have come to think of rhythm in terms of visual cues, such as watching the down and up of a guitarist's strum. There is *nothing* about rhythm that is visual. Rhythm is heard and rhythm is felt, but rhythm is not seen.

Another common misconception among novice players is the belief in *strumming patterns*, the idea that one constant unchanging series of down and up strokes produces music. Music without rhythm may be noise, but rhythm by rote, rhythm without heart, is just as sterile.

Yet one of the best ways to learn about rhythm is by reading notation. And one of the best ways to develop rhythm is to repeatedly get it into your system so that it's like a second skin. Quite the paradox, wouldn't you say?

Reading for the Ears

As you learned in Chapter 3, guitar tablature rarely gives you any indication of how the rhythm of a song, or even a short riff, is supposed to be played. Music notation, on the other hand, tells you both the notes needed to be played *and* the proper rhythm in which to play them. However, if you're strumming full chords, reading six notes stacked one atop the other can certainly be a daunting task.

Fortunately, there is a practical solution—rhythm notation.

At first glance, rhythm notation looks a lot like regular music notation, as you can see in this illustration:

Example of rhythm notation.

Note Worthy

Many books of guitar transcriptions from recorded music use lines of rhythm notation, usually placed over the vocal line (which is written in standard notation) and below the chord markings.

If you look carefully, you can see that instead of a regular note, the familiar little dot, there is a dash attached to the stem. Where this dash appears on the staff is irrelevant because the note itself isn't important. All you're interested in is the rhythmic value of that note.

In the preceding example, you also notice *Em* printed above the first note in the first measure. This indicates that you're to play an Em chord until you are told otherwise and that you are to strum it according to the rhythm specified in the notation.

While we're on the subject of rhythm, here are two new types of notes to learn:

Whole notes and half notes (and their rests) in standard notation and rhythm notation.

Whole notes, shown in standard notation in the first measure and in rhythm notation in the second, are four beats in length. In both standard notation and rhythm notation, whole notes look a lot like open holes, although slightly stylized. The note head is slightly larger than those of the quarter notes and eighth notes.

Half notes look like a cross between whole notes and quarter notes. The head of the half note is the same size as those of quarter notes and eighth notes but it is hollow, not filled in. The half note also has a stem like the quarter note but without the flag of the eighth note.

The corresponding rest symbols for half notes and whole notes look very much alike—a thin black box shape on a line. But look closely and you see that the whole rest (a rest of four beats in length) hangs below the line while that half rest (a rest of two beats) sits atop the line.

You might have noticed that while the whole note in the first measure is B (on the middle line of the music staff) and the two whole notes in the third measure are both As (second space from the bottom on the music staff), the rhythm notation in measures two and four are all squarely in the middle of the staff. Most music notation software does this and, again, that's why it's important to ignore where on the staff the slash of the rhythm notation is placed. The important information of rhythmic notation is the rhythmic shape of the note.

Basic Strumming

Now that you have a way to read rhythms, as well as two new rhythmic notes to remember, we should also get on the same page concerning strumming itself. Up to this point we've used fairly basic types of rhythm, just quarter notes and eighth notes plus their equivalent rests, but rock music can get fairly complicated, rhythmically speaking, so let's go over a few basics.

Make an Em chord and strum it down toward the floor four times. Count along out loud as you do so. Don't be shy! Counting is a vital part of rhythm, and you'll be amazed at how it can help you out. Tempo, meaning the speed at which you played these four quarter notes, is not a factor here. Keeping the beat steady is what you should focus on. Don't have the third and fourth beats be twice the speed of the first two.

Okay, you've made the chord and strummed it four times and by counting the beat, not to mention playing the chord on the beat, you can say that you've just played four quarter notes.

So what did you do on the upstrokes?

Upstrokes

You might be thinking, "I didn't make any upstrokes." But actually you did. You had to. Without an upstroke you would not have been in a position to play the second beat of Em as a downstroke. In other words, you made the motion of the upstroke but you didn't strike the strings while making the upstroke.

To put it more plainly, you *missed* the upstroke. This may seem overly simple but it's an important step to understanding how to play the guitar rhythmically.

Let's discuss strumming strokes for a moment. When you play a downstroke, you usually play from one of the three thickest strings down to the floor. On an E or Em chord, for example, you strum all six strings. On an A or Am you start with the A string and strum five strings down.

On an upstroke, you usually don't want to strum all the strings. Try playing an Em chord, strumming all six strings down and then all back up and listen to how much sound there is and how muddled it gets! Generally, you want to just catch two or three of the higher strings (high E, B, or G) on the upstroke.

The easiest way to ensure a shorter upstroke is have the wrist do the work. Think of it as cocking your hand for the next downstroke.

Getting More Musical

Track 33

It's time to become more musical in your strumming. The following illustration shows the two simple patterns used for practice so far (one measure of quarter notes and one measure of eighth notes) for two chords, Em and A7:

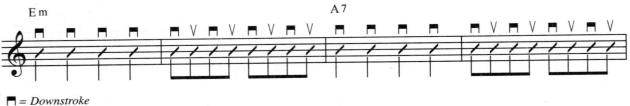

⊓ = *Downstroke*

v = *Upstroke*

Simple strumming of quarter notes and eighth notes.

I picked these two chords because switching between them shouldn't give you all that much trouble. Take a few minutes and get comfortable with the chords and with counting the beats.

Start with a slight variation of the "four quarter note" pattern, as shown in the next exercise. On the second beat, play two eighth notes instead of one quarter note.

Track 34

Be sure to count and keep the beat steady (as you can hear me counting on the CD) and use both a downstroke and an upstroke on this second beat. Using two quick downstrokes is certainly possible, but it might throw off your timing. And I'd like you to get accustomed to playing both types of strokes when strumming.

Mixing quarter notes and eighth notes in strumming.

Counting to Four

You can hear that this latest exercise sounds more musical than either of the patterns involving all quarter notes or all eighth notes. Here are some more simple strumming exercises using combinations of quarter notes and eighth notes.

Each of these four lines contains a different strumming pattern, and each sounds slightly different from the others. When you practice these, be certain to play the eighth notes using both downstrokes and upstrokes. Listen to the differences of the patterns when you play so that you can hear the beat and feel it as you strum.

Practice one pattern at a time until you can play it, with the chord change, steadily and evenly. Can you do it with your eyes closed? Can you strum the pattern, keep the beat, and hold a conversation without losing the beat? Then you've got it down.

Track 35

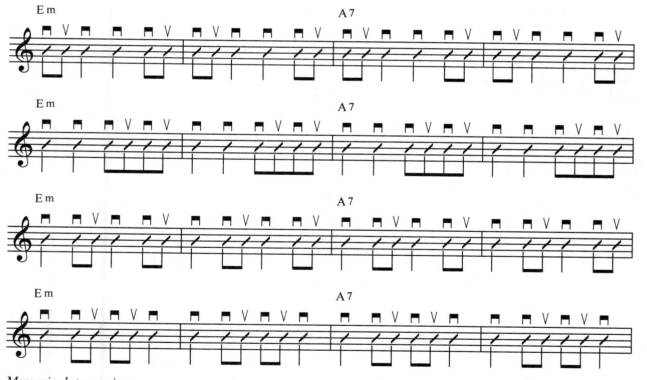

More mixed strumming.

Pattern Patter

The question now is "Which pattern is *right?*" That seems to be an absurd question, doesn't it? But that's what people are asking all the time when they want to know a "strumming pattern of a song."

Track 36

When someone talks about a song's strumming pattern, he or she is usually referring to the strumming of a guitar taken at the time of the recorded performance of a song. Pattern implies that there is one set of strumming throughout the song, but musicians rarely do that. It's one thing to practice patterns as those in the last exercise, but when playing live, it's a good bet that things will get a little mixed up, like this:

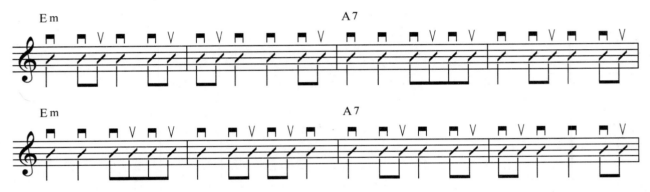

Combining strumming patterns.

There is a real danger in thinking of patterns as "downs and ups" instead of thinking of them in terms of beats. As you'll learn, we can subdivide beats into smaller units than eighth notes, into thirds of beats, quarters of beats, and even smaller pieces. And we haven't even started adding in tied notes or rests!

If you're concentrating on the beat and you change up your pattern by missing an up or down or moving it to a different place in the measure, as with this last example, no one is going to think twice about it because you're keeping the beat steady. Slight strumming alterations in a pattern, made while maintaining the beat, sound organic and real.

On the other hand, if you're concentrating on the pattern and you miss an up or down, chances are it's going to throw you off and it might take a beat or so for you to recover. It's hard for anyone not to hear that.

So instead of fixating on a pattern, focus your attention on the beat and you'll be able to play with good rhythm.

Taking a Giant Step

Up to now all of our strumming exercises have involved various combinations of quarter notes and eighth notes, and while they have been interesting, you've probably not found them to be very tricky. That's about to change.

I want you to take one of our earlier exercises and, for the moment, forget about the chord change. Just play this strum with only the Em chord for a few measures to get the beat into your head. Do yourself a favor and count it out loud:

Strumming the E minor chord.

At this point in your strumming, you probably don't even think twice about the fact that you're often missing the strings on some of your upstrokes. If you think about it at all, you might simply feel you're "skipping the up" on your way to the next downstroke.

Skipping a Down

This next exercise is almost identical to the previous one, except you're not going to play the third beat (notice the tied notes). Be sure to listen to the count on the CD:

Track 37

Skipping the downstroke in a strumming pattern.

Most beginners have trouble with this initially because they are thinking in terms of "downs and ups" and not thinking about the beat. In every exercise you've played so far, you've kept your wrist moving in accordance to the beat. Remember the imaginary string connecting your toe to your wrist? That hasn't broken!

Focus on keeping your wrist movement steady and count out loud until you can get this exercise down pat. Remember that if you miss "missing the down," the strum is going to sound just like the earlier exercise. Who besides you is going to notice?

More important, if you can grasp this concept of missing the beat and playing only on an offbeat, there is not a rhythm pattern alive that you won't be able to master, given the time to work on it.

More Rhythms to Practice

For the moment, though, let's work on some relatively simple rhythm patterns. Here are some that combine the ideas we've used so far.

Each line in this exercise has a separate pattern. When you can play each line well, try combining the various strums. The idea is that you are teaching your hand a variety of rhythmic strums so it will be able to shift from one strum to the next without you consciously thinking much about it. It's like walking on a crowded sidewalk—you're constantly making minor adjustments to avoid bumping into people or mailboxes or other objects while maintaining a steady, even pace.

Track 38

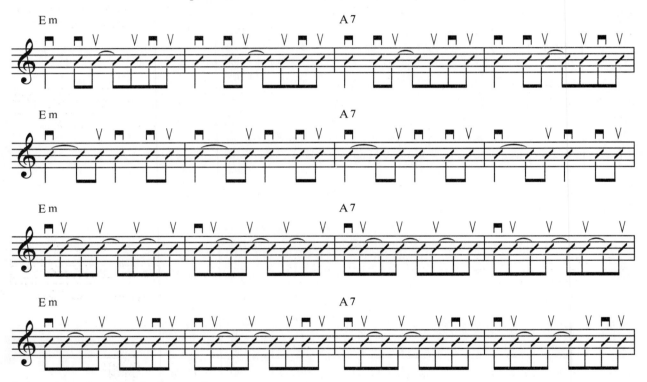

Strumming patterns for rhythm practice.

Swinging in Time

Rock 'n' roll rhythms, quite obviously, involve more than just eighth notes and quarter notes. Part of rock's history springs from the deep waters of the blues, so you will find many rock songs with blues rhythms. Jazz rhythms, too.

Listen to a song like "Paranoid" by Black Sabbath and compare its rhythm to a song like "Sweet Home Chicago." Remember that the rhythm, or pulse, is not about tempo (speed). You can play both of these songs at the same tempo, yet their rhythms sound quite different. "Paranoid" sounds steady, like someone running at a furious pace, but still keeping an even gait. "Sweet Home Chicago," on the other hand, has a lighter feel. You can almost imagine a person skipping along to it, albeit skipping quite rapidly!

This skipping feel is often called a *shuffle*, but most musicians refer to it as swing. And it comes from dividing a beat into thirds (or *triplets*) instead of halves (eighth notes).

The Triplet

As mentioned earlier, beats can be subdivided into all sorts of smaller units. When a beat is divided into even thirds, the resulting note is a triplet, which looks like three eighth notes beamed together with a little *3* written over (or under) the beam. The following illustration shows triplets in both standard notation and rhythm notation:

Triplets shown in standard notation and rhythm notation.

Playing triplets can be tricky, so it's good to figure out how best to approach them. Here are the two typical ways guitarists strum triplets:

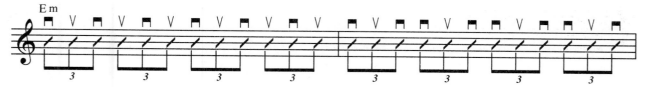

Strumming triplets.

The first method uses alternate picking (which we discuss in earnest later this chapter), switching from down to up with each note of the triplet. While this certainly works, it can get a bit tricky at faster tempos and your triplet could accidentally turn into four or more sixteenth notes (sixteenth notes, as you learn in Chapter 10, are a quarter of a beat in duration).

Track 39

The second method starts out each triplet on a downstroke. Doing so clearly helps to define where the beat is, but you have to get used to playing two quick downstrokes (the third note of the triplet and the first note in the ensuing triplet) one after another. That means developing a bit of a "hiccup" in your upstroke.

Whichever method you find works for you, practice with it so that you feel very comfortable with triplets. You run into them a lot in rock music, especially when it comes to soloing.

def•i•ni•tion

The rhythm style of most blues and blues-based rock songs is also often called a **shuffle**, but that can be confusing because a lot of books subdivide shuffles into blues shuffles and rock shuffles. Blues shuffles are played in swing eighths while rock shuffles are played in straight eighths.

Swing Eighths

If you listen closely to a blues shuffle, you might be wondering why we're discussing triplets at all. There are two notes played in each beat, they just aren't evenly dividing the beat the way eighth notes do.

Track 40

That's true. And the two notes of a blues shuffle or swing rhythm are created by starting with a triplet and then removing the middle of the three notes from it. In other words, you play only the first and third notes of the triplet, as shown in the following illustration (and CD example):

Triplet played without middle note = "Swing Eighths" (often written out as regular eighth notes)

Defining swing eighths.

Try this exercise without your guitar: Sit and tap your foot in a relatively slow, steady beat. While tapping your foot, place a hand on your knee and tap out triplets, counting out loud as you do so. Musicians usually count out triplets as "one and a, two and a, three and a, four and a," by the way. Your foot should be hitting the floor on the numbers (one, two, three, and four).

How are you doing so far? Now keep your foot steady and keep counting aloud but change your hand tapping so that you're tapping your knee on the numbers and the *a*s but not on the *and*s. Your hand is now beating out what's called *swing eighths*. This is the essential rhythm of the blues shuffle.

The difference between swing eighths and straight eighths (regular eighth notes) can be very striking. And for a lot of rock songs, this swing rhythm can define the mood of a song. "Midnight Rambler," by the Rolling Stones, has the same basic chord progression as "Sweet Home Alabama," but the feel is totally different because "Midnight Rambler" uses swing.

From Blues to Rock and Back

Most early rockers were heavily influenced by the blues, as well as gospel and country music. Many Chuck Berry songs, like "Roll Over Beethoven" or "Johnny B. Goode," are traditional blues chord progressions played in straight eighths instead of swing eighths. A lot of early rock music evolved this way.

But while many songs were pounded out in straight eighths rhythm, quite a few were still played in swing, only a high energy, electric guitar–fueled swing that combined elements of blues, country, and old Appalachian music that would later evolve into bluegrass, and even jazz. Rockabilly music grew out of this mix as well.

Both blues guitarists, such as Muddy Waters and John Lee Hooker, and early rock guitarists inspired a horde of young British guitarists who would soon bring the "British Invasion" to the United States.

The most basic blues form is the twelve-bar blues. Bar is another name for measure, so you can guess that a typical twelve-bar blues song is 12 measures long.

"Woke Up This Evening"

In the meantime, here's a practice song in twelve-bar blues format. If you find yourself thinking that it sounds a bit like "Nine Note Rock" from Chapter 2, you'd be absolutely right!

Track 41

"Woke Up This Evening"

Alternate Picking

All the talk this chapter of "down and up" applies to single note playing as well as to strumming. For some mysterious reason, beginners tend to play everything on the guitar as downstrokes. While dramatic, playing only in downstrokes can also be problematic, especially where rhythm is concerned. And soloists also have to be very much aware of rhythm.

Alternate picking is a technique you want to develop early in your guitar playing. Not that alternate picking is difficult (far from it), it's just that the longer you put it off, the longer it seems to take to get comfortable with it.

The easiest way to start in on alternate picking is to go back to your "one finger one fret" exercise from Chapter 2, this time being very careful about your picking as you play the notes. Remember that downstrokes are indicated by marks that look like heavy-duty staples (⊓) and upstrokes are indicated by tall, thin *V* shapes (ᐯ):

"One finger one fret" exercise with alternate picking.

As with most of our earlier exercises, start this one off slowly. Don't be worried about timing until you feel good about your alternate picking. Once you're comfortable with that, speed will come with repetition.

Speed is one of the by-products of alternate picking. Just as with strumming chords where you have to make an upstroke to make the second downstroke, you also have to make an upstroke in order to make a new downstroke on a single string. If you can hit the string on an upstroke as well as a downstroke, you're getting twice as many hits as someone who only strikes the string on a downstroke.

Economy of movement is a goal for most guitarists, but many people only think of movement in terms of the fretting hand. The picking hand moves quite a bit, too, often more than the hand on the neck, so getting twice the work for a simple down-and-up picking motion is a bonus.

Track 42

Here are a few more exercises to help you get in some more practice with alternate picking:

Alternate picking exercises.

"Shuffle Rock"

And here is a practice song to help reinforce the material we've covered in this chapter, paying particular attention to triplets and swing eighths:

Track 43

Swing Eighths ♩ = 100

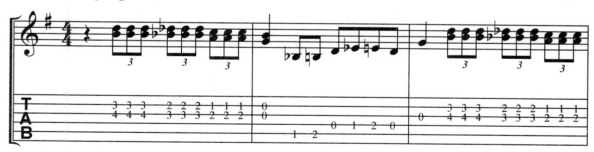

continues

"Shuffle Rock"

This song starts with a one beat rest, so don't just jump in! It also begins with a series of double stops, but these are a bit different from those you've played so far because the notes are on different frets. Use your middle finger for the notes on the G string and your index finger for notes on the B string.

Alternate picking will help you play the single note lines, such as those in the second measure, smoothly and cleanly. A good way to approach learning this song is by breaking the song into phrases, working them out individually, and then putting the pieces together.

There's a little bit of vibrato and a bend or two, just to keep you on your toes, and the song ends with a G6 chord (a little bit of a preview for Chapter 7), which is fairly easy to play. Your middle finger gets the note on the low E (sixth) string while your index finger is on the second fret of the A string.

The Least You Need to Know

- ◆ Rhythm is an essential part of music. Good guitarists play in rhythm.
- ◆ Rhythm notation uses the same rhythm shapes as standard music notation.
- ◆ Concentrating on the beat is better than thinking in terms of "down and up" when it comes to strumming.
- ◆ Blues, as well as jazz and even some rock music, is played in swing rhythm.
- ◆ Alternate picking provides both speed and accuracy to your playing.

7

Some of the Lowdown on Chords

In This Chapter

- ◆ Various open-position D chords
- ◆ C and G chords
- ◆ Working through chord changes
- ◆ More seventh chords and the moveable ninth chord
- ◆ Dotted notes

Chords are the lifeline of the guitarist. Guitarists, who may never play a chord on stage, need to know what chords all their other band mates are playing in order to solo in the right key. And even they may not be aware of it, but most of the scales they use to solo come from specific chord placement on the fretboard of the guitar.

Rock guitarists don't strum full chords as much as you might think (and regardless of what you may think you see at concerts and in videos). More often than not, hitting three or four strings provides all the harmonic punch a player needs. But you still need to know how and where to place your fingers to make the chord you want.

The signature riffs of many songs come directly from minor changes and adjustments to chord fingerings. And, being able to move smoothly and quickly from one chord to the next helps you acquire speed and accuracy in your playing.

Where Chords Come From

Chords are formed, as you've learned, by playing three or more different notes at a time. Two notes work, too, if you are okay with the concept of power chords (back in Chapter 5). In Chapter 13, you learn more about why different combinations are major or minor chords. Right now you just want to get playing some so you can make more music!

Before you dive into making chords, though, here are a few tips. First, at this stage in your learning, you'll benefit a lot from using the cleanest setting your amp has. Full distortion has a way of making everyone sound more like a rocker, but it also can cover up a lot of fingering mistakes. You want to be able to hear when you're not fretting a chord cleanly or, worse, creating an out-of-tune chord by fingering too hard.

Putting Your Finesse to Good Use

All the work you've put into developing a light but firm touch on your guitar helps you immensely when it comes to making chords. Beginners have a natural tendency to grab the neck of the guitar hard to begin with, and this can be disastrous when playing chords, particularly those in *open position*.

You have hopefully spent some time exploring and experimenting how the different ways you place your finger on a fret vary the sound of the notes you play. With chords, your fingers need to get the cleanest note possible without applying more pressure than needed.

Often, and quite by accident, a new guitarist grabs the neck hard and puts a lot of pressure on the fretted notes, sometimes actually pulling or pushing the strings in one direction or another perpendicular to the fretboard. Sounds like what happens when you bend a string, right? So imagine what happens when you have two to four notes of a chord correctly but you've got one or two others that have been bent up a quarter-tone in pitch?

Make the effort early on to finger your chords cleanly and with just as much pressure as you need. A lighter touch not only makes for better sounding chords, it also keeps you on your fingertips so you can change between chords more quickly.

def•i•ni•tion

Open-position chords involve using open strings on the guitar. All the full chords (as opposed to the power chords) that you have learned so far, such as E, Em, A, and Am, are open position.

Various open-position E and A chords.

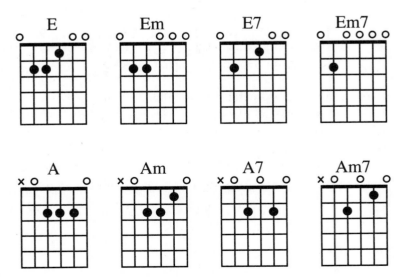

So far, you've learned eight "full" open-position chords.

Now it's time to learn the other open-position chords you run into quite a bit in your playing.

D and Friends

The D Major chord looks like it should be very simple to play.

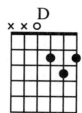

D Major chord.

The most common fingering for this is to use your middle finger for the second fret of the first (high E) string, your ring finger for the third fret of the B string, and your index finger for the second fret of the G string.

Many beginners have initial trouble getting a good sounding D chord. If that's the case with you, try approaching it in this manner:

1. Play an A7 chord.

2. Play it again, this time using your middle finger for the second fret of the B string and your index finger on the second fret of the D string. Check your finger position and try to line up these two fingers so that they are close to being right over one another on the frets. You may need to tip your wrist slightly so that the palm of your fretting hand is pointing more toward the body of the guitar (when you look at it) than toward you.

3. Shift both fingers one string closer to the floor (index finger is now on the second fret of the G string and the middle finger is on the second fret of the high E [first] string) and then add your ring finger to the third fret of the B string. Try to get just the tip of the ring finger on that string and don't let the first knuckle of that finger collapse, which flattens the finger slightly and inadvertently deadens the high string.

If you're having trouble getting the high E (first) string to ring out while playing a D chord, chances are that you are gripping the neck too tightly and pulling all of your fingers down, and the string is actually being muted by your hand along the edge of the neck closest to the floor. Relax, shake out your hand, and then try again, this time placing the middle finger first and testing the note you get before adding the other two fingers (index finger and then ring finger).

Hear How
George Harrison once said that there are more songs written (and to be written) on all the cool things you can do with the D Major chord. And it's true! Once you play a D chord yourself, you start recognizing its distinct voicing in many songs.

Getting Better

It may seem impossible to worry about which string to strum from while you're trying to figure out how to play the D chord, but make the effort from the start. You are developing muscle memory each time you play and all the practicing you're doing will pay off. Within a very short time you won't even notice that you're almost always strumming a D chord from the D string down, or an A chord from the A string. And that's what you want—to have it in your brain but to have it happen without having to think about it.

Hitting the Strings You Want

The root note of the D Major chord is D, so you want to strum this chord from the open D string down to the floor. If you hit the open A string, the chord sounds a little duller. If you hit all six strings, the open low E (sixth) string makes it sound dreadful! But because you've been working on being able to hit just the strings you want since Chapter 2, this shouldn't be too much of a challenge for you.

The D Major chord, as well as the other D chords you learn in a moment, are Root 4 chords, meaning that their root note (in this case, D) is on the D, or fourth, string (the open D string in this case). When you practice playing the D chord, you want to concentrate on only hitting the four thinnest strings with your stroke.

D7, Dm, and Dm7

Along with D, you also want to learn D7, Dm, and Dm7. Here are the chord charts for each:

D minor, D7, and D minor 7 chords.

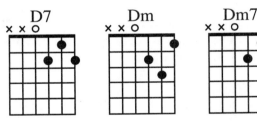

Even though these are all D chords, each one needs a slightly different fingering. For D7, your index finger plays the first fret of the B string while the ring finger is on the second fret of the high E (first) string and the middle finger gets the note at the second fret of the G string.

On Dm, your index finger frets the note at the first fret of the high E string and your middle finger plays the second fret of the G string. Guitarists seem split as to which finger plays the third fret of the B string. Some use the ring finger and some use the pinky. Try both ways and see which is more comfortable for you.

Dm7 is a little tricky. The easiest way to play it is to lay your index finger flat across both the high E and B string, much in the same way you played one-finger double stops back in Chapter 3. You can then use your middle finger for the second fret of the G string. Some guitarists use their ring finger for that note, but most use their middle one.

More Fun with the D

When you're comfortable with the D Major chord, you can also have fun "playing around" with it. While fingering the D chord, add your pinky to the third fret of the high E string (keeping your middle finger in place on the second fret) to make a *suspended chord*, referred to as Dsus4, or Dsus for short.

You can also totally remove your middle finger from the high E string, creating Dsus2. Here are chord charts for these two chords:

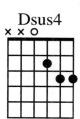 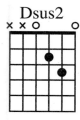   *D suspended chords.*

def•i•ni•tion

Suspended chords are created when the third note of the chord is replaced with a different note, most often the fourth. You read more on this in Chapter 13. Suspended chords, like power chords, are neither major nor minor. The difference between the two is that in power chords, the third is totally removed and not replaced by a different note.

This "playing around" with the D chord has led to the creation of many a song's signature riff. Plus, it's an excellent way to keep your pinky in shape. You're going to need your smallest finger a lot when handling other techniques, so it's good to give it something to do from time to time.

From C to Shining G

Along with D, the two other chords you're most likely to find in songs of all kinds are C and G. Both of these pose interesting challenges, but nothing you aren't capable of handling.

C Major is very close to Am, which you already know. Start by playing the Am chord. Then take your ring finger, which should be on the second fret of the G string and place it on the third fret of the A string:

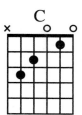   *C Major chord.*

It's important that you get a good clean note on the A string. Don't be afraid to "cheat" your fingers over in direction of the guitar's body to do so. Your index finger should be able to crowd the first fret of the B string and still get the note there to ring true as long as you keep your finger up on its tip.

The C Major chord spans across three frets, and it's the largest stretch on the neck you've tried so far, so don't give up if it doesn't happen the first time. Relax, give your fingers a good shaking out, and try again from the Am chord.

C, like A, Am, and the other A chords you know, is a Root 5 chord. So you want to strum it from the A string down. Don't hit the low E string when you strum it.

The G Chord

Like E and Em (as well as E7 and Em7), G Major is a Root 6 chord, so you can strum across all six strings. Like the A Major chord, the fingerings for G are many, so first take a look at the notes you want:

G Major chord.

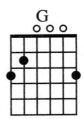

Getting Better

Beginners tend to put way too much pressure in fretting the low E string, often pushing or pulling it anywhere from a quarter tone to a half step higher in pitch. That makes for one sour sounding chord! Use only enough pressure to get a clean note and try to stay up on your fingertips as much as possible, unless you're also using that particular finger to mute an adjoining string.

The majority of guitarists finger the open-position G chord by using their index finger on the second fret of the A string, their middle finger on the third fret of the low E (sixth) string, and their ring finger on the third fret of the high E (first) string. It is certainly the more comfortable (for most) fingering of the many options.

But because C is one of the chords you often play after a G chord, some players finger the chord without using the index finger at all—pinky on the high E string, ring finger on the low E, and middle finger on the A. To change from this fingering of G to C, you simply shift the middle and ring fingers up a string (middle finger to the second fret of the D and ring finger to the third fret of the A) and then drop down the index finger on the first fret of the B string.

Another option is to use the "string muting" technique from playing octaves, back in Chapter 5. You put either your index or middle finger on the third fret of the low E string and flatten it just enough to deaden the A string. Place your ring finger on the third fret of the high E string and you're good to go.

Which Finger Moves First?

If you decide to play your G chord in the popular fingering, then you're going to find that changing from G to C involves a complete shift of all three fingers to different places on the fretboard. And that means that you want to pay special attention to how your fingers make that switch in chords.

Play a G chord and then slowly change from G to C and watch what, exactly, your fingers do. Most beginners find that their index finger is the first one to move and place itself at the first fret of the B string. What that usually means is that the guitarist is going to wait until all of his or her fingers are in place on the C chord before strumming it.

Much of the time the first strum of a new chord takes place on the beat, that is, on a downstroke. If you have to wait until all your fingers are in place before you can start to strum, you're going to create a rhythmic "hiccup," which needs to be corrected.

A Little Bass

Ideally, you want your ring finger to be the first that touches down (on the third fret of the A string) when you form a C chord, because that's the first string you hit.

One way to get into the habit of doing so is to practice using a "walking bass line" from the G chord to the C chord, like so:

Track 44

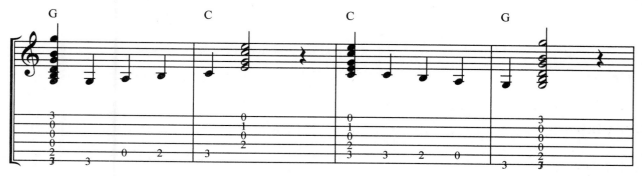

Walking bass line exercise—from G to C and back again.

Play the G chord once and then play just the root note, which is the note at the third fret of the low E string. Remove all your fingers from the strings and play just the open A string. Then place your middle finger on the second fret of the A string, play that note, and then put your middle finger on the third fret of the A string. As you play this last note, drop your middle and index fingers down onto their appropriate places and play the rest of the C chord.

Try out the first two measures of this exercise slowly and carefully several times. When you're good with it, then work through the third and fourth measures, which is essentially the same exercise in reverse (you start with C and then go to G).

If you get in the habit of playing your C chord by leading with your ring finger, as you have to in this exercise, it becomes second nature to you in a very short while. Likewise, switching from C to G becomes an easy task.

Getting Your Fingers Going

Watch a guitarist's hands on his or her guitar neck and you might think that all his or her fingers move simultaneously, in a single fluid motion from one chord to the next. In a way, they do. But at one point every guitarist started at the same place you are right now, trying to get his or her fingers to do something that seems impossible.

Part of getting better at chords, as has been mentioned earlier, is to not think of chords as "static" objects. The fingers of your fretting hand should always be itching to move someplace. When you pick up your guitar, do you just sit with it or do your fingers seek out a chord to play?

Getting Better

When changing chords, try to resist the temptation to let your fingers fly open with each chord change. The closer you keep your fingers to the fretboard, the sooner they can get back to it to fret a note.

As a beginner, you are rightly concerned about methodically getting your fingers onto the right strings at the proper fret, but you also have to push them to the point where they start to work as a unit. When you're playing, you can't wait for each finger to take its individual turn to get on the correct note of a chord.

How to Practice Changing Chords

The advice on changing chords back in Chapter 4 still holds. Pick any two chords and work on switching back and forth between them, strumming a specific number of beats as you do so, until you can do so without much of a pause between the chords. Then either pick two new chords to switch from or add a third chord to the original two and practice changing between the three.

Think about economy of movement. Whenever possible, try to move fingers as little as possible. If a finger (or fingers) can stay on the same fret and string, as with changing from Am to C, try not to move it when going from one chord to the next.

When you find yourself having particular difficulty with the switch from two particular chords, give that change special attention. Slow down your strumming, even to a crawling pace if you have to, until you can make the change at whatever snail-like speed without a hitch and then, only after having done so, gradually and incrementally increase the tempo of your practice.

And be certain to give yourself a break! Your muscles need time to absorb all the information you're giving them. Many players find that, after taking a complete break for a while, whether by focusing on a different technique (like bending or single-note alternate picking) or simply putting down the guitar for a while, the changing of chords gets easier. Rest and a cooling down period is an essential part of any exercise routine.

"Open Chord Rock"

Here is a practice song to help you work through your chord changes.

Track 45

Notice that this song contains rhythm notation as well as standard notation and guitar tablature, depending on whether you're playing full open-position chords or single notes.

Getting Better

Many beginners spend too much time watching their hands making the changes. For some, this constant state of surveillance can impede their progress. When you know where you want your fingers to go, and after making the desired chord change a dozen or so times, try not to look at your hands. Stare ahead or up at the ceiling or even close your eyes and imagine you're up on stage looking out at your audience. You might surprise yourself by making the chord changes more smoothly and quickly than you did before.

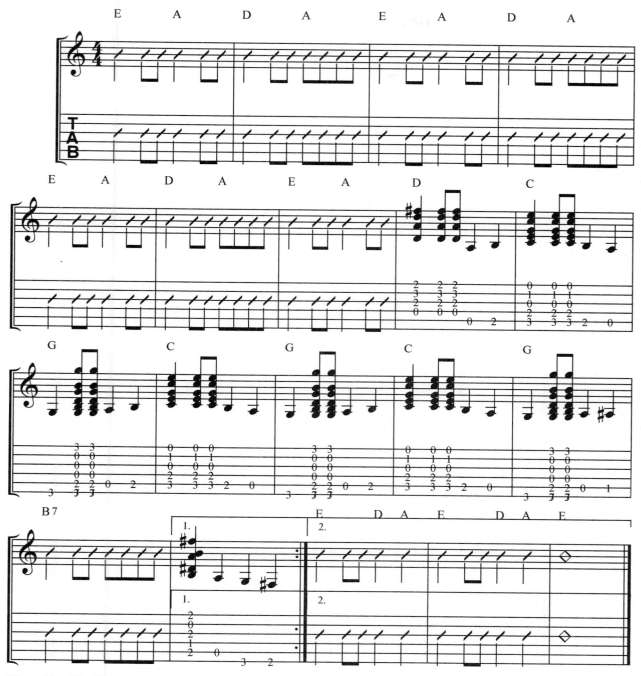

"Open Chord Rock"

Sevenths

You already know some seventh chords. Here are the chord charts for C7 and G7, plus a new chord, B7.

C7, G7, and B7 chords.

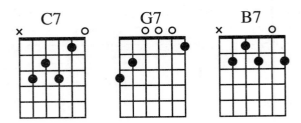

In music theory, the use of the number 7 to indicate a seventh chord is short-hand for the term *dominant seventh*. There are also *minor seventh* chords (you've learned Em7, Am7, and Dm7) and *major seventh* chords as well. As you'll learn in Chapter 13, dominant sevenths add the flatted seventh note of the major scale to a chord while major sevenths add the seventh note of the major scale. Here are the open-position major seventh chords of A, C, D, E, and G:

Various major seventh chords.

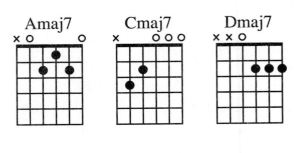

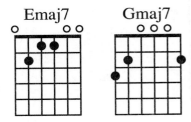

The only tricky one of this group is the Gmaj7. Using the string muting technique is probably the easiest way to play it. Place your middle finger on the third fret of the low E string and flatten it out slightly, muting the A string. Your index finger gets to play the second fret of the high E string.

We discuss more of the theory behind these chords in Chapter 13. Right now, though, you can benefit from listening to the differences between the various seventh chords you know.

The Flavor of Sevenths

Dominant sevenths have a distinct tonal quality. It could be called transitory or restless because seventh chords sound like they want to go somewhere, to another chord entirely. In many songs they do assume that function. You'll see many chord progressions where D changes to D7 and on to G, for instance, or a progression of E to E7 to A.

As with concepts as personal and vague as the feelings one gets from listening to certain chords, there are many ways to describe this quality of dominant seventh chords. One way that has stuck around for the better part of a century is "bluesy."

Back to Blue

It's pretty rare for a blues song *not* to contain at least one seventh chord. Sometimes every chord is a dominant seventh. Do you remember the "twelve-bar blues" format from Chapter 6? Here are two typical blues patterns using seventh chords.

These charts leave out the rhythm but, as you can hear on the CD, you can use the blues shuffle pattern you learned in Chapter 6 for these chords. Or you can review your power chord knowledge by playing the appropriate power chords instead of the seventh chords.

Track 46

> **Hear How**
>
> You hear dominant seventh chords in lots of rock songs. The haunting opening of "Born on the Bayou," by Creedence Clearwater Revival (as well as the rhythm guitar part during the solos) is an extended arpeggio of an E7 chord.

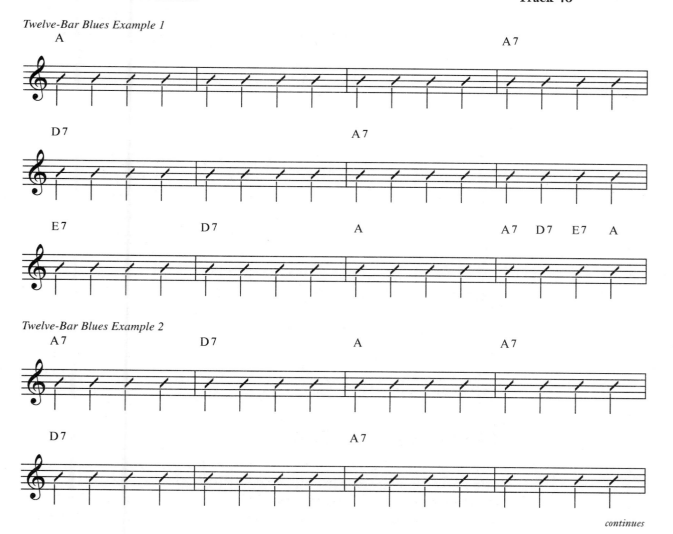

Twelve-Bar Blues Example 1

Twelve-Bar Blues Example 2

continues

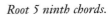

Two twelve-bar blues chord progressions.

How About Nine?

Ninth chords also figure prominently in blues. They sound, if possible, more bluesy than seventh chords! Start with the C9, the leftmost chord in the following illustration:

Root 5 ninth chords.

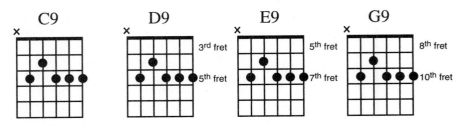

It looks a lot like a C7 chord, but involves a little more work from your fingers. Place your ring finger on the third fret of the A string and your index finger on the second fret of the D string. Finally, flatten out your ring finger across all three of the highest strings (high E, B, and G) at the third fret. You may find that angling your wrist slightly toward the body of the guitar (as you did with the D chord) helps you to do this cleanly.

This fingering of the ninth chord is a moveable chord and is also a Root 5 chord. So if you know what the notes are along the A string, you can create other ninth chords, as shown in the previous illustration.

One More Note to Take Note Of

So far you've learned about whole notes, half notes, quarter notes, and eighth notes. Whole notes last for four beats; half notes for two; quarter notes as a single beat; and eighth notes are a half beat. You also know, just from listening to music, that notes can last any number of beats. So how would one indicate a note that was supposed to last, say, three beats long? Or a beat and a half?

Tied notes are certainly one answer, but standard notation also has another, and that is the *dotted note*, such as the ones below.

dotted half notes (three beats)

dotted quarter notes (one and a half beats)

dotted eighth notes (three-quarters of a beat)

Dotted notes in standard notation and rhythmic notation.

When a dot is placed after a note, it means that you are to add half the original value of that note to the original note. That sounds a little complicated, but it's not hard to grasp. In the first measure, you see two dotted half notes. Because a half note is two beats long, the dot means to add one beat (half the length of a half note) to it, so a dotted half note is three beats long.

A dotted quarter note, as shown in measures three and four, is a beat and a half long because the dot indicates adding a half beat (half the rhythm value of the quarter note) to the quarter note. The dotted eighth notes in the last two measures are three-quarters of a beat in length, which is one half beat (the original eighth note) plus a quarter beat (half of an eighth note, as indicated by the dot).

Dotted notes, especially dotted quarter notes and dotted sixteenth notes, are used more than you can imagine in rock. The more complex the rhythm or the solo, the more likely you'll find some dotted notes as part of the rhythmic make up.

def•i•ni•tion

Dotted notes are a sort of shorthand of rhythm notation. The dot tells you to add one half of the original note value to the original note value, giving you a note one and a half times the original note's length.

"7 to 9 Blues"

Let's conclude this chapter with a blues piece to further practice various seventh and ninth chords. It also involves a liberal use of the dotted half note in its rhythm.

A common (and great sounding) thing to do with ninth chords is to play it one fret higher than intended and then move to the target chord, as you see at the end of the first measure and the beginning of the second.

Also be sure to note the new ways of playing A, Amaj7, and A7 at the very end of this song. They'll be coming up again before you know it!

Track 47

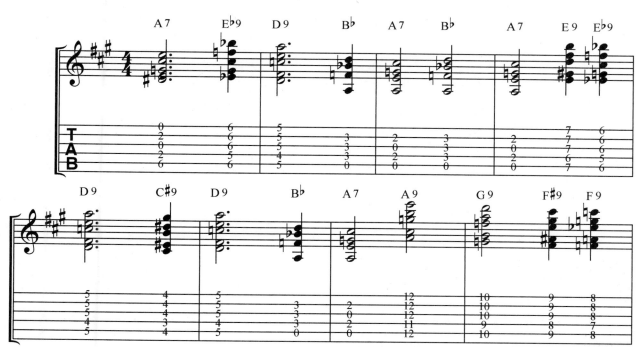

continues

continued

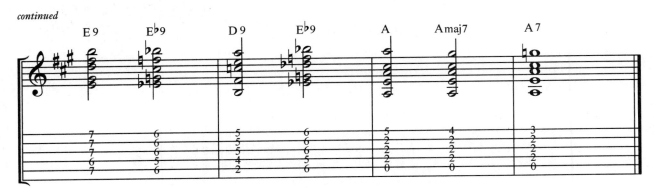

"7 to 9 Blues"

The Least You Need to Know

◆ Chords are made up of different combinations of notes.

◆ Open-position chords have open strings as at least one of their component notes.

◆ Practice, practice, practice, and more practice is the only tried and tested way of getting better at making chord changes.

◆ There are four different types of seventh chords.

◆ Seventh and ninth chords sound very cool in blues and blues-styled rock songs.

Chapter 8

Rocking in Bits and Pieces

In This Chapter

- ◆ Arpeggios, broken chords, and partial chords
- ◆ What strumming patterns really are
- ◆ Hammer-ons and pull-offs
- ◆ Slides
- ◆ Combining slurs with rhythm

With even just a few basic open-position chords under your belt, you can now play even more songs than you could with just power chords. You can also make a lot of the songs you played with just power chords sound fuller, which is great if you are the only guitarist in your band.

Playing chords though, just like playing rock guitar, is still a matter of touch. Depending on the chord, you can play all six strings, or just four, or even two or three, just like you do with power chords. The difference is that using full chords gives you a lot more notes to choose from, because full chords contain three or more different notes while power chords use just two.

Pieces of Chords

As mentioned in our last chapter, rock guitarists don't often use all the strings of a chord when playing. Instead they often play pieces of the chord, if you will—two, three, or four strings at a time. Adding volume, and more often than not a bit of distortion, makes these *partial chords* sound like a small orchestra.

Playing partial chords—or arpeggios or broken chords—instead of simply strumming full chords also gives the guitarist a chance to sound like an individual. Because each strike of the string can be so different than the next, each musician develops his or her own personal style. Picking patterns can be copied, but the individual nuances given each pick of the string are almost as unique as fingerprints.

Arpeggios

Play an Em chord, strumming it in one downstroke. Now play it again, this time hitting each string distinctly and slowly, letting it ring out as you do so. This is called an *arpeggio*.

Guitarists have been playing arpeggios since the very first guitars were made. The instrument is obviously very suited to playing chords in this manner because it's just a matter of strumming through the strings slowly enough to have each note sound out individually instead of being part of a quick, single strum.

Depending on which direction you're strumming, you can create either an ascending arpeggio or a descending one. When you strum down, the notes go higher in pitch, so that's an ascending arpeggio. Conversely, when you strum up, the notes get lower in pitch, so that's a descending arpeggio. No wonder any discussion of "up" and "down" tends to make a guitarist's head spin!

Skipping Around

You can, of course, decide to skip a string or two along the way or even change direction. That's when the fun starts. Using Em as an example, here is an illustration to show the difference between ascending arpeggios, descending arpeggios, and broken chords.

The first two measures here are ascending arpeggios, even though the one in the second measure does not use all six strings, instead skipping from the low E string of the first note to the E note at the second fret of the D string. The second two measures are descending arpeggios, with the arpeggio in measure four going so far as to skip two strings.

Getting Better

Arpeggios are also a great way to constantly check up on how well your fingers are fretting the individual notes of a chord. When you play each note string by string, you can't help but hear when you've pressed a note out of tune or when your fingers aren't setting properly and giving you either buzzing notes or "tunks." Be sure to listen to your arpeggios and adjust your fingers accordingly if you hear notes that are off or muted.

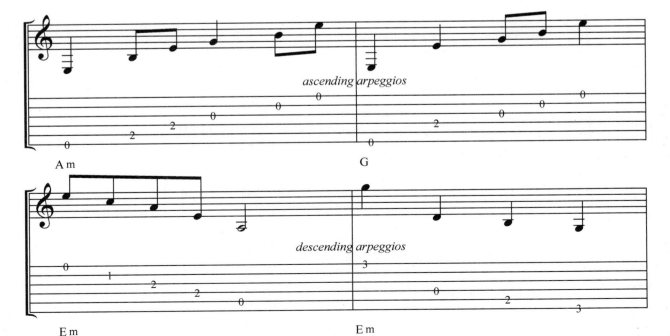

Arpeggios and broken chords.

Crosspicking

Measures five and six may look like arpeggios, but they are actually called broken chords. A broken chord is an arpeggio that changes direction more than once. When a guitarist plays broken chords, he is *crosspicking*, a term you find used a lot by bluegrass players, even though the technique is used in all genres of guitar music.

Guitarists crosspick broken chords in their own ways. Some use strict alternate picking (from Chapter 6) while others use the pick as many finger-picking players use their fingers—downstrokes on the three low strings and upstrokes on the three high ones. Most people tend to use combinations of these two approaches, depending on both the notes (and strings) involved and their own personal comfort zone.

Partially Scrambled Chords

Try as you may, you'll probably find yourself hitting more than one string when practicing crosspicking broken chords. The cool thing is, as long as you are fingering the full chord, it's still going to sound good. In fact, it may be just the sound you're looking for.

When you hit two or three (or the occasional four) strings of a full string chord, it's called a *partial chord*. And partial chords are the meat and potatoes of rock guitar.

def•i•ni•tion

> **Crosspicking** is the term used for the technique of playing broken chords. It refers to the guitarist jumping from one note of a broken chord to the next, sometimes on an adjoining string, sometimes skipping to a different string, possibly in a different picking direction.

Note Worthy

Guitarists often use the terms *arpeggios*, *broken chords*, and *partial chords* interchangeably, although there are technical differences between the three. Arpeggios and broken chords are chords played one note at a time while partial chords are just two, three, or four notes of a chord played at once. Arpeggios, by the classical definition, are played in either one direction or another. That is, you either strum down the strings (an ascending arpeggio because the notes go up in tone) or up the strings (a descending arpeggio). You can skip a string, but the minute you reverse direction you are either playing a new arpeggio or a broken chord.

You could say that you've already played partial chords before. Double stops, such as those in the exercises and song ("Double Stop Rock") in Chapter 3, certainly qualify as partial chords. The only difference is one of context as double stops are thought of as a "lead guitar" technique while partial chords are labeled as part of the rhythm.

The concept of broken chords is easy to digest. Playing them is even easier. Beginners do it all the time without thinking, simply because they don't know that's what they're doing.

But seeing broken chords written out in tablature is an entirely different matter:

An example of rhythm using partial chords.

Track 48

If you only listen to this last example without reading it, you'd probably say that it was just someone strumming a G chord in an interesting manner. And you'd be right.

The Illusion of Patterns

Broken chords, in reality, tend to be created on the spur of the moment, and usually they are not a conscious thing. And beginning guitarists, especially those who obsess about copying the guitar part from a recording note for note, don't always get this. They want to believe that by copying every strum and hitting only the same strings in the tablature that the original guitarist of the recording did, they will sound just like it. They call these rhythmic tablatures strumming patterns and believe they are the key to playing well.

But strumming patterns are only useful to a point. The reality is that the original guitarist didn't sit down and think, "Now I only want to hit the low E string here and then just the B and G strings on an upstroke and then the D string on a downstroke and then the high E and B strings on the upstroke," and so on. He or she simply sat down and started strumming a G chord. The result was an organic combination of single notes, full chords, and partial chords played in a rhythmic manner appropriate to the song.

You also can't forget that the original recorded rhythm guitar was also the result of that particular player's own practice habits, personal tastes, and individual style, developed for however long he or she had been playing guitar up to that point.

Instead of fixating on copying someone else's technique, use an original recording as a starting place or a template on which to create and develop your own style. Always keep in your mind that as long as you are fretting the full chord, you can't really hit a wrong note, or a wrong partial chord or arpeggio for that matter. Different notes of a chord almost always sound fine.

Bad rhythm, on the other hand, can't be covered up. It's the "strumming" part of a strumming pattern that's important, not the "pattern." Keeping the beat has to be your first concern.

Slurs

Other techniques are used by both rhythm and lead players alike, the most common being the use of *slurs*. Simply put, you create a slur by playing one note (or notes) in the regular fashion and then use your fretting hand to sound a new note (or notes). Bending notes, as you did in Chapter 4, is one type of slur. The other three guitar slurs are the hammer-on, the pull-off, and the slide.

In musical notation (and most guitar tablature), a slur is indicated by an arced line, at first identical to the tie, drawn over or under two or more notes. Unlike the tie, which connects two notes on the same line or space on the staff, the slur connects different notes, as shown in the following illustration:

The difference between a tie and a slur.

Different slurs are also identified in both notation and tablature by the appropriate letter. An *H* between two notes will mean to play a hammer-on to get the second note. Similarly, a *P* indicates the use of a pull-off and an *S* or *Sl* denoting a slide between notes.

Hammer-On My Wayward Son

If you ever should forget how to play any slur on the guitar, you don't have to go any further than the name to be reminded! Hammer-ons are played by hammering a finger of your fretting hand onto the proper fret for the note you want.

Track 49

To play this, place your index finger on the seventh fret of the G string. Strike that string with the pick (or fingers if you don't use a pick) and then slam the tip of your ring finger onto the ninth fret of the same string. Don't pick the string twice! The new note at the ninth fret is created by the ring finger of your fretting hand.

Hammer-ons are primarily used as a speed technique. Why pick a string twice when you only have to pick it once to get two notes? You have four fingers, so you can even pick a string once and get four additional notes through hammer-ons!

An example of a hammer-on in notation, plus an exercise to develop finger strength.

Here you want to start by picking the open G string. After you sound that note, hammer your index finger on the fourth fret of the G string and then hammer your pinky on the seventh fret of the same string.

Be certain to keep your index finger in place when you're making the hammer-on with your pinky. Otherwise you lose the first slurred note and the second one won't be as dynamic.

You may find it helps to overexaggerate the whole motion of hammering at first. Your fingers aren't used to performing this technique, so initially you want to simply get used to the mechanics involved. As your fingers get stronger, you'll find you actually need very little "hammering" to produce the note that you want.

Track 50

An example of multiple hammer-ons.

Pull-Offs

It's the *pull* of the pull-off you need to remember. Place your index finger (or any finger will do) on the third fret of the high E (first) string, play that note, and then take your finger off by lifting it straight up perpendicular from the neck. Chances are that you got the note of the open high E string to sound, but not that clearly or cleanly.

Try it again but this time, instead of *lifting* your finger up *pull* it down toward the floor, lightly catching the string with your fingertip and pulling it with you until it releases back into place. This downward release motion is the secret of a good pull-off.

You should hear a much more resounding note from the open high E string. By lightly pulling on the string, your fretting finger also serves the function of the pick and sounds the pull-off for you.

Now try it further up the neck. Place your index finger on the seventh fret of the G string and place your ring finger on the ninth fret of the same string, like this:

Track 51

An example of a pull-off in notation, plus an exercise to develop finger strength.

Perform the pull-off by pulling your ring finger down from the G string while keeping your index finger in place. The flesh of your fingertip will tug it downward and will help sound the D note (held at the seventh fret by your index finger). You can use the same old "one finger one fret" exercise you used to work on your hammer-ons for practicing pull-offs, only you obviously want to place a finger on first and then pull off to get the open strings.

And just as with the hammer-ons, you want to work on developing your fingers to handle multiple pull-offs. The secret to success in multiple pull-offs, as in multiple hammer-ons, is to keep your fingers in place as much as possible:

Track 52

An example of a pull-off in notation.

In this example, place *both* your index finger and your ring finger on the first string before you pick it. Then keeping your index finger on the fifth fret, perform a pull-off with your ring finger. After the note at the fifth fret sounds, then you can pull off your index finger to sound the note of the open high E string.

Combining Hammer-Ons and Pull-Offs

Many rock riffs and solos involve both hammer-ons and pull-offs used in combination. Here is an example:

An example of hammer-ons and pull-offs played in combination.

Track 53

The key to playing this riff is to keep your index finger on the fifth fret across all three strings involved (the G, D, and A strings). If you can lay it flat, covering those three strings, you only need to use your ring finger to play the rest of the notes.

Another option is to keep your index finger up on its tips and have your two fingers work along the three strings like a seesaw. If you've gotten good at your hammer-ons, you might even find that you only need to pick the very first note of this riff and you can get all the other notes as slurs.

With a surprisingly small amount of concerted practice, you should find yourself gaining speed with your hammer-ons and pull-offs. While that's a good thing, don't let your newfound quickness on the fingerboard erase all your knowledge of proper timing. Be sure to make note of when you're supposed to play a slur as a grace note and when it's supposed to be a note of specific timing, such as an eighth note or a quarter note.

The Trill of Victory

Track 54

A specific use of a hammer-on/pull-off combination is the *trill*, a repeated hammer-on and pull-off between two specific notes. You might recognize the following example as sounding a lot like the beginning of Stevie Ray Vaughn's cover version of "Little Wing," a song originally done by Jimi Hendrix:

Playing a trill.

This trill, four measures long, uses only two notes—the open D string and the E note at the second fret of that string. Just like vibrato (from Chapter 4), you can vary many aspects of the trill, making the change between the two notes regular or speeding them up or slowing them down. With practice on your hammer-ons and pull-offs, you can create changes of volume on your trills as well, not to mention accenting the attack of some of the hammers-ons. Many a rock song, especially one at a live performance, ends on a long, drawn out trill by the lead guitarist.

Tricky Tablature

While guitar tablature and music notation are great at explaining just about anything you need to know, both can be misleading when it comes to slurs, particularly when it comes to dealing with grace notes.

In all three of these examples, you start by playing a D chord and then immediately performing either the hammer-on (first measure), pull-off (second measure), or combination (third measure) indicated in the notation.

Every musical instrument has its own slurs, but most notation and tablature software do not adjust to the individual nuances of every possible slur for every musical instrument. You are the one who has to read the tablature and then decide what, exactly, the writer meant. Most times, thankfully, you can make an educated guess.

Sliding Along

While hammer-ons and pull-offs seem very dynamic and dramatic, slides (a slur created by fretting a note, striking the string and then sliding the finger fretting the note along the string to another fret along the neck of the guitar) are more graceful.

They can be just as dramatic, though. Think of Jimi Hendrix's slides between the short phrases at the start of "Purple Haze" or the one almost right at the beginning of "Little Wing."

Switching to Glide

Sliding between notes, simply gliding your finger up or down the fretboard from one note to another, seems to be the easiest thing in the world. That is, until you try it for the first time! Then you realize that there are a lot of factors involved in this *simple* technique.

Track 55

It's all about pressure, really. You start out with enough pressure to fret the initial note with a finger (any finger) of your fretting hand. Then as you start your slide, you have to slightly ease off a bit. Too much pressure and you won't be able to navigate the frets and find your finger catching on them. Too little pressure and you totally lose the sound of the slide.

An example of various slides in notation.

Slides are a prime example of the need for finesse we discussed back in Chapter 4. Don't be surprised (and don't be discouraged) if it takes you more time than you imagined you might need to develop the touch to slide effortlessly along the neck of your guitar.

And it truly is a matter of touch—and practice and repetition. And more practice.

Fortunately, this is also one of the many things you can practice without plugging into an amplifier. Just sit with your guitar, choose a string and a starting point, and then choose a target fret for the note you want to slide to. Keep repeating this procedure until you get the result you want—a clean, clear sounding slide with definitive beginning and end points.

And then keep repeating it until you aren't surprised that you can do it. And repeat again until you get what you expect every time.

To (or From) Nowhere

Occasionally, slides in tablature have no apparent starting or ending point, such as those in the following example:

Track 56

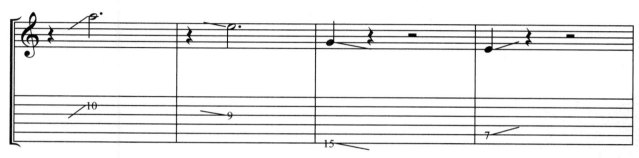

Slides without apparent starting or ending points.

When sliding up or down to a note from a nonspecific starting point (as in the first two measures), the convention is to begin one, two, or three frets away from your target.

To play a slide that seemingly ends nowhere, as in the third and fourth measures of the last example, start with the given note and let your finger simply trail off as you slide in the indicated direction. The sound of the slide should fade off as you move further from your starting point.

Adding Pizzazz with Slurs

Adding slurs to your playing opens up a whole world of expressive possibilities for your guitar, whether you're playing a single note lead or riff (think of the beginning of the Eagles's "Life in the Fast Lane") or full or broken chords ("Fly Like an Eagle" by Steve Miller or "Beast of Burden" by the Rolling Stones). At this point, you want to experiment and try adding these little touches whenever and wherever possible, just so you can get to know them well.

Hammer-ons and pull-offs go especially well with open chords, whether strummed fully or played as arpeggios or partial chords. A little riff to help demonstrate is found on the next page.

When you are learning a new riff such as this, one that involves multiple slurs as well as a number of chords and some single note lines, it's best to first break the riff down into components or *phrases*. Ignore the timing and concentrate on the fingering, and don't even look at the second phrase until you are absolutely certain you can play the first one cleanly and clearly.

> ### Note Worthy
>
> Quite often, a slide serves a technical function as well as being a musical slur. It is a way of moving smoothly from one place on the fretboard to another. Nonspecific slides especially are used in this manner, to get your fingers from one place to the next. Keeping this in mind can help you determine where best to start or finish a nonspecific slide.

Track 57

An example of adding slurs to a rhythm part.

def•i•ni•tion

A **phrase**, musically speaking, is a relatively short grouping of notes. Melodies of songs are generally sung in phrases, usually the length of one line of lyrics. Phrases can contain any number of notes, possibly even a single note played in a distinct rhythmic fashion.

This is important because the last thing you want to be doing is wondering how your fingers are going to get from the first phrase to the second one. You have to *know* what you want your fingers to do to play.

Look at our previous example. The first measure centers around an open-position A Major chord, but hammering-on that A chord with just the index finger (and being very careful to not hit the high E string) would probably give the rest of your fingers the best chance of playing the following pull-offs. How about one more example, this time combining slurs with partial chords?

As with the example in the previous section (slurs with open chords and arpeggios), begin simply by getting comfortable with the techniques needed for each phrase. Don't worry about the timing until you feel you can handle the various hammer-ons and pull-offs. Then work on getting the timing of each individual phrase played correctly at a slow tempo. Once all the pieces are in place, play the whole thing, again as slowly as necessary to play it correctly and cleanly.

Only after you've gotten through all these steps should you go about playing this exercise (a typical rock guitar riff, by the way) at a faster speed.

Track 58

An additional example of adding slurs to a rhythm part.

"Velvet Noir"

Our practice song to close this chapter combines many of the techniques we've just discussed, as well as those from our past chapters. Naturally, you'll find hammer-ons, pull-offs, and slides, and there will also be some power chords, full chords, arpeggios, and broken chords, not to mention some bending and some vibrato. Oh, and there are triplets, and it's also in swing eighths time! Hopefully we didn't miss anything!

Track 59

"Velvet Noir"

The Least You Need to Know

◆ Arpeggios are chords played one note at a time in either an up or down direction.

◆ When you change direction more than once in a single arpeggio, it becomes a broken chord.

◆ Most strumming is full of partial chords.

◆ Hammer-ons, pull-offs, slides, as well as bends are slurs.

◆ Combining slurs with other aspects of playing makes the guitar part a lot more interesting and fun to listen to.

Part 3

Rocking the House

It's time to open up and expand your abilities even further with barre chords, sixteenth notes, and string muting (with both the left and right hands). You work out rhythms and techniques used in metal, punk, and even funk guitar and you also learn about creating cool sounding guitar riffs on your own.

Speaking of rhythm, you also see how easy it is to work out the strumming of any rhythm you hear. It's simply a matter of writing it down by the beat.

Chapter 9

Breaking Through the Barre-ior

In This Chapter

- Playing barre chords
- Learning the E- and A-shaped barre chords
- Using half (or partial) barre chords
- The "thumb over" grip
- Left-hand string muting

Between all the power chords and open-position chords you know, you have a lot of options when you're playing guitar. When you factor in the various techniques you've learned—the arpeggios and partial chords as well as the various slurs—you might think you've got everything a rock guitarist could possibly need.

And you'd be close to being right. As you already know, you can move your power chords all up and down the neck. Some of them are the same notes, just in different places, like the A5 whose root is found at the fifth fret of the low E string and the A5 with its root on the open A string (our example back in Chapter 5). And some are different octaves of the same notes, such as the E5 using the open low E string as its root and the E5 whose root note is at the seventh fret of the A string (again, from the examples we used in Chapter 5). Logic would dictate that a guitarist should be able to find chords everywhere, at any place on the fretboard.

Open and Closed Cases

The Root 5 and Root 6 power chords you learned in Chapter 5 are *moveable* chords. The trick to moving them is remembering that, aside from the Root 5

A5 and the Root 6 E5 (whose root notes are the open A and open low E string, respectively), you have to have a finger on the new root note, depending on whether that note is on the A or low E string. To create C♯5, for example, you need to first find C♯, either at the fourth fret of the A string or at the ninth fret of the low E string. Place your index finger on either of the two locations and the second note of your power chord will be two frets higher on the next higher string.

Notice, too, that you are only picking the strings that your fingers are on. Because there are no open strings used in this chord, it is called a closed position chord, or a closed chord for short. All closed position chords are moveable chords, and that means you can find them anywhere on the neck that you can make the same shape using the same strings.

Think of the *barre chord* as the ultimate closed position chord. Barre chords ("barre" is pronounced "bar," just like the place where you're likely to get a gig) are made by laying a single finger, usually the index finger, across the strings at a particular fret. In a *full barre*, the finger lays across all six strings, just as if you've laid a small bar there. If you lay your finger across any other number of strings, from two to five, it's called a *half barre*. You will hear some rock guitarists refer to the half barre as a *partial barre*. Most guitarists also think of five-string barre chords as full barres.

If you watch a rock guitarist playing, you'll see that he or she plays barre chords at least half of the time, if not more. Not only are barre chords a staple of rock guitar music, they also are the foundation of many riffs, fills, and solos, as you find out in Chapter 17.

To the beginning guitarist, barre chords are like a spooky story told over the dying embers of a summer campfire. But like all the techniques you've studied so far, barre chords get less scary—and easier!—with practice and repetition. And the good news is that you've already had some essential practice without even knowing it!

The work that you did with double stops back in Chapter 3, particularly on the exercise where you played double stops using one finger to cover two strings, was the first of several steps leading you up to playing barre chords. So were the exercises in Chapter 5 with three- and four-string power chords. So don't worry—you're practically there!

Making the Barre

The main component of any barre chord is laying your finger flat across the neck of the guitar and fretting the necessary strings. That may sound easy, but take a look at your index finger. Unless you were in a bizarre ironing accident, chances are very likely that your finger, with its creases and joints, is anything but flat. Beginners will try to overcompensate for this lack of flatness by either gripping way too hard in order to get a lot of pressure on the strings or by jamming as much of the index finger onto the neck as possible.

def•i•ni•tion

Barre chords are closed position chords, formed by laying the index finger across all six strings, usually while one or more of the other fingers fret additional notes. **Half barre chords** involve laying the index finger across two, three, or four strings.

Because you've gotten this far in this book, it probably won't come as too much of a surprise to learn that playing barre chords is also a matter of finesse and touch. Like power chords, it's usually easier to start off a little higher up the neck. Try the seventh, eighth, or ninth fret for your first attempt.

First, line up your index finger so that the tip of it just passes beyond the far edge of the neck. The crease of the first knuckle should fall between the G and D strings, but that obviously depends on the size of your finger. If it doesn't, try to position your finger so that the crease is poised between the strings and that the meat of the finger lies on the strings when you lower it into place. Your thumb should simply be there for the neck of the guitar to rest upon, as shown in the following illustration:

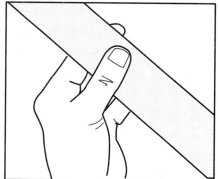

How to place your index finger for a barre chord.

Try not to jam your whole hand against the far end of the neck. Doing so hinders you from getting a good fretting position for your other fingers.

Keeping Straight

Also do your best to keep the index finger parallel to the fret. Many guitarists find their sweet spot by feeling the fret along the inner edge of the index finger. If you're having a hard time doing so, go back and check your posture. Sit or stand straight and remember to keep the neck of the guitar angled so that the fretting hand is level with your chest. It may not look the coolest, but once you're comfortable making barre chords, you'll find that you can get away with holding the guitar a little lower. For now, though, give yourself the best chance to play by paying close attention to your posture.

When your finger is set, strum across all six strings, striking them one at a time and making sure you're getting a nice clean note for each string. Remember that this is something new to you and that you might not get it the first time! If you're having trouble, try laying out your index finger one string at a time. First fret the high E string and play that note. Then place your index finger across the high E and B strings and play each of those notes separately and then together. Repeat this process with the remaining strings, making certain that you get good notes with each additional string covered by your index finger.

Getting Better

Some guitarists find that rolling the index finger slightly on its edge helps them to play cleaner barre chords. If you find that rolling your finger helps, try to keep it as parallel to the fret as possible.

E and Em Shapes

Placing your index finger is obviously just the first step. Your other fingers have to be involved, too. Relax for a moment and shake out your fretting hand, getting it loose and ready to go. Now form an open-position E chord but without using your index finger to fret a note. In other words, put your middle finger on the first fret of the G string, your pinky on the second fret of the D string, and your ring finger on the second fret of the A string. Strum it across all six strings to make sure your fingers are doing their job.

Now slide the entire chord up the neck so that your middle finger is on the eighth fret of the G string and your pinky and ring fingers are on the ninth fret of the D and A strings, respectively. Play through the chord again to make certain that your three fingers have got the notes clean and clear.

Once you're set, lay your index finger across the seventh fret, barring all six strings, as shown in the following illustration:

Making a full barre chord.

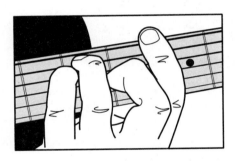

B Major chord.

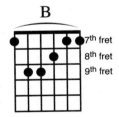

Congratulations! You have just played B Major. You should notice in the chord chart that there is an arc across all six strings. That arc denotes a barre chord, and it indicates both full barre chords and half barres, as you'll soon see.

And whether you know it or not, you also can play Bm, B7, and Bm7, simply by using the shapes you learned in Chapter 5:

Bm, B7, and Bm7 chord charts.

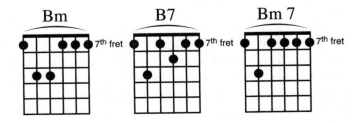

All of these are *Root 6 barre chords* because the root note is found on the low
E (sixth) string. So you now can play all 12 major and minor chords, as well
as their corresponding seventh chords, by finding the chord's root on the low
E string and forming the appropriate Root 6 barre shape. To make F7, for
instance, barre the first fret (that's where F is on the low E string) with your
index finger and then make the E7 shape with your other fingers.

A and Am Shapes

As with power chords, learning both the Root 6 and Root 5 forms of barre
chords will give you almost any chord you could ever hope to use as a rock
musician. Typically, Root 5 barre chords use the A and Am open-position chord
shapes. Here is B Major played as an A-shaped barre chord:

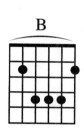

B

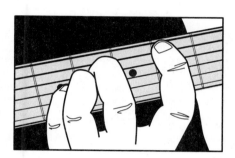

*Making a Root 5 (A-shape)
barre chord.*

Just like the open-position A chord, you can finger this chord in a number of
ways. Most guitarists have problems cramming all three fingers into the same
fret on three adjacent strings and so instead deal with this barre chord by laying
their ring finger across the first four strings and then being very careful not to
strum the high E string when playing the chord. Some people have ring fingers
that naturally (and conveniently!) bend slightly backward at the second joint,
allowing them to cover just the necessary strings. Others use two fingers, one
fretting two strings and the other, the remaining string.

Once you can play this Root 5 "A shape," you can also use the Am shape as well
as A7 and Am7 in barre chord form, as shown here:

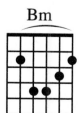

Bm

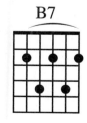

B7

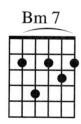

Bm 7

Learning the barre chords is, of course, just part of what you have to do. You
want to get used to switching between these two basic shapes (the various
E shapes and the various A shapes) and you also want to practice switching
between open chords and these new barre chords. Here are some sample chord
progressions to help get you going on that:

Hear How

To hear the dramatic difference in voicing between
an open chord and a
barre chord, listen to the
beginning of "Brown Eyed
Girl" by Van Morrison.
The first measure of rhythm
guitar is an open-position
Em chord and the second
measure is another Em
chord, but played as an
Am-shaped barre chord at
the seventh fret.

Track 60

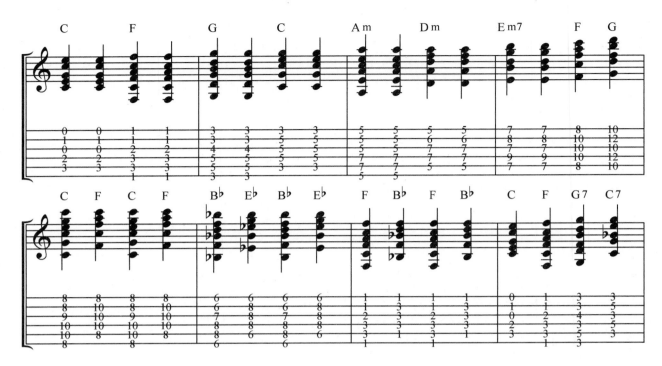

Barre chords are an essential part of playing rock guitar. With the foundation you've developed so far with this book, it shouldn't take long for your index finger to comfortably and smoothly barre across all six strings. And it shouldn't take your other fingers long to work out the shapes they already know.

Take your time and work through practicing changing between barre chords as well as between open chords and barre chords until you feel confident playing them.

C Shape

C Major is another Root 5 chord you know well, and it can be used as a moveable chord shape as long as you take the open G string into account. For example, the following illustration shows an F Major chord, played as a C-shaped barre chord at the fifth fret. Note that the entire chord, including the barre, spans across four frets. The index finger covers the first three strings of the fifth fret while the index finger is on the sixth fret of the B string, the ring finger is on the seventh fret of the D string, and the pinky sits on the eighth fret of the A string:

Making a C-shaped barre chord.

F

Making an F-shaped barre chord.

5th fret
6th fret
7th fret
8th fret

While the C-shaped barre is a good one to know, most rock guitarists don't use it all that much. Rather, they use *most* of it, playing the Am7 shape and being careful to only strum the four highest strings of the guitar. The low root note doesn't get played.

Half a Barre

As noted previously, half barre chords are barre chords in which anywhere from two to five strings are barred by one finger (almost always the index finger). The most common half barre chords use a barre on the highest strings and, like full barre chords, it's easiest to remember them by their open-position counterparts: E, Em, Am, and D.

Here are some examples of E-shaped half barres:

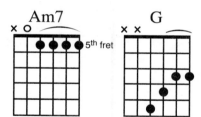
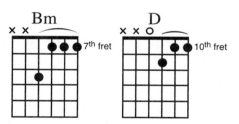

E-shaped half barres.

The E- and Em-shaped half barre chords can be found in the same way as the Root 6 full barres. Remember that the notes on the low E string have the same note names as those on the high E string! So to find the C chord, the first chord in the previous illustration, you find the C note at the eighth fret of the high E string and then barre across two, three, or four strings with the index finger. Add your middle finger to the ninth fret of the G string and your ring finger to the tenth fret of the D string and you're good to go.

Am-shaped barre chords are quite often played as partial barres. The Am7 shape, in fact, uses the same fingering as the high four strings of the full C barre, so many guitarists use it as a substitute, as mentioned earlier.

As an added bonus, the Am7 half barre chord can function as two different chords. The following example shows this half barre chord at the fourth fret:

Hear How
Probably the most recognized half barre chord in rock music is the very first notes of "Stairway to Heaven," which is an Em-shaped half barre version of the Am chord.

Getting Better

With many half barre chords, you will want to think ahead and use your index finger to cover one or more strings than you need for the current chord. This is especially true when switching from Root 5 A-shaped barre chords to Root 6 E-shaped chords. The less you have to adjust your index finger, the smoother the chord change will usually be.

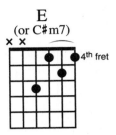

E
(or C#m7)
4th fret

The notes played in this chord (from high to low: G#, E, B, and G#) are the three notes of the E Major chord, but they are also three of the four notes used in C#m7, which has the notes C#, E, G#, and B. Many chords share common notes; getting this idea into your head will help you find more chord voicings along the fretboard.

You will also run into the Am7 shape quite a lot when playing rock in Open G tuning, which you'll read more about in Chapter 19.

The "Thumb Over" Option

If you have large hands, you may want to try an alternate way to play E-shaped barre chords. Start with a half barre E chord, using your index finger to cover the first two or three strings. Then play the root note on the low E string by wrapping your thumb over the top of the neck of the guitar. You don't need to get a lot of thumb on the string, just enough to sound the needed note:

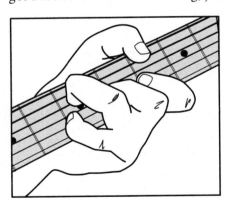

Because most electric guitars have small, slender necks, even people with normal or small hands can usually make this shape. It takes a little getting used to, but having a second option for six-string full barres can help keep you from tiring out your fretting hand.

With a little practice, you probably will also develop enough finesse to play the note at the low E string and simultaneously mute the A string with your thumb. That can be very handy.

Combining Barres and Slurs

Both the "thumb over" approach and half barres work well when combining chords with slurs. Having the ring finger or pinky free enables you to ornament your chord with additional notes.

Many riffs and fills, not to mention the signature hooks of numerous rock songs, come from just playing around with a half barre chord, using a free finger to add a hammer-on or a hammer-on / pull-off combination.

Hammer-Ons and Pull-Offs

In the following example, inspired by the classic rock of Chuck Berry, start with either a partial E shape at the fifth fret or a "thumb over" that also mutes the A string:

Track 61

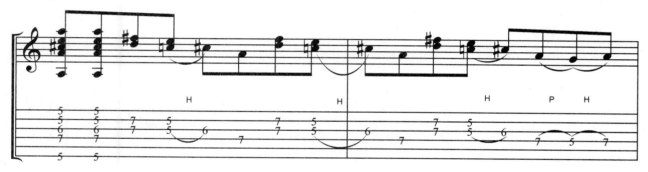

Half barre riff.

Play the first chord twice, and then use your ring finger to fret the necessary notes at the seventh fret while keeping your index finger on the notes at the fifth fret. After playing the second double stop (at the fifth fret), use your middle finger to hammer-on for the note on the sixth fret of the G string. Your ring finger is then free to get the note at the seventh fret of the D string.

After you've got the hang of this, work on being able to sound that last note (seventh fret of the D string) just by hammering your ring finger into place. That will also help you pick up a bit of speed in your playing.

Sliding Barres

When playing barre chords, you have to remember to keep a light touch. Initially, you will use a lot more pressure than you need to get the chord to sound clearly, but as you gain confidence you'll discover that the chords sound even better when you use just enough pressure.

Plus, you'll find that with less pressure and a light touch, you'll be able to slide your barre chords up and down the neck with ease. And that's a good thing, because you can come up with a lot of fun riffs and fills when you manage to slide your full barre and half barre chords around, as the following exercise demonstrates:

Track 62

Sliding barre riff.

Getting Chunky with Left-Hand Muting

One unexpected benefit of learning barre chords is that you learn about *left-hand muting* in the process. You did a little bit of muting back in Chapter 5 when you learned about playing octaves. That may have been a bit tricky, but full left-hand muting is very easy. Start by playing a Root 6 barre chord, say G, as in the following example:

Track 63

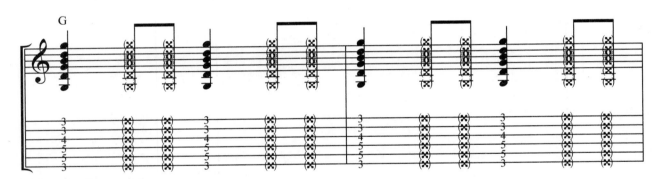

Left-hand muting example.

def•i•ni•tion

Muting occurs when using either the left hand or right hand to deaden some, or all, of the sound of the guitar strings. Left-hand muting, done on the fretboard, is traditionally called *string muting* while right-hand muting, usually done near the bridge of the guitar, is known as *palm muting.*

Remember that note heads that look like an *X*, or any *X* on the guitar tablature staff, are symbols for muting. Here, you play the full barre G chord and then slightly raise all your fingers but still keep them in contact with the strings. You only want to deaden the sound. Too much pressure and you'll end up with a fretted note. If you lose contact with any string, you'll get the note of that open string.

Another common way of left-hand muting is to simply lay two, three, or even all four fingers across the strings, with just enough pressure to effectively dampen the individual notes.

Left-hand string muting is a very effective technique that adds a bit of personality and variety to an ordinary rhythm. With practice, it can also be used to cover up moving from one barre chord to another while still strumming!

"Chunky Barre Rock"

Our "practice song" for this chapter concentrates on full barre chords, just the E and A shapes (both major and minor) in order to keep it relatively easy for starters. It also has quite a bit of left-hand muting, which gives it a very dynamic rock style.

You'll note that some of the chords are labeled with a *2* after them, such as E2, F2, and G2. These indicate different voicings for these barre chords. Here is a chart to help you out:

And here is the song:

Track 64

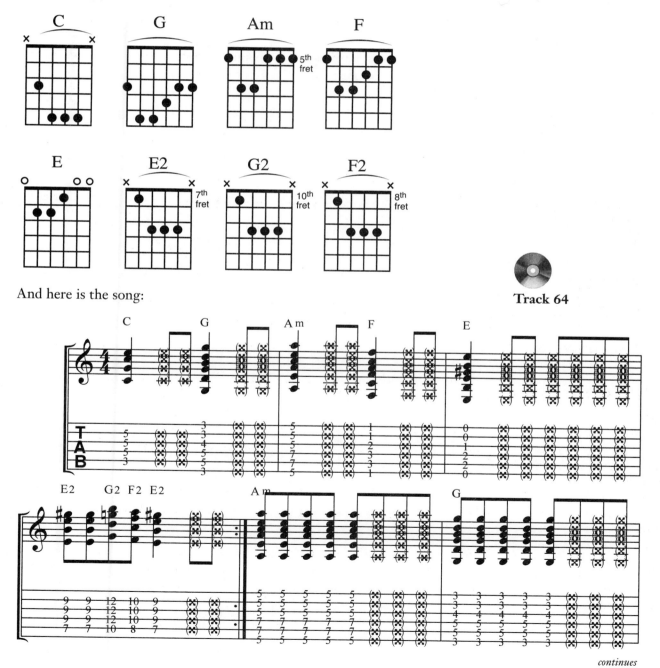

continues

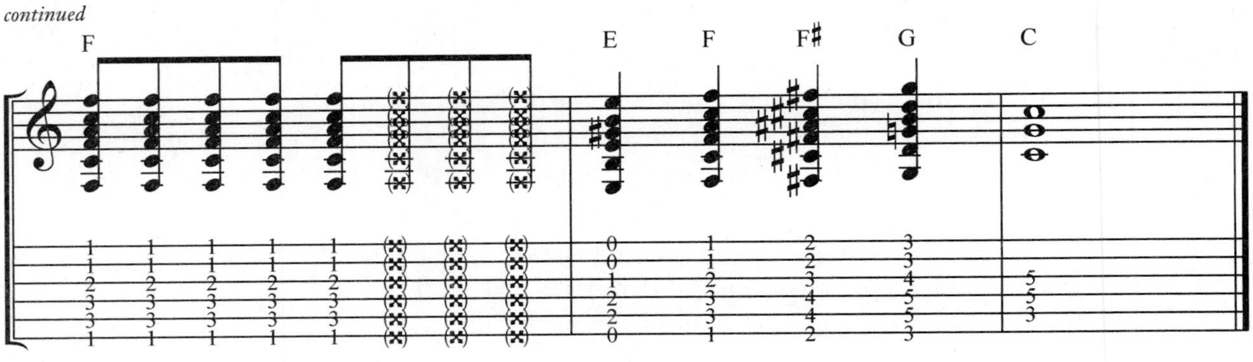

continued

"*Chunky Barre Rock*"

You've covered a lot of ground in this chapter, so take extra time to make certain you are comfortable before moving onward.

Barre chords are an essential tool of the rock guitarist, possibly even more important than power chords, so practice them until you feel you can make smooth changes while keeping a steady rhythm.

The Least You Need to Know

♦ Chords, like scales, can be open or closed position.

♦ Barre chords are closed, movable chords.

♦ Rock guitarists primarily use E- and A-shaped barre chords.

♦ You create half barre chords when you barre four or fewer strings with your index finger.

♦ Left-hand string muting is an important rhythm technique.

Chapter **10**

Serious Metallurgy

In This Chapter

◆ Understanding sixteenth notes

◆ Palm muting

◆ Finding natural harmonics

◆ Playing artificial harmonics

◆ A few words on tapping and sweep picking

Sometimes learning guitar seems like a contest between your left and right hands. If you've been keeping score of such things, you've already learned a number of left-hand techniques, such as hammer-ons and pull-offs, that have helped you develop speed in your fretting hand. You've also been working on your alternate picking, which certainly gives you a lot more speed in the right hand. The previous chapter definitely focused more on your left hand and now, with barre chords and left-hand muting techniques in your pocket, it's time to work some more on your right-hand technique.

Hopefully, concentrating on one hand at a time reinforces your sense that playing the electric guitar is a matter of touch and finesse. Hopefully, too, you are developing an appreciation for rhythm and its vital role in playing rock music. You're definitely going to need both your sense of touch and your feel of rhythm for these next two chapters!

Sixteenth Pack

Up to now, most of our work has been with either eighth notes (both "straight" and "swing") or triplets. We can subdivide any beat into even smaller portions. A *sixteenth note* is equal to one quarter of a beat. In other words, it's half the length of an eighth note. In notation, sixteenth notes look like eighth notes but they have two flags on their stem instead of one or are joined by two beams when connected together, like the example on the next page.

Sixteenth notes in standard notation.

Counting sixteenth notes out loud can be tricky. The conventional practice is to go "one ee and ah, two ee and ah, three ee and ah, four ee and ah." As you might imagine, this is pretty hard to do when playing at even reasonably moderate tempos!

A great way to acclimate yourself to playing different note values is to play one measure of each (quarter note, eighth notes, triplets, and sixteenth notes) and then try stringing together a few measures that have single beats of each type of note, as shown here:

Strumming notes of different timing values.

Track 65

Picking or strumming sixteenth notes while counting off eighth notes usually works for most people. But it does take some getting used to. And it should go without saying that you want to use alternate picking to play sixteenth notes, as shown in the previous illustration.

Fast and Furious

However you decide to count sixteenth notes, it's important that you do count, and preferably out loud to start. Many beginners find themselves playing too fast simply because they are playing a lot of notes. As you heard in the previous example, the tempo, the "one, two, three, four" of your count, remains constant, whether you're playing quarter notes, eighth notes, triplets, or sixteenth notes.

Track 66

In rock music, you'll play mostly eighth notes and sixteenth notes. The best way to develop good rhythm is to practice. Write out a few different measures, making sure to have a mix of eighth notes and sixteenth notes, and you're on your way. Here are a few you can use to start out:

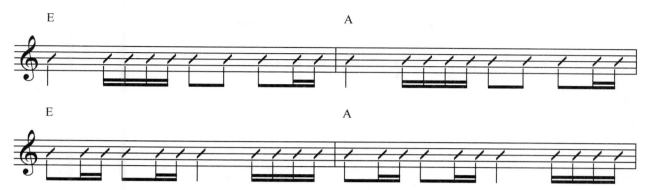

Rhythm patterns to practice.

Taking a Rest

Sixteenth rests look a lot like eighth rests, only they have two flags on the stem, just like sixteenth notes themselves:

Sixteenth rests.

You want to make certain to include both eighth rests and sixteenth rests in your practicing, such as in these examples:

Track 67

continues

continued

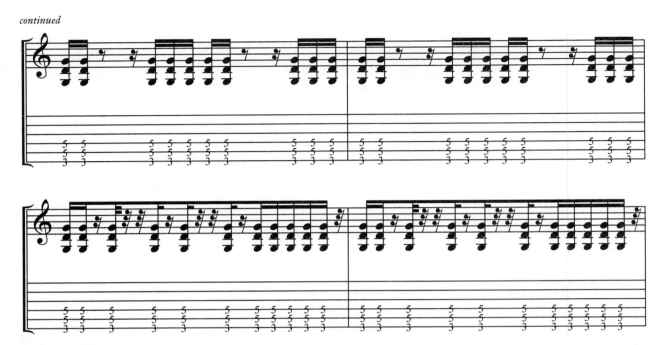

More rhythm patterns to practice (with sixteenth rests).

Muting the strings for a sixteenth rest requires practice and patience. At slower tempos you can get by with doing most of the muting with your left hand, simply by raising the fingers off the neck but not off the strings, which will effectively dampen the note you've played.

But you'll probably find yourself using your right hand or even both hands to mute strings for tricky rhythms, and that's perfectly okay to do.

In the Palm of Your Hand

Right-hand muting is used for many different rhythmic aspects of playing the guitar. *Palm muting*, along with power chords, is one of the signature sounds of rock guitar. It's slightly misleading in its name, in that you don't really use the palm of your hand as much as the heel, or far edge of your hand that runs along the pinky to the wrist.

You are already aware of the importance of keeping your picking hand close to the strings.

Palm muting takes this one step further, literally putting the heel of your right hand in contact with the strings as you pick them. The following illustration demonstrates proper positioning for palm muting:

def•i•ni•tion

Palm muting is a right-hand technique that uses the heel of the picking hand to partially mute the strings as they are picked. It's one of the signature sounds of rock guitar playing.

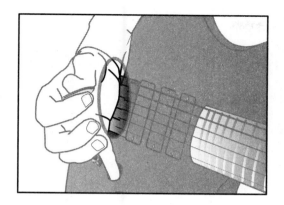

Palm muting.

Single Strings

Begin by placing the heel of your hand close to the bridge of your guitar. Play the low E string, keeping the heel of your hand on the string and applying just enough pressure to *slightly* mute the string.

Track 68

Low E string palm muting.

It truly is a matter of touch. You control the amount of muting that occurs, so the tone of your notes will vary according to how much pressure you apply with the "palm." It can be anything from a barely noticeable softening of the open string to a barely heard percussive thumping.

Also, varying your hand's position in relation to the bridge will greatly influence your control (the closer you are to the bridge, the less pressure you need) as well as the tone you produce.

Getting Better _____

If you use a lot of arm motion to pick the strings, you will find palm muting to be a bit of a challenge. It's important to keep the heel of your hand relatively still and to let most of the picking motion come from your wrist and thumb.

Two, Three, and More

When you feel comfortable using palm muting on a single string, the next step is to try it with double stops—two adjacent strings. Then move on to three-note power chords. You can even use the exercises from Chapter 5 to practice palm muting!

With palm muting across several strings, you want to ease off the pressure enough so that you can readily pick the two or three strings you want. Occasionally, you'll find yourself shifting your palm along the strings as you readjust your picking. That is perfectly fine to do.

Applying Pressure

Track 69

Palm muting can add a lot of texture to your rhythm playing, especially when combined with regular strumming. Metal rock guitar constantly switches from palm-muted notes or chords to full strums, using this dynamic shift in tone to punctuate the music:

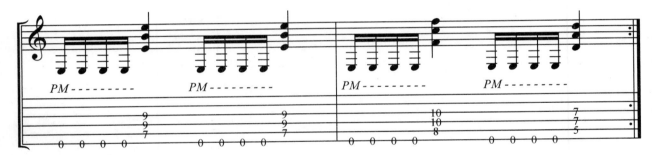

Combining palm muting with regular strumming.

Don't kid yourself into thinking this technique is something you can do without practice. At first, palm muting might seem impossible. You will probably be too tense and choke the notes off completely. That's okay. As with all the other techniques you've learned so far, steady practice and repetition will bring you the confidence you need, and before long you'll find yourself using palm muting without even thinking about it. And you'll sound even more like a rock guitarist than before!

Anticipations

Rhythm, steady rhythm, is essential to rock music. But sometimes it's good to break things up a bit, or at least to make it sound like you are!

Anticipation involves coming in slightly ahead of a given beat, usually a half beat ahead. This can be done with a single note or a whole chord, by one player or a whole band. And though it might seem to run contradictory to all the advice about rhythm that you've gotten so far, anticipation is also a very important part of rock rhythm playing.

The Illusion of Speed

If you listen to a song like "Franklin's Tower," by the Grateful Dead or "Three Marlenas" by the Wallflowers, you can hear that while the beat seems steady, the music seems to be picking up speed, gathering momentum all through the song. This is because the chords are changing a half beat ahead of time. The drums (and sometimes the bass) keep constant and the guitars hit the chord change on the last half of the fourth beat on any given measure. With "Three Marlenas," there is an anticipation on the last half of the second beat as well.

This seeming tug-of-war between the guitar and the drummer creates the feeling that music is speeding up, while in reality it's staying steady. Anticipations are used in all kinds of music, but they probably occur in rock music more than any other genre.

Unfortunately, many beginners are likely to totally lose track of the beat when playing an anticipation. This is understandable as they are used to chord changes occurring right on the beat.

More Ties

Obviously, then, it's important to work through rhythms that involve anticipations. Being able to hear and feel the way the chords change during anticipations will keep you from losing the beat and floundering along.

Usually, an anticipation on the last half of the fourth beat of a measure will carry through at least the first half of the first beat of the next measure, so the note will be tied from one measure to the next. Here are two simple exercises to help you recognize and play anticipations:

Track 70

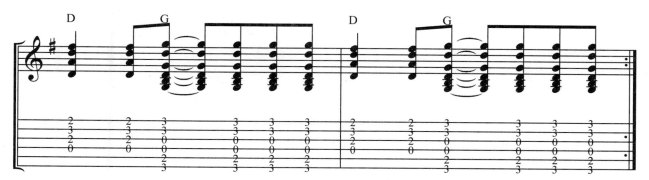

Examples of anticipation.

Notice that in these two examples, the anticipation chord changes occur on an upstroke. This is not always the case, especially with more complex rhythm patterns. But for most simple rock songs, thinking of the anticipation as a chord change on the upstroke before a first or third beat will often do the trick.

Finding Harmonics

Ultimately, finesse requires you to use both your hands, working together to produce music. *Harmonics*, which are chimelike tones, can be produced on your electric guitar using a variety of two-handed techniques. Played cleanly, they are almost like bells. Add some distortion and they can positively scream.

Harmonics are primarily used in soloing, but can also be part of the rhythm backing of a song. Guitarists tend to classify harmonics as either "*natural*" or "*artificial*," depending on how they are executed.

def•i•ni•tion

Harmonics are clear, almost bell-like tones that can be played through one of several two-handed techniques. **Natural harmonics** are located at specific places on the guitar's fretboard and, depending on the guitar's tuning, correspond to a specific group of notes. **Artificial harmonics** can be produced for any note at any location on the neck of the guitar.

Natural Harmonics

Track 71

Playing natural harmonics is easy if you know where to find them and, fortunately, your fretboard makes it very simple. Place your index finger on the twelfth fret of your high E (first) string, as shown in this illustration:

Playing natural harmonics.

You want to take note of two things. First, your finger should be positioned *over* the wire fret, not in the space between the frets as if you're playing the normal note at the twelfth fret. And you want to be on the metal fret closer to the body of the guitar.

Second, you want your finger to be as light on the string as possible, almost as if you're trying to not be on the string at all. When you pick the high E string, you should hear a clean, clear, crystal tone.

Natural harmonics can be found all over the fretboard of your guitar, but the easiest places to play them are at the twelfth, seventh, and fifth frets.

Squealies!

While natural harmonics are found at specific spots on the fretboard, artificial harmonics can be produced anywhere. The most common type of artificial harmonic is the pinch harmonic, usually notated as "P.H." or just "PH" in music and tablature.

Pinch harmonics are created by striking the guitar string almost simultaneously with both the pick and the thumb. The thumb touching the string deadens the fundamental note and enhances one of its harmonics. You want to choke up a bit on your pick so that when you strike the string, it feels like you're hitting both pick and thumb at the same time.

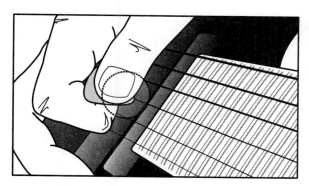

Playing pinch harmonics.

The pinch harmonic played on the CD is located at the ninth fret of the B string, but you can play them anywhere. They add a lot of punch to a solo.

Track 72

It should go without saying that this technique involves quite a bit of experimentation and trial-and-error on your part. Once you have the technique down, play around with the tones and controls on both your guitar and amplifier. You'll be astonished at how powerful a sound you can get with such a light touch on your guitar.

"Metal Mettle"

Let's take a moment and try a little practice song to help go over both the sixteenth note timing and palm muting covered earlier in this chapter, and we throw in some harmonic techniques for good measure.

Remember that even though this song is full of sixteenth note rhythms and single lines, the general tempo is still on the slow side. That should make counting and timing easier!

Track 73

"Metal Mettle"

Further on Down the Road

This is probably as good a time as any to stress that just playing around with your guitar, experimenting with how to create different sounds, is an important part of learning. As mentioned way back in the introduction, this book is meant to get you started as a rock guitar player. There is no way to cover every possible technique in these pages, but with a solid grasp of the basics, coupled with some knowledge of how music works (which you read in Part 4), you should be set to go quite far.

Very briefly, I'd like to touch upon a few other techniques that you've undoubtedly seen, heard, or read about. As beginners, some of them are quite a bit beyond you at present. But most of them are simply, in some way or another, more advanced versions of techniques you already know. Some you may be able to get very quickly and some may take weeks or months.

Whamming the Vibrato Bar

If your guitar has a vibrato bar, then you automatically have an additional way to create both vibrato and bends, including full bends of chords that you could never do "the old fashioned way."

The vibrato bar is attached to the guitar's bridge section or tailpiece assembly. Depressing or pulling up the vibrato bar will slacken or tighten string tension, in turn lowering or raising the pitch. The difference between using the vibrato bar and using your fingers is that the bar works all six strings at once.

By controlling the force and speed with which you manipulate the bar, you can create all sorts of effects, from the "dive bomb," a drastic and dynamic drop in pitch, to a short, hurried vibrato to a light rise or fall much like a Hawaiian guitar or pedal steel.

Tapping

At its heart, tapping on the guitar is essentially hammering-on and pulling-off done, pardon the pun, on a grand scale. The right hand is used to hammer, or tap, a note high up on the fretboard while the left hand is set at a certain note (or notes) that will be sounded after the initial tap.

In the illustration on the next page, the left hand is positioned with the index finger (labeled "3") on the fifth fret of the G string and the ring finger ("2") on the seventh fret of the same string.

Hear How

Jimi Hendrix, of course, was a master at using the vibrato bar, but for a good example of its use in a more casually mannered way, check out "Walk Don't Run," a classic surf rock instrumental by the Ventures, courtesy of Bob Bogle on guitar.

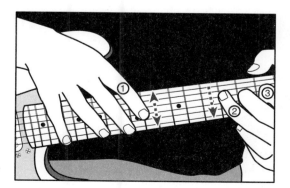

Tapping.

The tap is started by the index finger of the right hand (1) producing a note by hammering on the twelfth fret of the G string. When the note is played, the finger then performs a pull-off, in either an inward (up) or outward (down) direction, which sounds the note at the seventh fret, where the ring finger is sitting in position. Once this note is sounded, the ring finger then performs a pull-off (downward) that in turn sounds the note at the fifth fret of the G string.

Because of the amplification, tapping is a technique tailor-made for rock guitar, but it also has its drawbacks, particularly for a beginner. Excessive string noise is bound to happen when making the initial tap, so you have to be fairly adept at muting with both hands. And making certain that the initial tap is also a pull-off ensures the second note comes through clearly. The simple pull-off motion of the tapping finger can make all the difference when it comes to producing clean notes instead of an undefined blur of sound.

Sweep Picking

To the uninitiated, sweep picking may seem just like strumming a chord, or like playing an arpeggio very, *very* fast. And in theory, they are close to being right. Sweep picking is, essentially, playing an arpeggio while gliding the pick first downward and then back up. But unlike a chord or a typical arpeggio, in sweep picking you don't want the notes to ring out. They are played evenly and separately. You should be able to clearly hear each note as it is played without hearing the ringing of the last note.

Saying this isn't easy is a bit of an overstatement. Technically, you want your fretting hand to move from note to note (and deaden the previous note as well) as quickly as your strumming hand makes its stroke in one direction or the other. It involves incredible coordination, exceptional pick handling, and a lot of skill at muting with both hands (and pick).

The good news is that the skills you are developing now as a beginner will, one day down the road, help you to perform this technique. So don't stop practicing your basics!

The Least You Need to Know

- Sixteenth notes are one quarter of a beat in length.
- Palm muting is one of the essential rhythm parts of rock guitar.
- Harmonics can add spice to both soloing and rhythm playing.
- The vibrato bar can bend all six strings at once.
- The basic techniques you are learning will help you one day use more advanced techniques, such as tapping and sweep picking.

Chapter 11

Punky and Funky

In This Chapter

◆ Developing an accent

◆ Keeping rhythms steady and true

◆ Writing out rhythms

◆ Sixteenth note and quarter note triplets

◆ Building a funk riff from scratch

The addition of sixteenth notes to your musical knowledge opens up almost endless possibilities, particularly when it comes to rhythm. When you add string muting—either left hand, right hand, or both—to the mix, the idea of coming up with a single "strumming pattern" for any song seems like a waste of resources!

Two genres of rock music, punk and funk, both tend to use rhythm to its fullest potential. Funk, with its slinky combination of chords and single note riffs, probably seems obvious. Punk music is more straightforward in its attack, but uses palm muting, string muting, and accenting to give its rhythm some real bite.

And this brings up another important point: *all* music has something to teach you, even if it's a style that you're not particularly a fan of. For example, you will find both punk and funk guitar stylings in more mainstream rock bands from the Police to the Red Hot Chili Peppers. One of the greatest ways to bring new dimensions to your own playing is to listen to music outside of your usual interest areas. It will almost always be worth your while.

Punching It Up

Accenting a note or a strum means giving that note or strum a little more punch in the stroke. In music notation or in tablature, accents are indicated by ">" symbols placed over or under the note. Usually it's over a number in

Track 74

tablature and either over or under a note in notation, depending on whether the stem is upturned or downturned.

Here is an example of a typical use for accenting in rhythm:

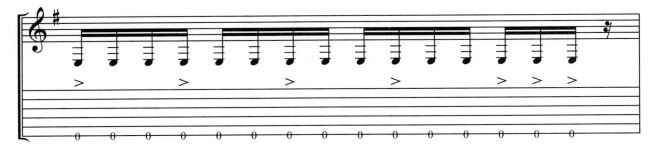

Using accents in rhythm playing.

As you can hear on the CD, there is no one single right way to accent. You can stress the accent slightly, giving it just a little more edge than the rest of the "normal" strumming, or you can go over the top, pounding it out so hard that you make people stop in their tracks.

More times than not, especially if you're just going off of chord sheets for your music, accenting a particular note or chord is up to your discretion as a player. Ultimately, accenting becomes part of your own personal style. And even though it's one of those techniques most guitarists seem to do instinctively, it's important to give it some concentrated attention in practice at this early stage.

Flawless Rhythm

If you don't practice good rhythm, then you could easily be practicing bad rhythm without even realizing it. And once a false rhythm is in your head, it's harder to get it out than you might think.

As mentioned numerous times earlier in this book, counting aloud can certainly help. So can using a metronome. But it's just as important to have a firm grasp of what rhythm entails and not be fooled into thinking that it's merely as simple as moving your arm down and up.

Making "Down and Up" Work

Well, actually, it can be that simple, but you also have to think about what you're doing. When you play quarter notes, timing seems easy enough. Eighth notes get a little trickier and sixteenth notes trickier still.

You probably remember the following exercise from the previous chapter. This time, though, I've added the "count" to each measure:

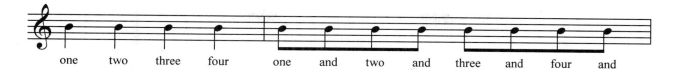

one   two   three   four   one   and   two   and   three   and   four   and

one and ah two and ah three and ah four and ah   one ee and ah two ee and ah three ee and ah four ee and ah

Notes with counting.

If you can remember to keep your strumming hand in motion and always hit each beat of a downstroke (each half beat if sixteenth notes are involved), then you have a great chance of keeping a steady rhythm throughout a piece of music.

Reading Between the Notes

The real test, as you learned in Chapter 6, comes when rests or tied notes are involved. But the same principles of "constant motion" still apply. Here are four moderately complicated rhythms involving sixteenth notes. At the beginning of the track, you will hear me count out four beats and you will also hear me "clicking" the strings with my pick in sixteenth notes:

Track 75

Practicing rhythms with sixteenth notes.

I deliberately play this slowly so you can follow along. By giving myself a "template" of sixteenth notes to start with, I can hear in my mind just how fast a sixteenth note is going to be at this particular tempo. If I keep my picking hand in a constant motion at that pace, there is little chance of having my rhythm derailed.

You can use this method even if you don't have sheet music for a song. Just write out the beats and half beats on a piece of paper like this:

```
1     +     2     +     3     +     4     +
```

Or also include the sixteenth notes, like this:

```
1  *  +  *  2  *  +  *  3  *  +  *  4  *  +  *
```

When you listen to a song, get the beat firmly in your head and then listen to when a chord is strummed. Place an *x* under the appropriate beat, or fraction of a beat. For instance, you may hear this kind of rhythm in a heavy metal song:

```
1  *  +  *  2  *  +  *  3  *  +  *  4  *  +  *
x  x  x  x        x  x     x  x  x  x
```

Your strumming hand should already be in constant motion, playing downstrokes on any beat (the numbers 1, 2, 3, and 4) as well as the "+"s, and upstrokes in between (on the "*"s). But if you're hung up on the up and down aspects, then write those in as well and you have this:

```
1  *  +  *  2  *  +  *  3  *  +  *  4  *  +  *
x  x  x  x        x  x     x  x  x  x
D  U  D  U  D        U  D     D  U  D  U  D
```

There are very few rhythms that you won't be able to figure out if you think about counting first. If you think visually, only in terms of downstrokes and upstrokes, then you're more likely to lose the rhythm and get lost.

Triple the Triplets

Fortunately, rock rhythms are fairly steady most of the time, and keeping your picking hand in a constant, even motion will do the trick. But you sometimes come across anomalies. Just as you can divide a beat into thirds by using triplets (which you should remember from Chapter 6), you can also divide a half beat into thirds. These are called sixteenth note triplets.

You will come across sixteenth note triplets in all kinds of rock music, particularly in guitar solos. Remember to keep the triplet even, with each note equally spaced within that half beat, as shown in the following illustration.

Sixteenth note triplets are often used in solos as very fast hammer-ons and/or pull-offs. The temptation is to get through one as quickly as possible, but that often results in picking up the overall tempo of a song. Guitarists who begin playing at speed usually tend to pick up even more speed when confronted with a sixteenth note triplet.

Getting Better

Sometimes learning a tricky passage of a solo or a complex rhythm is best done beat by beat. Don't hesitate to "dissect" a measure into single beats in order to work through complicated music.

Track 76

Playing sixteenth note triplets.

So whenever you find yourself working on a riff or part of a solo that uses sixteenth note triplets, start by taking the tempo slowly enough so that you can make certain of the timing of each note. Beginning at a slower pace will help you hit the notes cleanly and distinctly.

You can also divide two beats into a set of triplets. These are *quarter note triplets* and they can be especially tricky to play at first. Here are two examples:

Track 77

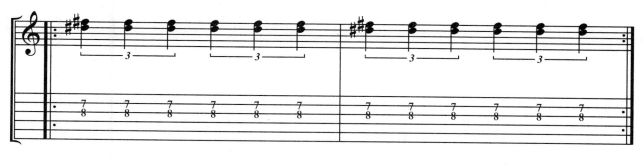

Playing quarter note triplets.

The first four measures are a steady stream of quarter note triplets, and you can hear how there is a distinct tension between the rhythm of the drums and the rhythm of the guitar. Even though they work together nicely, it sounds (and feels) as if either instrument could run off on its own at any moment.

Jazz and blues guitarists use this "three against two" feel quite often, and you will also hear it in blues-based rock music, such as ZZ Top's "La Grange."

The second example (the second line of four measures) mixes things up a bit more, combining dotted quarter notes, eighth notes, and two sets of quarter note triplets. It's a very similar rhythm to "Seven Nation Army" by the White Stripes. And again, you can hear how the clashing of the rhythm between the drum and guitar makes the music much more dynamic than if it were simply eighth notes and/or eighth note triplets.

From Chord to Riff to Groove

Track 78 (0:00)

As you learn in Chapter 17, riffs and fills are easy ways to spice up simple strumming rhythms. This is especially true with rock music and even more so with funk-based rock. The cool thing is that most of the riffs make use of notes that are either part of the chord you're strumming or that can be found relatively close by, such as this one:

Funky single note riff.

This single line riff uses notes found in the Em-shaped Dm barre chord, formed at the tenth fret. Like most funk riffs, not to mention rock riffs, it's surprising how cool it sounds using a limited number of notes.

Making Space

Track 78 (0:16)

Using this riff as a starting point, let's have some fun with the various techniques you've learned in the past three chapters. First, let's add some string (left hand) muting to it:

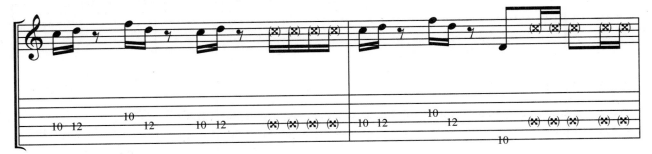

Adding string muting to funky riff.

If you're keeping your picking hand in motion, playing a measure of sixteenth notes in continuous fashion isn't all that hard. And you don't have to hit the same muted strings each time or even catch them on the same beats from measure to measure. The rhythm sounds and feels very organic.

Now try adding some pinch harmonics for a bit of a change:

Track 78
(0:32)

Adding pinch harmonics to funky riff.

Smooth Moves

Finally, try adding in a few partial chords, double stops, and pull-offs to flesh it out even more.

There's plenty of interesting things to listen to in just this two-measure riff in its current form, but just as important, you can make all sorts of minor variations as you repeat the riff over and over again. By mixing things up, neither you nor your listeners get bored.

Track 78
(0:48)

Complete funky riff.

And remember, even though we've used a funk-style riff here as an example, you can create riffs of all styles and genres in the same manner. We take a longer look at this in Chapter 17.

The Least You Need to Know

- ◆ Accenting single notes or chords adds interest to strumming.

- ◆ Keeping your strumming hand in constant, even motion helps you maintain a steady rhythm.

- ◆ Writing out a rhythm, beat by beat, is a great way to work out strumming patterns by ear.

- ◆ Any duration of beats can be divided into triplets.

- ◆ Funk riffs often combine single notes, muted strings, and chords.

Part 4

From Scales to Solos

Playing a mesmerizing rock solo is the dream of many guitarists. With the skills you've worked on so far, it's not beyond your capabilities. All you need is a little bit of musical direction.

Here you learn the basics of music theory, about notes and how scales and chords are created, about keys (in order to know which scales and chords to use), and about one scale in particular, the pentatonic, that is music's gift to the soloing guitarist. You also get some advice on how to come up with ideas for creating your own solos.

Chapter 12

A Little Music Theory Goes a Long Way

In This Chapter

♦ The twelve different notes

♦ Making any major scale

♦ Open and closed scale patterns

♦ Moveable Root 6 and Root 5 major scale patterns

♦ Where to find intervals on your fretboard

You don't have to read music to play guitar. You also don't have to know music theory. You can also live in a foreign country and never learn to speak the native language. But you might find yourself making better progress if you at least know how to say "hello."

Rock guitarists usually fall into two camps—those who know some music theory (*some* can fall anywhere between "enough to figure out how to play what needs to be played" and "puts most college music majors to shame") and those who don't know what they know. The fact of the matter is that anyone who plays any musical instrument does know some theory, simply by virtue of playing music. Often, though, they don't know how to tell you what they know. Worse, they don't know how to go about accessing that information in order to become better musicians.

You can only decide for yourself which camp you want to be in. But if you want to be able to hear a song and quickly figure out a guitar part for it, then you definitely want to opt for a bit of knowledge. Contrary to what you may have read anywhere else or heard in interviews, there's nothing about "rock guitar" that implies you need to pretend you don't have a brain. Don't make the divide between "emotional" and "intellectual." No one is going to notice how emotional your solo is if you play it in the wrong key!

The cool thing is that you don't have to tell anyone you know theory. Or you can be even cooler by helping other musicians tap into what they already know but don't know they know.

Do? Si, Do!

Better still, music theory can be as simple as "do, re, mi." Somewhere in the recesses of your brain, you can probably remember the song "Do, Re, Mi," either from *The Sound of Music* or from your childhood or early schooldays. The notes do, re, mi, fa, so, la, ti, and do, sung as they are in this song, make up the pattern of the *major scale*, and the major scale is the basic building block of music theory. Virtually everything about chords, keys, and other scales is described in terms of the major scale. That makes the major scale, as Julie Andrews would sing, "a very good place to start."

We'll begin by laying out the major scale as we learned it in childhood:

Do   Re   Mi   Fa   So   La   Ti   Do

Notice that there are *Do* notes at both ends. This means that you've gotten back to the note name you started with, but that note is now an *octave* (eight notes) higher in pitch. Of course, you do remember discussing octaves back in Chapter 5.

For the sake of using "real" note names instead of "do, re, mi, etc.," let's replace *do* with C and then lay out our other notes in order. Remember that the note names go from A to G and then start at A again. Our major scale should now look like this:

C   D   E   F   G   A   B   C

So far, so good, but now we need to take a few steps sideways in order to understand what this really means.

Twelve Frets, Twelve Notes

Western music (*Western* meaning music of the Western Hemisphere and not Roy Rogers's songs) is made up of half steps. On the guitar, the note found at each fret is one half step either higher or lower than the neighboring note at the adjacent fret.

You also already know that there are more notes than just the seven (A, B, C, D, E, F, and G) written out above, because you've run into *flats* and *sharps*. These *accidentals* fall in between some of the notes, like this:

C	C#/Db	D	D#/Eb	E	F	F#/Gb	G	G#/Ab	A	A#/Bb	B	C

Not every note is spaced a whole step from the other. B and C are only a half step apart, as are E and F. All the other "regular" notes are one whole step away from their neighbors.

Note Worthy

Technically speaking, there is such a thing as E#. Raising the E note one half step in tone turns it into F. Likewise, Fb is another name for E, B# is the same as C, and Cb is B. It's very rare for these notes to be used in rock guitar music, but it is possible you may run into them at some point.

I started with these notes in this particular order to give you a little visual aid. Look at all 12 notes again and picture a piano or keyboard in your mind's eye. The "regular" notes (the ones without flats or sharps) would be the white keys while the accidentals (the notes that are either flat or sharp) would be the black keys. If you've ever seen a piano, then you might remember that the black notes come in sets of two and three, just as with the groupings of accidentals above.

Putting Things to Scale

Now that you have all the possible 12 notes on your palette, you want to have a way to arrange them. That's what scales are for. A *scale* is a specific pattern, usually a combination of half steps and whole steps, beginning from one note until you reach that same note once again. You start with *do*, whatever note you choose *do* to be, and your scale must end at *do*.

def•i•ni•tion

A **scale** is a specific series of steps, half steps, or larger intervals. Scales are usually given a name of two parts, such as the C Major scale, or the E minor pentatonic scale or the F# melodic minor scale. The first part of the name is a single note, namely the root note, which starts (and ends) the scale. The second name is more descriptive, such as major, minor, diminished, and so on. You will learn that each of these descriptive names is shorthand for a specific combination of half steps and steps that make up that particular scale.

def•i•ni•tion

To make any note **sharp** is to raise that note a half step in tone. When you lower any given note by a half tone, you make it **flat**. An **accidental** is a note that has been made either flat or sharp. Some accidentals share names and are called *enharmonic*. For example, the note that is a half step between G and A is called G# because it is a half step higher than G, *and* it can also be called A♭ because it is a half step lower than A.

Scales can begin at any of the 12 possible notes. Suppose I told you to start with the A note and then told you that the pattern for the *chromatic scale* was to move one half step at a time until you reached your starting note again. You would be able to figure out that the A chromatic scale is this:

A	A#/B♭	B	C	C#/D♭	D	D#/E♭	E	F	F#/G♭	G	G#/A♭	A

If you think the A chromatic scale is exactly like the fretboard map of the A string shown in Chapter 5, you'd be absolutely correct.

The Major Scale

There are more scale patterns than you can ever hope to remember. Fortunately, most of playing rock guitar involves only a handful of scales. And as mentioned earlier, they are all described in relation to the major scale.

The pattern for any major scale is as follows: You start with whatever note you want. This will be the *root note*. From the root note, take the following pattern of whole steps (W) and half steps (H):

Root   W   W   H   W   W   W   H (the root note again)

Try it out! Start with C. One whole step from C is D. One whole step up from D is E. Next you want a half step, and that is F. One whole step up from F is G. A is the next note (whole step up from G) and then B (whole step up from A). Finally, you go up one half step from B, which takes you to C again, completing the major scale pattern.

Don't stop there. Now that you know how to do it, work out several, if not all 12 possible major scales. Starting with A, for instance, the A Major scale would be as follows:

A   B   C♯   D   E   F♯   G♯   A

You see that we have to start using the accidentals in this scale because C♯, not C, is a whole step up from B. It turns out that each possible scale has a specific number of either flats or sharps (not both). You read all about that in Chapter 14.

Mapping Things Out

It's one thing to set this all down on paper. Working scales out on the guitar is another matter entirely. But it's worth it for you to do so for a number of reasons. First, it gets you more familiar with how to find the notes on your fretboard. And once you get to know how to find where the notes are, you're on your way to simply *knowing* where they are.

Another plus is that you start hearing how the notes of a scale work together, and that's a big plus when you start to improvise solos on your own because you can try to play what's going on in your head instead of being a slave to a scale pattern.

Scale patterns, as you've probably guessed, are moveable patterns that can be played at any place up and down the fretboard. They are incredibly important for guitarists, particularly as tools for practice and learning (as well as soloing and creating riffs).

Finding the Notes

Scales, just like chords, can be open or closed. An open position scale uses open strings for some of its notes. Here is the C Major scale in open position:

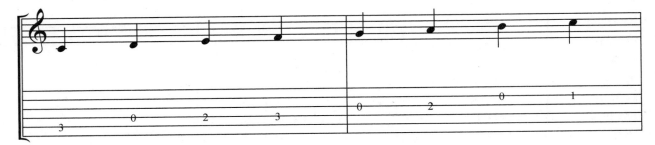

The C Major scale in open position.

It's important to mention here that scales, just like notes, extend both higher and lower than the selected portion. When learning scales on the fretboard, it's good to extend the scale in both directions across all six strings, like this:

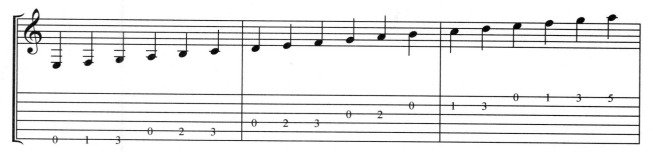

The C Major scale in open position, extended across all six strings.

You see that this last example includes notes of the C Major scale found on the low E (sixth) string, which are the open E as well as F and G. It gives us the D note on the B string, and the E, F, G, and A notes on the high E (first) string as well. Just as important is that all the notes are within a comfortable span of frets. You're not stretching your fingers at impossible angles or over a huge number of frets to go from any one note of the scale to the other.

Closing Down the Pattern

Turning an open position pattern into a closed position pattern means taking all the notes played on open strings and finding another place to play them. In the first example of the basic open position C Major scale, there were three such notes—D, G, and B. Back in Chapter 2 you learned there were other places to place those particular notes in the section on "relative tuning." The note at the open D string is also found at the fifth fret of the A string. Another place to play the note of the open G is at the fifth fret of the D string, and playing the fourth fret of the G string gives you the same note as the open B string.

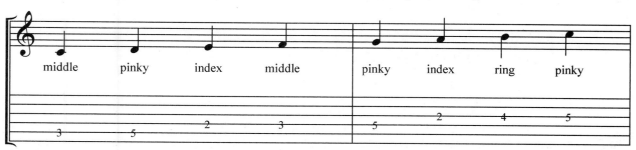

The C Major scale in closed position (with suggested fingerings).

Substituting these notes for their open position counterparts, you can play the C Major scale in the manner above.

Because this scale pattern covers four frets, you can play it reasonably easily, assigning each finger a fret and letting it take whatever notes fall on that specific fret.

Taking this one step further, you can also expand your closed position C Major scale across all six strings:

The C Major scale in closed position, expanded.

This is a little trickier to play, owing to the F note at the sixth fret of the B string. The best way to deal with this note is to play the E (fifth fret of the B) with your pinky as you did with the previous example and then slide the pinky up the neck one fret to reach this note. This shift of fingers means playing the G note (third fret of the high E) with your index finger and the A note (fifth fret of the high E) with your ring finger.

Moveable Root 5 and Root 6 Major Scale Patterns

Most guitarists find it easier to remember both chords and scale patterns by root positions, meaning they use whatever string the root note is on as a starting point of a particular pattern. For instance, this closed position C Major scale that you've been using as an example would be a Root 5 scale, because you used the C note at the third fret of the A string to start the initial closed position scale. Once you learn this scale pattern, you can use your knowledge of the notes on the A string to create major scales all up and down the neck. G, for example, is located at the tenth fret of the A string, so the G Major scale, in Root 5 position, would be as follows:

The G Major scale in Root 5 closed position, expanded.

Any note can be found on any string, so knowing that G can also be played at the third fret of the low E string means that you can first figure out the notes of the open position G Major scale (once, of course, you've determined what notes are in the G Major scale). Your findings will probably give you this:

The G Major scale in Root 6 open position.

The Root 6 position scale is interesting because it gives you two complete octaves, plus one additional note (possibly two depending on where on the neck you play it). There's not all that much expanding of notes to do.

Converting this open position G Major scale to a closed position gives you this:

The G Major scale in Root 6 closed position, expanded.

As long as your guitar is in standard tuning, you can move both of these major scale patterns anywhere on the neck. You will probably find you stop thinking in terms of individual notes and concentrate instead on the pattern itself. That's normal. When you're playing a lead, chances are you're not thinking "okay, first G, then A, then skip down to E," and so on. But knowing where the notes are on the neck gives you a place to start.

Scale patterns are usually shown in generic terms, like this:

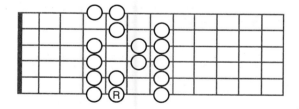

Generic closed position Root 6 major scale.

Here each dot represents a note of the scale. The dot with the *R* inside it is your root note. Rather, it's one of the root notes, but being on the sixth string, that's the one that helps you best identify where to begin. Suppose you want to play the C♯ Major scale. You know that C♯ is at the ninth fret of the sixth string, so you line up your root note there. The second note of the scale is at the eleventh fret, the third note is at the eighth fret of the A string, and so on.

The Root 5 moveable major scale would be as follows:

Generic closed position Root 5 major scale.

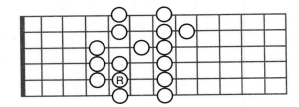

Knowing these two positions of your major scale gives you two distinct places on the neck for riffs and soloing and is a good start to better knowing the notes on your fretboard.

An Interlude on Intervals

When you know your major scale, you also have a start on recognizing intervals. Intervals are the distance between one note and another, and they are named according to the positions in the major scale. The root note is always "one" and the other notes are seconds, thirds, fourths, fifths, sixths, and sevenths.

Going from C to E, for instance, is a major third. So is going from A to C♯, because if A is our starting point (root note), C♯ is the third of the major scale.

Naturally, it's not all that cut-and-dry, but it's very easy to learn. And it's also important to know how to go from one note to any possible interval on your fretboard, especially if you want to be a good soloist. Here are all of the various types of intervals that you can create.

Major and Minor Seconds

The major second is the second note of the major scale. It is one full step higher than the root. You find it two frets further up the neck from your root note.

Major and minor seconds.

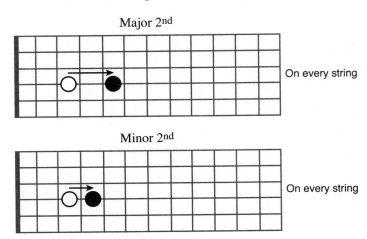

Going only a half step higher than the root is called a minor second. It is located at the next fret higher than your root note.

Major and Minor Thirds

As you learn in the following chapter, the note at the third interval is the one that determines whether a chord is major or minor. So it's a vital interval to know. The major third is two whole steps higher than the root, while the minor third is a step-and-a-half higher.

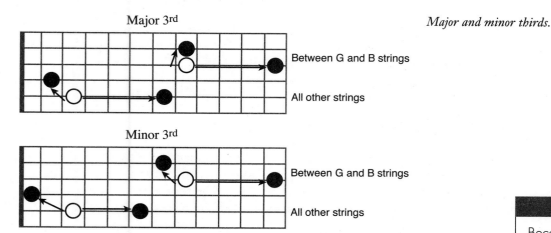

Major and minor thirds.

Two full steps translates to a reach of four frets, so many guitarists opt to find the third on the next string higher. The major third will be one string higher and one fret lower and the minor third is one string higher and two frets lower, as shown in the preceding diagram.

Fourths

Fourths are also commonly called perfect fourths, at least by musicians who've studied theory in school. Just plain old fourths is fine for most rock guitar players!

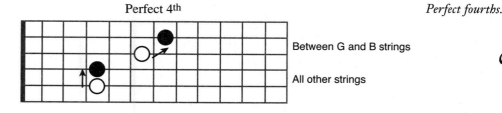

Perfect fourths.

Fourths are two and a half steps higher than the root note. On most strings, you find the fourth on the same fret as the root note, only one string higher. If your root note is on the G string, then the fourth may be one fret higher on the B string.

Three Fifths: Perfect, Diminished, and Augmented

Fifths come in three flavors. The perfect fifth (usually called the "major fifth" or just simply the "fifth") is three and a half steps higher than the

---

Note Worthy

Because of the standard tuning of a guitar, intervals that span the B string in some way will not be the same as intervals not involving the B string. This is because the B string is a major third (four frets) higher than the G string while all the other strings are tuned in perfect fourths (five frets higher).

def•i•ni•tion

The **diminished fifth**, also called the *tritone*, is exactly halfway between the root note and its octave. Its striking quality has been associated with evil and menacing connotations for centuries, even to the point of being described as "the devil in music" since the 1800s. Often the tritone is marked in music as *TT*.

root. The *diminished fifth*, which can also be called a "flat fifth" or the "tritone," is three full steps higher. The augmented fifth, or "sharp fifth," is four whole steps higher.

The fifth, as you remember from the appropriately numbered Chapter 5, is the second note necessary to make a power chord. Unless your root note is on the G string, the perfect fifth is always one string higher and two frets higher than your root. The diminished fifth is one string higher and one fret higher as well, while the augmented fifth is three frets higher on the next string.

Perfect, diminished, and augmented fifths.

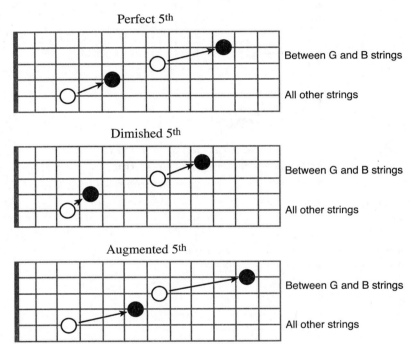

Perfect 5th

Between G and B strings

All other strings

Dimished 5th

Between G and B strings

All other strings

Augmented 5th

Between G and B strings

All other strings

If you're on the G string, the diminished fifth is two frets up on the B string, the perfect fifth is three frets higher and you'll find the augmented fifth four frets away.

Major and Minor Sixths

The augmented fifth, four whole steps up from the root as previously mentioned, is also the minor sixth. The major sixth is four and a half steps higher than the root.

Because of the way guitars are tuned, you will find the major sixth in different places depending on which string you have your starting note. If your root is on the low E (sixth) or A string, the sixth is two strings higher and one fret lower than the root note. If you're playing a root note on the D string, then the major sixth will be found on the same fret of the B string. When your root note is on the G string, the sixth is also two strings higher (the high E string) and on the same fret. But if your root note is on the B string, you're probably going to have to make quite a stretch as the major sixth would be four frets higher on the high E (first) string.

Hear How

The opening measures of "Purple Haze" by Jimi Hendrix consist of the tritone of E and B♭ being played by both the bass and guitar.

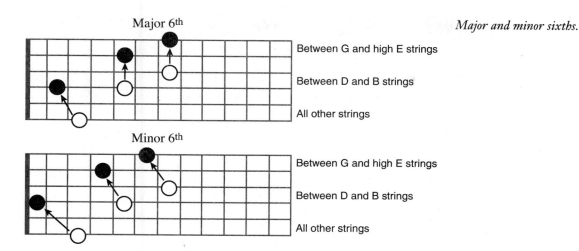

Major 6th

Between G and high E strings

Between D and B strings

All other strings

Minor 6th

Between G and high E strings

Between D and B strings

All other strings

Major and minor sixths.

Major Sevenths and Flatted Sevenths

Major sevenths are five and a half steps higher than the root note. If you prefer, and it's certainly easier to remember them in this way, think of them as being a half step below the root note, or better yet, the octave of the root note. Flatted sevenths are one whole step lower than the root's octave.

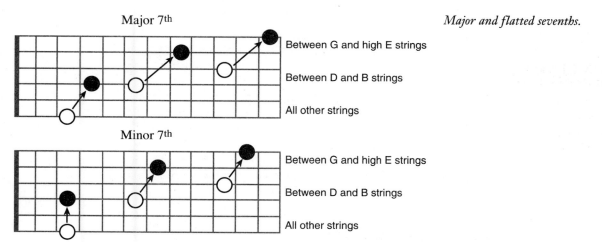

Major 7th

Between G and high E strings

Between D and B strings

All other strings

Minor 7th

Between G and high E strings

Between D and B strings

All other strings

Major and flatted sevenths.

Like sixths, finding a major seventh relies a great deal on what note you're starting with and what string that note is on. For the low E and A string, the major seventh is two strings higher and one fret higher and the minor seventh will be found on the same fret as the root, two strings higher.

For notes on the D and G strings, the major seventh is two strings higher and one fret higher and the flatted seventh is two strings higher and one fret higher.

And it's safe to say that both these sevenths are probably out of your reach if your starting note is on the B string, being either five frets (flatted seventh) or six frets (major seventh) higher up on the high E string.

Hear How

Being able to distinguish musical intervals helps you to learn guitar parts from recordings, not to mention any other instrument you may want to learn from. It's easier to practice your ear training with intervals when you have a sense of the interval to start with. Many people use easy familiar songs to help. For instance, the first two notes of "Somewhere Over the Rainbow" are an ascending octave, while the first two notes of "O Canada" are an ascending minor third. If you Google "musical intervals," you find all sorts of free websites that offer help and advice with interval ear training.

The Least You Need to Know

◆ The major scale is the cornerstone of music theory.

◆ There are 12 possible different notes, each one half step from its neighbor.

◆ Scales are created by using different combinations of half steps and whole steps.

◆ Closed position scales can be used anywhere on the fretboard.

◆ Intervals are the distances from one note to another.

Chapter

13

The Rest of the Lowdown on Chords

In This Chapter

◆ Making the four basic types of chords

◆ Suspended chords

◆ All sorts of seventh chords

◆ Very strange chords

◆ Slash chords

So far you've learned power chords, open-position chords, and barre chords. You've also learned that chords can be played at different positions along the neck.

Now it's time to take a moment to discover how chords are made. You may think this step unnecessary. After all, you already know enough chords to play most of your favorite songs for the rest of your life. Why go back now to learn why a C7 chord is a C7 chord or what notes go into making Dm?

I can only answer this with more questions—what kind of guitarist do you want to be? If all you want to do is play power chords (and there are enough guitarists out there who do just that), then you don't have to worry about chords all that much.

The Four Basic Chords

If you want to start exploring more of the possibilities your guitar has to offer, chords make an excellent starting point. Chords are the harmony of a song, and you can get very creative with chords by using chord substitutions or different chord voicings to make a song more interesting.

Play an open-position A Major chord. Now play it again, only remove your finger from the B string. This chord, as you learn later in this chapter, is Asus2. Listen to the difference between the two chords. It's subtle, but changing the C♯ at the second fret of the B string to B (open B string) creates a very interesting mood.

Now take your index finger and place it on the sixth fret of your G string and then put your middle finger on the seventh fret of the D string. Strum this chord down from the A string, using the note of the open A as your root. You have just played the Add9 chord. This last chord puts the C♯ note (sixth fret of the G string) back into the A chord and also adds the B note (open B string) and gives even more of a pronounced difference. It's a very cool sounding chord!

I highly encourage you to learn how chords are made. This knowledge will help you to come up with your own style of playing chords and it will also make it possible for you to make substitutions for chords that you might initially find hard to finger.

So to get you started, here are the four basic types of chords and how each are made:

- **Major chords** have the root, third, and fifth taken directly from the major scale of the root note.

- **Minor chords** have the root, minor third (the note of the third is lowered one half step), and the fifth.

- **Augmented chords** have the root, third, and augmented fifth (the note of the fifth is raised one half step).

- **Diminished chords** have the root, minor third, and diminished fifth (the notes of both the third and fifth are lowered one half step).

Constructing Triads

To get creative with chords, it helps to know where chords come from. As you've probably already guessed, chords are built from notes based on their position in the major scale. The harmony of Western music is based on *triads*, or thirds. Take a look at the notes of the C Major scale again:

C   D   E   F   G   A   B   C

The C Major chord is made by taking the root note and then adding the third and the fifth notes of the major scale to it. So the notes of the C Major chord are C, E, and G.

It gets even more interesting if you think of these notes as intervals. From C to E is a major third, as you learned last chapter. The interval of C to G is a major fifth.

Now consider that the interval from E to G is also a third, but it is a minor third, because G is one and a half steps higher than E. So you can also say that the C Major chord is created by starting with the root note (C), adding a major third (E) to the root note, and then adding the minor third higher than E, which would be G.

Stacking the thirds on top of one another like this gives you a *triad*, three notes that are thirds of each other. Because there are both major and minor thirds, you have four possible ways of combining triads, and these different ways give you the four basic types of chords:

- ◆ Root note + Major third + Minor third = Major chord
- ◆ Root note + Minor third + Major third = Minor chord
- ◆ Root note + Major third + Major third = Augmented chord
- ◆ Root note + Minor third + Minor third = Diminished chord

These four basic types of chords all contain a root, third, and fifth. The root note cannot be changed, because you'd obviously need to rename the note! It's the slight changes to the third and the fifth that determine which of the four basic chords you have.

Note Worthy

Knowing the four basic chords (major, minor, augmented, and diminished) can help you out in a pinch. Suppose you are playing from a chord sheet and the upcoming chord is A13. If you don't know how to play A13, you do know that this is a major chord (there's no *m* for minor, *aug* for augmented, or *dim* for diminished), so you can play an A Major chord and get away with it, particularly if you're playing with another musician. If the chord is Am11, for example, you can substitute regular old Am and things will still sound okay.

Majors and Minors

The greatest number of chords you will run into playing rock music will either be major chords, minor chords, or power chords.

Major chords are made by taking the root note, the third note, and the fifth note from the major scale positions. Changing the third into a minor third, that is, lowering the note by a half step turns a major chord into a minor chord. The fifth of the minor chord is still the same as the fifth of the major chord.

Power chords are made up of only the root note and the fifth and are neither major nor minor. It is possible, though, to have augmented and diminished power chords, as you read in just a moment.

Augmented and Diminished

Both augmented and diminished chords sound very transitory. When you hear one you almost want it to quickly become another chord, preferably something definitely major or minor.

Note Worthy

Whether the third of the chord is a major or minor third determines if the chord is major or minor. It's important to know that whenever you see the symbol *m* on a chord, that *m* is always letting you know about the third of the chord and no other note.

In augmented chords, the root and the third are the same as the major chord but the fifth has been raised a half step higher. This is why some musicians call augmented chords "#5" chords. The symbols most commonly used to denote augmented chords are the plus sign ("+") and the abbreviation *aug*.

Lowering the third and the fifth each by a half step gives you a diminished chord. These chords are very dark sounding, and it's surprising they are not used more frequently in rock music. One possible reason is that they are not that easy to play in standard tuning. Either the abbreviation *dim* or the degree symbol ("°") denote this chord.

You will, though, come across diminished power chords as well as augmented power chords. They will usually be labeled "#5 (no third)" for augmented power chords and "♭5 (no third)" for diminished power chords.

Suspension of Belief

In Chapter 7, you got a brief introduction to suspended chords. In a suspended chord, the third of the major chord is replaced by another note, usually the fourth note of the major scale.

Suspended chords are like power chords in that they sound neither major nor minor because they have no third. Technically speaking, without having a third they cannot be any of the four basic chords, so suspended chords ("sus" for short) are a special category all their own.

Sus4

As mentioned, the fourth usually serves as the replacement note for the third and is generally written as "sus4" in a chord chart or musical cheat sheet or fake sheet. You would construct a sus4 chord like this:

> Root   perfect fourth   perfect fifth

Sus2

Occasionally, the major second is used as a substitute for the third, as shown here:

> Root   major second   perfect fifth

This chord is commonly referred to as "sus2" even though people who have studied music theory very seriously will tell you there's no such chord. They are right, of course, but so many musicians use the term "sus2" that it's become a moot point. Don't worry about this because most musicians that you deal with will know exactly what you mean if you say "sus2."

Make It a Double

Because of the tuning of the guitar, it is possible to create "sus2sus4" chords, particularly with open-position D and A chords, like this:

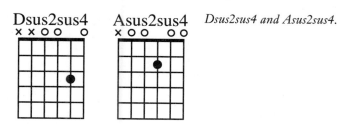

Dsus2sus4 and Asus2sus4.

Suspended chords, as a rule, are used to make long passages of single chords more interesting. They can help to brighten or accentuate a rhythm pattern as well as to push it along by constantly flipping from a chord to its suspended counterpart.

Making Sense of Sevenths

Most other chords that you will come across involve adding additional notes to the root, third, and fifth of your four basic chords (major, minor, augmented, and diminished). Seventh chords appear constantly in rock music (as well as blues, jazz, and country), and that may not be surprising when you consider that the seventh is the next interval of a third up from the fifth.

There are all sorts of seventh chords, and each one has a distinct feeling or mood of its own, so you definitely want to get familiar with each one.

Dominant

The dominant seventh, which also goes by just 7, has a bluesy feel and sounds transitory, though not to the extent that the augmented and diminished chords do. You create the dominant seventh by adding a minor third up from the fifth. Most people find it a lot easier to think of it in terms of adding the flat seventh from the major scale. So the formula for dominant seventh is:

Root   major third   perfect fifth   flat seventh

As you learn more songs and chord progressions, you may pick up on the fact that the chord that most often follows a dominant seventh is the chord one fourth up from the root of the dominant seventh. For example, C7 would more likely than not be followed by F, because F is the fourth of C (four notes up from C in the C Major scale).

Another way to look at it is this: F is the fourth of C, but C is also the fifth in the key of F (C being the fifth note in the F Major scale). In music theory, the fifth position of the scale is also given the name *the dominant*, from which the term "dominant seventh" comes.

All chords are interrelated, and many musicians use the "Circle of Fifths" to help remember how close these relationships are. You learn more about this in Chapter 14.

Major Sevenths

Major sevenths are made by starting with the major chord (root, third, and fifth) and then adding the note an interval of a major third higher than the fifth to it. This note turns out to be the seventh note of the major scale, so you might prefer to think of it this way:

> Root   major third   perfect fifth   major seventh

Remember that the term *major* is a default position. You never see the word *major* used on a chord sheet because you're supposed to assume a chord is major unless told otherwise. You'll always see *m* for minor, *aug* or "+" for augmented, or *dim* for diminished. But if you see a chord marked *G*, for example, you can correctly assume it's meant to be G Major.

The use of the abbreviation *maj* for major is used only when denoting the major seventh chord. This is easy to remember and helps to distinguish a major seventh from a regular or plain seventh. You may occasionally find major seventh chords denoted by "delta" symbols, or triangles ("Δ"). Cmaj7, for instance, may also be written as CΔ7.

Minor Sevenths

Keeping that little tidbit about the use of *maj* for major comes in handy when you see a minor seventh chord. Remember that the *m* for minor means that the third has been changed. So any minor seventh has a minor third but still keeps the dominant seventh (the flatted seventh of the normal dominant chord). In other words, the minor seventh would be made in this fashion:

> Root   minor third   perfect fifth   flat seventh

Minor sevenths are denoted by using the *m* of the minor chord and the 7 of the dominant seventh. E minor seventh, for instance, would be written out as Em7 on a chord chart.

> **Hear How**
>
> It's surprising how many minor seventh chords you hear in rock music once you train your ears to recognize them. Carlos Santana's version of "Black Magic Woman" is all minor seventh chords.

Minor Major Sevenths

The distinction between minor and major is important because, believe it or not, there is such a thing as a "minor major seventh." You would start with the minor chord and then add the major seventh to it, like so:

> Root   minor third   perfect fifth   major seventh

Minor major sevenths are denoted with the *m* of minor and the *maj*7 of the major seventh, usually the latter encased in parentheses, as in "Gm(maj7)" as an example.

Augmented Sevenths

Dominant sevenths are often added to augmented chords. They are denoted as regular sevenths with "(♯5)" added to the notation, such as "D7(♯5)." You construct them in the following way:

Root   major third   augmented fifth   flat seventh

Diminished Sevenths and Half-Diminished Sevenths

Diminished chords are a special case. When you see the term *diminished seventh*, you are adding a dominant seventh to a diminished chord and then also taking the added step of diminishing that dominant seventh. As crazy as it sounds, you're flatting a flatted seventh note!

However, lowering a flatted seventh note one additional half step gives you the sixth, so many folks prefer to think of diminished seventh chords in this manner:

Root   minor third   diminished fifth   flat   flat seventh (sixth)

Diminished sevenths are also called "full diminished sevenths" and are usually indicated by *dim*7 or a degree sign with the 7, as in E°7.

Things get a little more complicated because you can also add just a dominant seventh to a diminished chord, like this:

Root   minor third   diminished fifth   flat seventh

These are called "half-diminished chords," and you commonly see them written out as minor sevenths with "(♭5)" attached. "Am7(♭5)" is an example. A degree sign ("°") with a vertical slash through it is also used in some music notation.

If Six Were Nine

Things get a lot easier after you've gotten a handle on the various types of seventh chords. You either add individual notes to the basic triad or continue to stack up thirds on top of the seventh chords.

A sixth chord, for instance, means that you want to add just the sixth note of the major scale to the original major chord, like this:

Root   major third   perfect fifth   sixth

Sixth chords are a little sassy and are often used to give a little flair to a final chord, such as the last chord of the Beatles's song "Help."

Nines and Add Nines

If you see a chord that says "add9," you simply follow the instructions. First, you have to figure out that the ninth note of the scale is the same as the second one, but once you make that realization, you put together an add9 chord this way:

Root   major third   perfect fifth   major ninth

Chords like C9, though, require one more step. Any number higher than seven with just the number without the word *add*, implies that the dominant (flatted) seventh is still part of the chord. The word *maj* implies that the major seventh is the chord you're giving another note to.

So any 9 chord would be made:

Root   major third   perfect fifth   flatted seventh   major ninth

And maj9 chords would contain the following notes:

Root   major third   perfect fifth   major seventh   major ninth

Piling It On

The same principle applies to eleventh and thirteenth chords. If you see an *11* after a chord, assume that *both* the seventh and ninth are in this chord. A *13* means that seventh, ninth, *and* eleventh are present.

This becomes a bit of a problem, as you might imagine. After all, there would be seven notes in any thirteenth chord but you've only got six strings on your guitar!

More to the point, on the electric guitar the more complicated the chord, the more likely it's going to be very muddy. This is why very complicated chords tend to be played using four strings, five at the most, so that you don't end up with a sonic mess.

It's also why more complicated chords tend to be moveable bar chords, so that you only worry about a particular shape and where to find the root note of the chord.

Hear How

A lot of rock 'n' roll uses only three or four basic chords, but a guitarist can have a lot of say in how those three or four chords come across. Listen to Andy Summers of the Police on "Every Breath You Take" or "Message in a Bottle" to hear how he uses add9 chords to make a routine chord progression just reach out and grab you.

The Freaky Stuff

A good example of this is the 7(♯9) chord, which rock guitarists think of as the "Hendrix chord" because it's used so prominently in the song "Purple Haze." Here is E7(♯9):

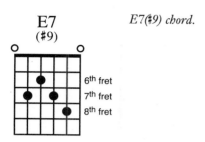

E7(♯9) chord.

Technically, there are five different notes in the E7(♯9) chord—E (the root), G♯ (the major third), B (the fifth), D (the flat seventh), and F "double sharp" (F♯ is the ninth and the instruction is to raise that note a half step)—but only four are being played in this chord. Both open E strings (first and sixth) as well as the seventh fret of the A string are all E notes. The sixth fret of the D string is G♯ and the seventh fret of the G string is D. The note at the eighth fret of the B string is F♯♯, which we'll call G, just to make matters easier.

Because this is E7(♯9), you can play both open E strings. But if you wanted to play B7(♯9), for example, or G7(♯9), you would want to shift the chord until you found the root note on the A string and then only play the middle four strings, not touching either E string with your strum.

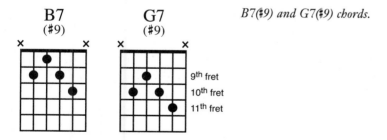

B7(♯9) and G7(♯9) chords.

Follow this strategy whenever you come across a fairly complex chord. Find a moveable shape that gives you the important elements of the chord and then play it someplace on the neck that also allows you to move to the next chord with relative ease.

Creative Voicings

Knowing what notes make up any given chord allows you to choose where to play a chord. Even simple chords can take on more depth and dimension when played in a different position along the fretboard.

And things get even more interesting when you start adding open strings to the mix. For instance, here are three different ways of playing Em9 and Am7:

Various chord voicings.

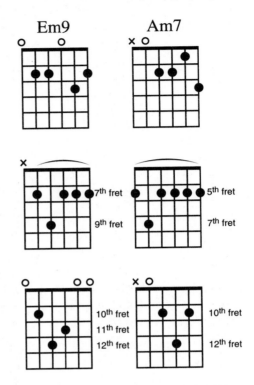

The first two are open position and the second pair features barre chords in the middle of the neck of the guitar. The last two voicings make use of open strings to give them an eerier feel. With the Am7, you could make a cool sounding substitution by taking a finger off the B string, giving you an Am9 instead of Am7.

Slash Chords

Sometimes a guitarist might want a note other than the root as his or her lowest note on the guitar. These are indicated by *slash* chords and look like two notes or chords divided by a slash symbol (/). The desired chord is on the left side of the slash and the new bass note is on the right side.

For the rock guitarist, slash chords tend to occur a lot with open-position chords, particularly when played as arpeggios and/or broken chords. When things get raucous, the bass player usually gets the job of nailing down the bass note.

Various slash chords.

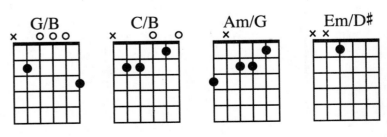

"Jazzing It Up"

To put all this chord knowledge to practical use, here is a jazz-style rock number. Don't worry! It's going to be a lot easier than it looks!

You want to first learn the chords so you can easily move from one to the next and then practice putting the pieces together.

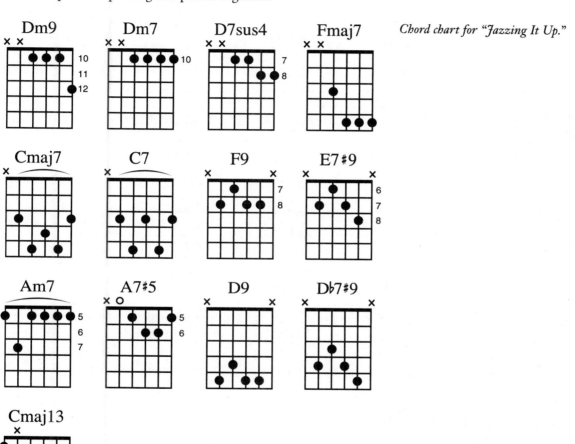

Chord chart for "Jazzing It Up."

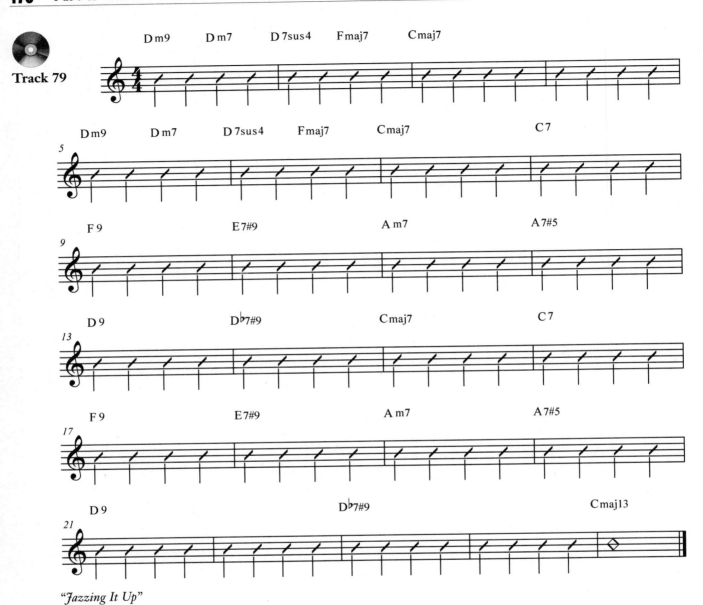

"Jazzing It Up"

The Least You Need to Know

◆ The four basic types of chords are major, minor, augmented, and diminished.

◆ Suspended chords are neither major nor minor.

◆ There are sixth, seventh, ninth, eleventh, and thirteenth chords.

◆ The more complicated the chord, the more you need to find a simple way to play it.

◆ Slash chords are chords that indicate a different bass note than normally played.

Chapter 14

Key Personnel

In This Chapter

- ◆ Discovering keys
- ◆ The 12 different major keys
- ◆ Creating diatonic chords
- ◆ The Circle of Fifths
- ◆ Common rock chord progressions

Knowing all the chords in the world won't help you at all if you're constantly guessing which ones to use! It's perfectly okay to follow along with a chord chart or "cheat sheet," but you may not even get that much help when you're asked to sit in and play on a song. All the instruction you might get from your fellow musicians may be, "We play this song in E Major."

As you play more songs (and *songs* is the important word here, not just scales or exercises), you pick up that many chords seem to go together. They just sound good when played in certain combination. Even the practice songs you're using in this book will help you hear that.

This isn't by accident. Songs, more than 95 percent of them, are composed of chord progressions, which are simply patterns of specific chords that are repeated throughout the song. Learning the guitar part of many songs means simply remembering its chord progression.

Better still, even if you don't know a song, you can often make some educated guesses as to its chord progression just by listening to it once or twice. You can do even better once you know what key a song is played in.

Keying In on Keys

Key, like many musical terms, has many meanings, some starkly specific and others fairly vague. And also like many musical terms, most individual musicians have their own highly personal interpretation of what a key really means. It can get more than a little confusing!

def•i•ni•tion

The **key** of a song is the tonal center, the note or chord that gives the song a feeling of resolution and completeness when played. Keys are usually, but not always, determined by the **key signature,** the number of flats or sharps (not both) at the very left of any staff of music. Each of the 12 possible keys has its own individual key signature.

In simplest terms, the key of a song is its *tonal center*, the note or chord that all the other notes and chords revolve around. Play a C Major scale:

C Major scale.

Now play it again, only this time stop on the B note and don't play the final C. The sound of that B really leaves you hanging, doesn't it? You can't help but want to play the C note so you can finish the scale and feel a lot better.

Chords work in the same way. Play the following chord progression:

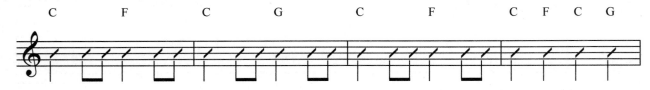

Sample chord progression.

You don't want to end on that G chord, do you? Doing so makes the music seem incomplete somehow, as if there's unfinished business that needs to be taken care of.

From Scale to Key

It probably won't be that big a surprise to you that all you can learn about keys starts (yet again) with the major scale. Play the C Major scale one more time, just to get it into your head. Now play the notes of the C Major scale, but this time start with the G note at the third fret of the low E (sixth) string:

Not quite the G Major scale.

Until you reached the seventh note, which is F (third fret of the D string), you probably thought you were playing the G Major scale. But that F note certainly made you think otherwise!

Note Worthy

You can often make an educated guess as to the key of a song if you only have a chord sheet instead of sheet music. Just look at the chords, particularly the ones that begin and end the song in question. If a song starts on G Major, for instance, there's a good chance it's in the key of G Major. If it ends on G, your odds are even better, and they are better still if the song both begins and ends on G.

Fortunately, you've learned your major scale and you know that the interval of the seventh should be a half step lower than the root note. So change that F to F♯ (fourth fret of the D string) and give it another try:

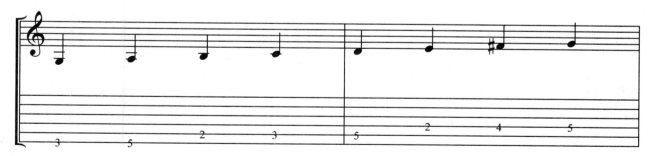

G Major scale.

That sounds much better! You probably have already written out the G Major scale for your own study and practice purposes, so why not compare the notes of both the C Major scale and the G Major scale?

C Major: C   D   E   F   G   A   B   C

G Major: G   A   B   C   D   E   F♯   G

You can see that they share six of seven notes. It's only the F and F♯ notes that make these scales different.

Twelve Signatures

Because there are 12 different notes in Western music, there are 12 possible major scales. Each one has a specific number of either flats or sharps, which distinguishes it from the other keys.

If you look at a song or a piece of music written in music notation, one of the first things you see is the *key signature*, which is a number of sharps or flats (never both) written onto the staff just to the right of the G clef. Here are the 12 possible key signatures, along with their keys and their scales:

The 12 different key signatures.

Diatonic Chords

Now comes the fun part! Knowing what key you are in also gives you a huge clue as to which chords you're most likely to play in that key.

Start with the C Major scale again but don't worry about the last C. Write it out both horizontally and vertically, like this:

C	D	E	F	G	A	B
C						
D						
E						
F						
G						
A						
B						

Do you remember making the C Major chord in our last chapter by taking the root, third, and fifth from the C Major scale? Write out the *E* and *G* beside the *C* in the vertical scale. Then add a note to remind that those three notes are the C Major chord:

C	D	E	F	G	A	B	
C	E	G		= C Major chord			
D							
E							
F							
G							
A							
B							

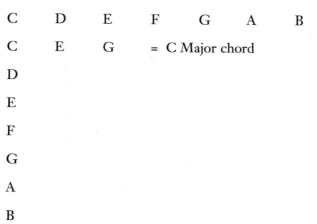

Getting Better

Learning the diatonic triads of each key is easier than you might think and reinforces your knowledge of major scales. Remember that the chords at the first, fourth, and fifth degrees of the scale are always major chords and that the ones at the second, third, and sixth degrees are always minor chords. The seventh diatonic triad is always a diminished chord.

So far, so good! The next note in the vertical scale is D, so start with D and then add the next third and fifth up from D, using just the notes of the C Major scale. It should look like this:

C	D	E	F	G	A	B	
C	E	G		= C Major Chord			
D	F	A					
E							
F							
G							
A							
B							

What you are doing is creating *diatonic triads* in the key of C. You start with each note of the C scale and add the next third and fifth up from your starting note but you can only use the notes from the C Major scale. Continue on now, using E as the new starting note. You should add G and B to that line.

Finish out the chart, filling out the triads at each note of the scale. Remember that when you want notes beyond B, you simply start with C again. Your chart of diatonic triads should end up looking like this:

C	D	E	F	G	A	B
C	E	G		= C Major chord		
D	F	A				
E	G	B				
F	A	C				
G	B	D				
A	C	E				
B	D	F				

Naming Numbers

Now let's examine the triads in your chart. This is actually a great way to re-inforce what you learned about chord construction in the previous chapter!

The notes D, F, and A make up a D minor chord, because F is a minor third (one and a half steps) higher than D and A is D's perfect fifth. Both the triads beginning with E and A are also minor chords while those starting with F and G are major chords.

The triad of B, D, and F is a diminished chord, because D is a minor third up from B and F is the diminished fifth (the tritone, which is three whole steps higher).

Write out your findings on your charts and also include the following numbers and Roman numerals as you do so:

	1	2	3	4	5	6	7
	C	D	E	F	G	A	B
I	C	E	G		= C Major chord		
ii	D	F	A		= D minor chord		
iii	E	G	B		= E minor chord		
IV	F	A	C		= F Major chord		
V	G	B	D		= G Major chord		
vi	A	C	E		= A minor chord		
vii	B	D	F		= B diminished chord		

The regular numbers appearing over the horizontal scale indicate the *scale degrees* of the C Major scale. They are simply to help you remember that A is the sixth of C, for instance.

The Roman numerals give you the traditional generic name for diatonic triads that can be found in any major scale. They become very important when discussing chord progressions (as we do later this chapter) and even more important when you are playing with other people.

Finding Clues

The important thing to know right now is that this combination of chords holds true in *every major key*. If you're playing in the key of A, for example, here is the A Major scale as well as the seven possible diatonic chords made from that scale:

	1	2	3	4	5	6	7	
	A	B	C#	D	E	F#	G#	
I	A	C#	E					= A Major chord
ii	B	D	F#					= B minor chord
iii	C#	E	G#					= C# minor chord
IV	D	F#	A					= D Major chord
V	E	G#	B					= E Major chord
vi	F#	A	C#					= F# minor chord
vii	G#	B	D					= G# diminished chord

For any song in any major key, the three chords you are most likely to use are going to be the I, IV, and V chords. You can see where this knowledge might come in handy!

You can also use this knowledge in reverse. Suppose you're asked to play a solo for a song you've never heard before, but you know that the chords for the song are D, G, and A. Odds are good that the song is in D Major and you can use the notes of the D Major scale as a good starting place for your solo.

Circling the Fifths

Knowing which chords are likely to come up in a particular key is not the same thing as knowing *all* the possible chords. The truth is that almost any chord can show up in a song written in any key. But it's also true that most won't simply because some chords just don't sound good when played in some keys.

There are exceptions, naturally, but even these exceptions are very likely to follow certain musical expectations. Go back and play the chord progression in the second example in this chapter, the one that starts with C and ends with G.

Note Worthy

In major keys, every major chord is a I, IV, or V chord in one of the 12 keys. C Major, for example, is the I chord in the key of C, the IV chord in the key of G, and the V chord in the key of F. These inter-relationships of the major chords are at the heart of the Circle of Fifths.

You've already heard that ending with G leaves the progression feeling incomplete. Try adding one last C chord at the end and see if that sounds better.

In the key of C (where C Major is the I chord), G Major is the V chord and the relationship of V to I is very special and crucial in music. A *cadence*, or short chord progression, made up of the V chord followed by the I chord, is called the *perfect cadence* because it leads our ears to rest at a tonal center. In other words, the V-to-I chord progression cements the feeling of being in a particular key.

Every major chord is the V chord in one key or another. And if you look at the possible keys and arrange them so that each key where a particular chord is the I chord is next door to the one where that same chord is the V chord, you'd end up with what's called the *Circle of Fifths* and it would look like this:

The Circle of Fifths.

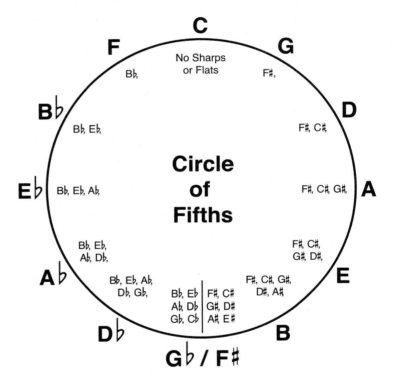

You see the key of C Major, right at the top in the 12 o'clock position of the circle. C is, of course, the I chord in the key of C Major. It is also the V chord in the key of F, the next key to the left at the 11 o'clock position. F, in turn, is the V chord in the key of B♭, which is at the 10 o'clock position, and so it goes.

The Circle of Fifths can be used as a tool to help remember how many sharps or flats are in each key. Notice that, from the top (C Major), each key to the left adds an additional flat until you reach G♭ at the 6 o'clock position. And each key to the right adds an additional sharp as it moves from the key of G to F♯ (which, because F♯ and G♭ are the same note, also sits at the 6 o'clock position).

But you can also use the Circle of Fifths to make an educated guess as to which chord is likely to follow another. Most chord progressions tend to pull the ear in terms of the perfect cadence. So if you are playing in the key of C and all of a sudden an A Major or A7 chord pops up, the chances are very likely that your next chord will be either D or Dm, because A is the V chord of both those keys. It's not foolproof (not much in music ever is), but it's right more often than wrong.

Typical Progress with Chord Progressions

There are a finite number of chords, even though right now it may seem like there are millions of them! Likewise, there are a finite number of chord progressions, especially when you take into account that not all chord progressions sound all that good. It's kind of amazing, when you think about it, that there's so much different music based on a very small number of chord progressions.

As a rock guitarist, this means you can learn to play a lot of songs very quickly, especially songs that repeat the same chord progression over and over and over. It also means that if you learn to listen to songs in terms of their chord progressions then you will be able to play along with songs you've never played before with surprisingly little preparation.

I – IV – V

Far and away, most rock songs involve three or four chords. And most songs using three chords have chord progressions that are some combination of the I, IV, and V chords. And that makes a lot of sense, especially knowing that the music of rock's closest descendents, namely most country and old-time mountain music, as well as almost all blues songs, rarely stray from these three chords.

You hear these various I-IV-V combinations in a lot of early rock 'n' roll, although you do have to look out for the occasional substitution of a seventh or ninth chord to the overall picture. "Be-Bop-A-Lula," for instance is in the key of E and uses E, A, and B7, which is a typical substitution for B. "Blue Suede Shoes," in the key of A, can be played with only the A, D, and E chords, although the original tosses in some D7 and E9 chords. Listening for both the "straight" chords as well as the possible substitutions is excellent ear training.

Three-chord rock spans the generations, even when it only involves power chords, as with "All the Small Things" (C, F, and G power chords) by Blink-182.

> **Hear How**
>
> Another common rock progression involving the ♭VII chord is I-IV-♭VII-IV. The Romantics's hit "What I Like About You" goes from E to A to D to A and so on for the entire song. John Mellencamp's "ROCK in the USA" is another song that uses this progression, in the same key in fact. It does, occasionally throw in the B chord right before the chorus.

I – vi – IV – V

If there's going to be an additional chord added to the I-IV-V mixture, it's typically the iv chord. "Good Riddance (Time of Your Life)" by Green Day (G, C, D, and Em chords), Tom Petty's "Learning to Fly" (C, F, G, and Am), or "Welcome to My Life" by Simple Plan (same as Tom Petty's but up a half step—C#, F#, G#, and A#m) all use these four particular chords.

And there are literally hundreds of songs that use this chord progression in the order of I-vi-IV-V, from the teen ballads of the fifties through present day.

I – ♭VII – IV – I

Another typical rock progression involves adding the major chord of the flatted seventh note of the major scale. That's sounds more convoluted than it actually is! If you're in the key of D, for example, where D Major is the I chord, the ♭VII chord is C Major. On paper, you might not think these two chords would go together, but people have been using this progression for centuries now.

In fact, going from I to ♭VII to IV and back to I again is practically a staple of rock music. You only have to think of songs like Bachman Turner Overdrive's "Taking Care of Business" or most of the Rolling Stones's "Sympathy for the Devil" to lock this progression into your ears.

You've Got Change Coming

You've read over and over again in these pages that listening is one of the greatest skills a musician can develop. You don't realize it right now, but you've been listening to chord changes all your life. A lot of what you need to do now is to discover how much you already know.

Listen to the music that you like and practice hearing the chord changes as they happen. Don't worry about exactly which chords are being played, but instead just try to pick them out. Once you can do that then try to work out the rhythmic pattern of the progression. Is it every two beats? Every four? You will soon be able to discern the structure of a song in terms of its rhythmic chord progression, and that's a huge start.

From there, add your interval and chord progression ear training to the task and listen for the generic (or numeric, if you will) progressions. Start small. Is the first change I-IV, I-V, or something else? By taking each single chord change as a test to your listening skills, you will start to acquire a sense of the "big picture" of song progressions, meaning that when a song takes a weird turn with its chords, you will have a good idea of where it's going.

On top of all this, you will also be developing a sense of harmony that will be a big help to you for soloing and making rhythmic riffs, not to mention the good it will do you should you take up songwriting.

The Least You Need to Know

- ◆ Keys are the tonal centers of songs.

- ◆ There are 12 different major keys but most rock music is played in half of them.

- ◆ Knowing the diatonic chords of a key helps you play songs you've never heard before.

- ◆ The Circle of Fifths is a helpful tool for learning keys or for following unfamiliar chord progressions.

Hear How

Sometimes a song totally changes keys. This quite often happens at the very end of a song in order to make a very dramatic finale. The last repeating chorus of Bon Jovi's "Living on a Prayer" jumps from G Major to B♭ Major. "My Generation" by the Who was one of the first rock songs to incorporate multiple key changes.

15

The Rock Guitarist's Best Friend

In This Chapter

◆ Pentatonic scales

◆ Finding the relative minor of any major scale

◆ The five positions of the pentatonic scale

◆ Combining major and minor pentatonic scales

◆ The blues scale

At one time or another, *everyone* has dreamed of playing a big guitar solo. It's okay to admit it. Who hasn't grabbed his or her favorite air guitar and played a completely rocking solo to an imaginary crowd of adoring fans?

One great thing about being a legend in your own mind, you never worry about the little things, like dropping your pick or not coming in at the right place or even thinking about what key you're playing in.

In reality, solos are usually well thought out and prepared for. Even improvised solos are the result of a lot of practice and repetition. As much as you want your first real solo to be as good as the imaginary ones you've already played, you're going to have to start out with little steps.

But the rock guitarist has a few tools that can help make even simple solos sound very artful. You've already learned a number of techniques—from bends and slides to vibrato and hammer-ons and pull-offs—that are very useful for solos.

You've also learned about the major scale and keys, which are invaluable when it comes to creating solos. It's time to put your scale knowledge to even better use.

Five Notes and the Truth

Back in Chapter 12 you learned about scales in general and the major scale in a bit more detail. You might remember the definition of a scale as being a specific series of half steps and whole steps beginning with the root note until reaching the octave of that root note. You might even remember learning the *chromatic scale* as an example of one type of scale.

def•i•ni•tion

Pentatonic scales have five notes instead of the seven of the major scale. The **major pentatonic** scale is made up of the root, second, third, fifth, and sixth notes of the major scale. The **minor pentatonic** scale is composed of the root, minor third, fourth, fifth, and flat seventh.

There are 12 notes in a chromatic scale, and that is the most possible notes any one scale can have because there are only 12 different notes. The major scale has seven notes.

And as you learn in this and upcoming chapters, there are quite a few more scales that a guitarist can use as soloing tools.

Chief among these scales is the *pentatonic scale*. As you might infer from its name, the pentatonic scale has five different notes. That's not much smaller than the seven of the major scale, but it's enough to make a difference in terms of playability.

The *major pentatonic* scale, defined in terms of the major scale, uses the root, second, third, fifth, and sixth notes of the major scale. Remembering that the C Major scale has the notes:

C   D   E   F   G   A   B   C

You then can figure out the C Major pentatonic scale to be:

C   D   E   G   A   C

**Track 80
(0:00)**

Here it is, written out in both notation and guitar tablature. Be sure to listen to it on the CD as well:

C Major pentatonic scale.

It's All Relative

There are, as you know, major and minor chords. It only makes sense that there are both major and minor scales. Not only are there minor scales, but every major scale has a *relative minor* scale. The relative minor scale has all the same notes of the major scale, but its root note is the *sixth note* of the major scale.

Using C Major as an example again, you would start at its sixth note, A, and write it out like this:

A   B   C   D   E   F   G   A

This is the A natural minor scale, and it is the relative minor scale to C Major.

This is actually a very convenient shortcut as you wouldn't normally describe the A natural minor in terms of C Major, but rather in terms of the A Major scale and in order to do that, you should put them side by side. Then you will be able to write out the step and half-step sequence for the natural minor, as well as describe any natural minor scale in terms of its major scale:

A Major:	A	B	C♯	D	E	F♯	G♯	A
A natural minor:	A	B	C	D	E	F	G	A
Sequence:	Root	W	H	W	W	H	W	W
Any natural minor:	Root	2nd	♭3rd	4th	5th	♭6th	♭7th	Root

> **Note Worthy**
>
> Every major scale has a relative minor, whose root note is the sixth note of the major scale. In the five "guitar friendly" major keys, the relative minors are these:
>
> | Major | Relative Minor |
> |---|---|
> | C | Am |
> | G | Em |
> | D | Bm |
> | A | F♯m |
> | E | C♯m |

It's probably a good idea to also come up with a Root 6 closed position version of the major pentatonic so that you can play more than just the C Major pentatonic:

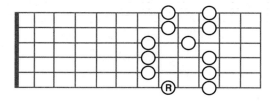

The C Major pentatonic scale in closed position—Root 6 form.

The Minor Pentatonic Scale

And just as any major scale has a relative minor scale, any major pentatonic scale also has a relative minor pentatonic scale. Remember that everything is still in terms of the full major scale, so the A note of the C Major pentatonic, though it's the fifth note of that scale, is still considered the sixth of C. In other words, every major key or scale has only one possible relative minor. The relative minor of C will always be A minor.

You can work out the A minor pentatonic scale in the same manner that you worked out the A natural minor. For now, though, why don't I save you a little trouble by setting it out for you:

C Major pentatonic: C   D   E   G   A

A minor pentatonic: A   C   D   E   G

In terms of any given major scale, you work out the minor pentatonic like this:

Minor pentatonic: Root ♭3rd 4th 5th ♭7th

This may seem like a lot of hocus-pocus right now. After all, both these scales have the same notes, right? It's when you map out the Root 6 closed position of the minor pentatonic that things become a little clearer:

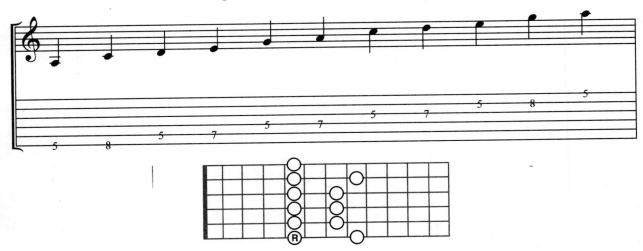

The A minor pentatonic scale in closed position—Root 6 form.

Even a beginner can see that this is a very easy pattern to learn and to remember. And that is both the beauty and the appeal of the minor pentatonic scale to guitarists as a soloing tool. There are only two notes per string. No two notes are more than three frets apart and, when you learn the Root 6 position, you don't have to shift your index finger at all from whatever fret the root note is on at the low E (and high E) strings.

Some people think of this form of the minor pentatonic scale as "the guitarist's best friend." And it's small wonder! There are many, many guitar leads and signature riffs from rock songs that are all snugly secure in this fingering, from Dave Davies's solo on "You Really Got Me" to Steve Miller's opening riff to "Fly Like an Eagle" to the solo in the middle of Weezer's "Beverly Hills."

Position Playing

Another important aspect of the pentatonic scale, whether you prefer to think of it as major or minor, is that it has only five notes. You have just learned it in Root 6 position, meaning that the root note is on the low E string. The last illustration used was an example specifically for the A minor pentatonic, but you can easily shift it around to whatever root note you'd like.

For the C minor pentatonic, for example, you place your index finger on the eighth fret of the low E string because that's where the note C is located on that string. For the second note of the C minor pentatonic scale, you place your pinky on the eleventh fret of the low E strings. The next two notes are at the eighth and tenth frets of the A string (use the index and ring fingers), and the next two pairs are on the same frets of the D and G strings. The last four notes are on the eighth and eleventh frets of the B and high E strings.

Just a little while ago, though, you looked at the closed position Root 6 form of the C Major pentatonic. And you know that C is the second note of the A minor pentatonic scale. Both scales have the same notes, you'll remember.

Shifting to Second Position

You could just as easily think of the Root 6 form of the C Major pentatonic as the "second position" of the A minor pentatonic scale. When you lay them out together, you can see that they share a note on each string:

Hear How

Listen to the beginning of the electric guitar solo in "Stairway to Heaven" for a great example of position playing. The first long note, as well as all but the last note of the first phrase of the solo, is done in the first position (Root 6) of the A minor pentatonic scale. The second phrase, most of whose notes are located at the eighth and tenth frets of the high E and B strings, is played in the second position of the A minor pentatonic.

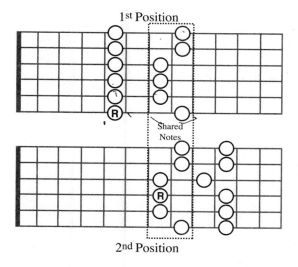

The A minor pentatonic scale—"first" and "second" positions.

Now think about how guitarists like to use economy of motion. Why deal with a stretch of three frets when you have the option of working with a stretch of two, or possibly even one? Granted, there's the three fret stretch of the first two notes on the low E string, but remember that the second note, C at the eighth fret of the low E, is also at the third fret of the A string, which is only two frets away from the fifth fret.

Bearing this in mind, here is a way to use a couple of slides in order to combine both the first and second positions of the A minor pentatonic scale. I've taken the liberty of writing this out in notation and tablature, as well as making suggestions for fingering.

The A minor pentatonic—"first" and "second" positions combined.

Getting Better

Many guitarists seem to develop more speed when practicing scales in a particular direction. For instance, some are faster playing ascending scales while others find descending scales more their speed. Whichever camp you may fall into, it's still important to work in both directions, up and down, until you feel you can do either direction at the desired speed.

If you start with your ring finger on the fifth fret of the low E string, your index finger is automatically in position for the second note, C (third fret of the A string). You can then use your ring finger to get the D note at the fifth fret and then slide your ring finger up two frets for the E note. This puts your index finger in perfect position so that your index and ring finger get the next four notes at the fifth and seventh frets of the D and G strings.

After playing the D note at the seventh fret of the G string with your ring finger, slide it up to the ninth fret of the same string to play the E note. Then use either your index or middle finger to play the G note at the eighth fret of the B string and complete the pattern.

You can, of course, use your index finger instead of the ring finger to make both slides. The first slide would be from the third fret of the A to the fifth fret. The second slide would be from the fifth fret of the G string to the seventh. You may find that you slide with one finger when you ascend the scale and with a different finger when you descend.

Positions Three Through Five

There's no sense of stopping with just two positions! The pentatonic scale has five notes, so there have to be three more!

Here, individually, are the fretboard maps for the third, fourth, and five positions of the A minor pentatonic scale. The root note of each is marked so you can use it as a moveable marker for other minor pentatonic scales.

While it's fun to go flying all over the fretboard, be sure to practice each pattern until you feel you can do it in your sleep. Sometimes your fingers might need to be in one place and it will be good to know they know what notes to play.

3rd Position

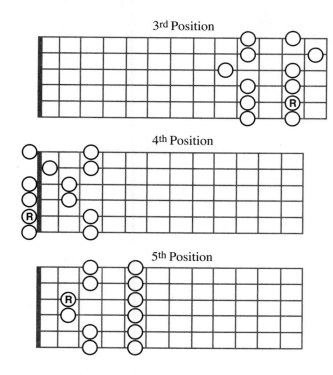

4th Position

5th Position

The A minor pentatonic—"third,"
"fourth," and "fifth" positions.

Connecting the Dots

Track 80
(0:12)

When you feel very comfortable with each position of the minor pentatonic scale, then experiment and mix the positions around a bit. You might try something like this:

The A minor pentatonic scale—"first" and "second" positions.

It's good to try sliding from position to position with different fingers. Being able to effortlessly glide from one place on the fretboard to another takes practice and patience, so take the time to make certain you're moving exactly where you want to go.

Notice, too, how a simple change of direction, or jumping over the notes of a scale instead of playing each note one after the other in sequence, makes your playing sound more natural. Think of the melodies of songs you know. It's extremely rare that they simply go up and down, following the notes of a scale.

You are now well on your way to making your dreams of soloing a reality. In fact, it's time to start playing your own solos!

Just a Phrase

The idea of soloing is probably filling your mind with all sorts of questions. "What notes do I play?" "When do I play them?" "Will they sound good?" "What if I play a wrong note?"

Relax and, if possible, don't worry about the notes just yet. The notes that you play are just one aspect of a solo. Equally important as the notes are the rhythm and the dynamic quality that you give each note. This is part of what is known as phrasing.

Phrasing is what makes a solo sound like a solo and not like someone practicing a bunch of scales. Truly memorable solos are usually ones you can sing along with. They have long, held-out notes as well as the occasional outpouring rush of short, quick ones.

Most beginning guitarists are so concerned with speed that they never develop a sense of phrasing. As a consequence, many of their solos sound similar to one another, almost cookie-cutter in style.

Your First Big—Okay, Little—Solo

To concentrate on the aspects of phrasing and dynamics, you're going to start off soloing by playing only two or three notes. And you're getting off lucky! Some teachers give their students only one note to use for their first solo.

As to which notes to play or which are the right ones, an advantage of using the pentatonic scale is that all the notes usually sound good. It's close to impossible to play a "wrong" one.

Track 81

You can use any three notes of your choice for the upcoming practice song, "Minimal Rock," as long as they come from the A minor pentatonic scale.

The practice songs for this and the next few chapters have a different slant to them. You should consider these more as "backing tracks" or "play along songs." They are here for you to practice your fledgling soloing skills.

When you listen to this one, "Minimal Rock," you will first hear the band go through the basic chord progression of the song and then you'll hear the lead guitarist play a short bit of a solo, using only three different notes, in this case, G and A at the fifth and seven frets of the D string, and the C note at the fifth fret of the G string. It will sound like more notes because he will also bend the C note up to D, E♭, and even E.

After this short lead, the band will stop and then start up again. This is your practice space.

I cannot stress enough that the point here is *not* to copy the first lead. In fact, that's why it's not tabbed out in the book. Your task is to come up with your own lead line, several of them in fact, using only these three notes (or three different notes of your choosing) taken from the A minor pentatonic scale.

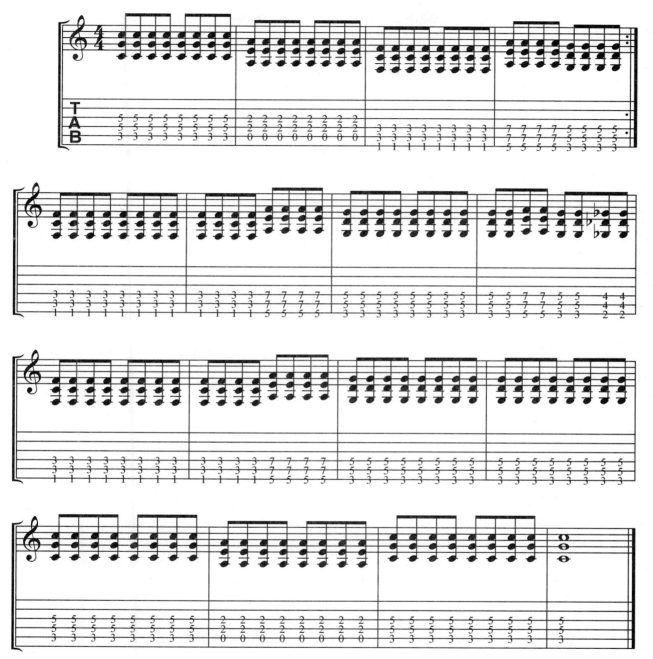

"Minimal Rock"

There is no right or wrong to this exercise. It's all about exploring rhythm and phrasing. Above all, have fun!

After you feel you've exhausted your possibilities with various combinations of three different notes (and don't forget to try them out in different places on the fretboard), then try four or even go with all five of the notes of the A minor pentatonic scale.

Work out some solos at each of the various positions along the neck. Finally, try soloing while shifting from position to position. Remember as you add notes and change positions that the whole purpose of this exercise is to work on your sense of phrasing. It's not about speed.

Why They Call It the Blues

The minor pentatonic scale has long been a favorite of blues guitarists, so it shouldn't be surprising to find it used so much in rock music. Jimi Hendrix developed his style while working as a backing guitarist to numerous blues, soul, and R&B musicians, most notably the Isley Brothers and Little Richard. Rock guitar icons such as Clapton, Page, and Richards constantly cite blues legends like Muddy Waters, Buddy Guy, Elmore James, and B. B. King as major influences.

When these rock guitarists were practicing copying the riffs and solos of their heroes, they added their own personal touches, but you can still hear a lot of blues in rock 'n' roll. And the prominent use of the pentatonic scale in rock music is a big part of the reason why.

Blue Note Special

All of music, no matter what style or genre, involves tension. You could hear, probably even feel, the tension when you did the first two exercises in Chapter 14, the ones where you played the major scale up to the seventh note or played the chord progression which ended on G. This constant interplay between tension and resolution, coming to a pleasant musical resting place, makes songs organic and gets you involved with the music.

In blues music, tension is developed by playing certain notes from outside of the major scale over major chords. These are called *blue notes* and, usually, they are the minor third, flat seventh, and diminished fifth. When these notes are sung or played over a major chord, they create a palpable tension. It's this particular style of tension that gives songs what we call a "blues feel."

The guitarist, like the vocalist, can punctuate these blue notes even more by use of vibrato and/or bending notes. The "not quite on target" quality of a quarter-bend or a large vibrato emphasizes the blue notes and makes a very dramatic and dynamic impact on the listener.

Three Chords—One Scale—Five Blue Notes

The minor pentatonic scale plays right into the tension of blue notes. The notes of this scale are already blue notes for most of the chords you use in a blues song.

Most blues songs use only three chords: the I, IV, and V chords of any major key. Using the key of C Major as an example, you know that a blues song in C uses C (the I), F (the IV), and G (the V). Write out the notes that make up each of these three chords and you will see:

def•i•ni•tion

Blue notes are notes from outside the major scale that, when played or sung, bring an emotional aspect of dissonance to a song. Resolution occurs when these blue notes are followed by the note from the major scale, releasing the feeling of tension. The minor third, flat seventh, and diminished fifth are blue notes.

```
C  =   C   E   G
F  =   F   A   C
G  =   G   B   D
```

To make the C minor pentatonic scale, you want the root (C), the minor third (E♭), the fourth (F), the fifth (B♭), and the flat seventh (B♭). If you examine each of those notes as possible blue notes, you find that E♭ is a blue note of both C (minor third) and F (flat seventh), F is a blue note of G (flat seventh), and B♭ is a blue note of both C (flat seventh) and G (minor third).

Now you have another reason why so many guitarists love this scale. If you are playing a blues song, or a blues-style rock song, in any major key, using the *minor* pentatonic scale of that same major key creates a wonderful blues feeling and helps you create a very cool sounding solo.

Major-Minor Combo Platter

Some guitarists stress the tension of the blue notes by trading off between both the major pentatonic and minor pentatonic scales when soloing. This is very easy to do if you can remember your relative major and minor.

Suppose you're playing a blues number in the key of C. You've just learned that using the C minor pentatonic scale gives you a boatload of blue notes to work into your solo. You also know that A minor is the relative minor of C Major, so your C Major pentatonic and A minor pentatonic scales have the same notes. Mapping both the C minor and A minor pentatonic scales in Root 6 position shows you something very interesting:

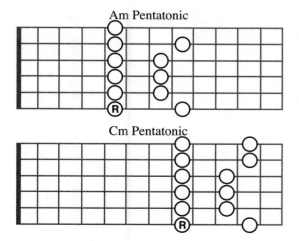

Using both major and minor pentatonic scales together.

See how both scales share notes at the eighth fret? By a wonderful coincidence, this is where the root note, C, is found on both the high and low E strings. That certainly makes remembering where the positions are a lot easier.

Track 82

Here are a few blues and rock riffs that combine elements of both the minor and major pentatonic scales.

Hang onto these riffs and try them out in the upcoming practice song that ends this chapter. You can certainly come up with a lot of your own, too.

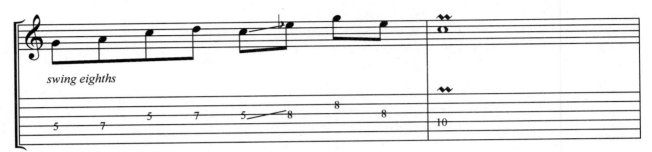

A few riffs that combine both the minor and major pentatonic scales.

The Blues Scale

Two out of three blue notes isn't enough for some guitarists. So they add the diminished fifth to the minor pentatonic scale to make the *blues scale*.

The blues scale.

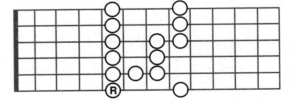

Getting a handle on the blues scale isn't all that difficult in terms of fingering. But it does take some practice to get used to the various blue notes that you hear.

Also, it's important to realize that the added blue note (the diminished fifth) is only the blue note of the I chord, and many people don't like the way that one particular note sounds when played over the IV or V chord. Some guitarists who love the sound of the blues scale deal with this by switching root positions with each chord change. For example, if playing a blues song in C, they use the C blues scale when C is being played and then switch to the F blues scale or G blues scale when each of those chords come up.

Hear How

You would never confuse Chuck Berry's style with that of Jimi Hendrix, but both guitarists used the blues scale quite a bit in their solos.

If you still haven't found all the notes you want for a blues solo, then you might want to try combining the major pentatonic with the blues scale. Be warned! It's a bit of a handful:

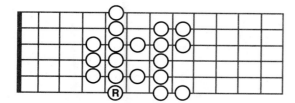

Combining the blues with the major pentatonic scale.

With so many notes to choose from, you might find yourself thinking that the minor pentatonic is a wonder of simple elegance.

"Bucketful of Blues"

Here is a blues-style rocker to help you practice using this chapter's scales as soloing aids. As with the previous song, start small, maybe just using a handful of notes to begin with.

Track 83

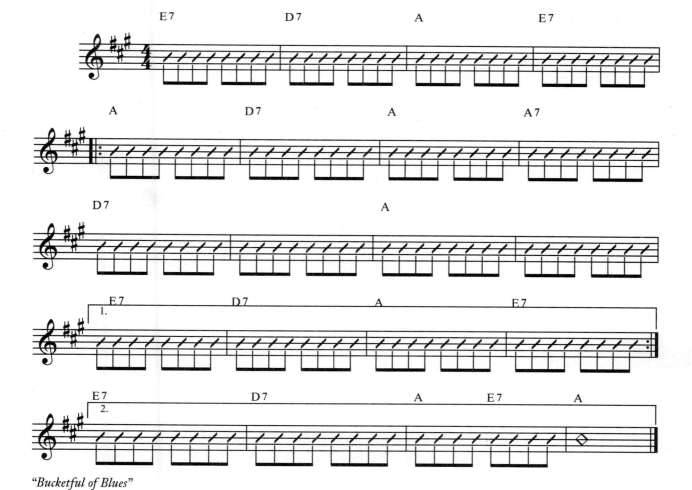

"Bucketful of Blues"

Don't forget about the other techniques you've learned—vibrato, slides, bends, and other slurs. And chord arpeggios, especially using sevenths and ninths as substitutes, make great starting places.

The Least You Need to Know

- ◆ Every major scale has a relative minor.

- ◆ Pentatonic scales have five notes and are very easy for guitarists to learn.

- ◆ You can find five different positions along the fretboard for each pentatonic scale.

- ◆ You want to play the minor pentatonic scale to solo over blues-style songs in a major key.

- ◆ When soloing over blues-style songs, you can also use the blues scale or a combination of the major and minor pentatonic scales.

Chapter 16

Choosing Colors

In This Chapter

◆ An introduction to target notes

◆ The seven modes of the major scale

◆ Three different minor scales

◆ Clues on which scale to use

◆ Using more than one scale for soloing

You've reached another point in your rock guitar studies where you could easily say, "Enough." There are thousands, if not hundreds of thousands, of guitarists who never use more than the basic pentatonic scale when soloing. Just as millions of songs are made up of a comparatively small number of chord progressions, there are millions of solo possibilities within your grasp with the minor pentatonic scale, especially when you combine it with the various techniques you learned in Parts 2 and 3 of this book.

Limited Options

Study the following chord progression and then listen to it on the CD and use that track as accompaniment while you work out some solos.

Track 84

This progression is in C Major, so you can use the C Major pentatonic scale (also the A minor pentatonic if you've decided you prefer to think of it in those terms) for your solo.

C   Dm   F   *Repeat four times*   C

C Major progression for soloing practice.

You probably sounded fine but perhaps you found something a bit lacking in your solo. Take a look at the notes that make up the chords involved:

C	=	C	E	G
Dm	=	D	F	A
F	=	F	A	C

The C Major pentatonic scale, made up of C, D, E, G, and A, has five of the six notes used in the chords of this progression. With only five notes to work with, a pentatonic scale will rarely contain all the notes of any chord progression. Usually that's not a problem but here the missing note, F, is vital because it is the root note of the F chord and the third of the Dm chord. And the root and the third are two of the more important notes of any chord.

Back to Basics

Go back to the last progression and solo over it again, this time using the entire C Major scale. Listen closely to what you play and see which scale you like better when soloing.

Most people find they prefer soloing over this progression with the full major scale. They may never touch the B note, but the added F is good to have when the chords are either Dm or F.

Target Practice

When you are soloing, your ears (and consequently your fingers) are constantly seeking *target notes*. Think of them as safe havens, if you will, notes where you can rest for even a moment and not worry that you've ended up on a clunker.

Usually a target note is one of the notes of the chord being played at that moment in time. Beginners especially find this to be the case. If your scale doesn't contain enough target notes for the chords involved in a progression, then it's a good idea to use a different scale.

Shifting Centers

Or you could use the same scale in a different manner. Go back to our last CD example and practice it again using the C Major scale. Get really comfortable with using the C Major scale for soloing. Then when you're ready, try using the same C Major to solo over the following progression.

Track 85

You might have had some difficulty getting started. Many of the important target notes from the last example aren't present in these two chords, particularly the C and E of the C chord.

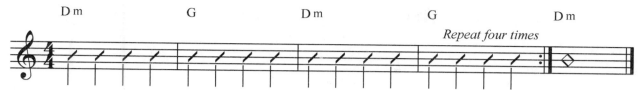

D minor progression for soloing practice.

Once you had a few go 'rounds with it, though, you probably settled in and managed to come up with some very passable lead lines. First your ears and then your fingers made the necessary adjustments, allowing you to solo with a little more confidence.

What happened here is that your tonal center changed from C Major to D minor. The scale you used for soloing (C Major) stayed the same. You just got a little better at picking your target notes. Another way to look at it is that you've just learned how to play a *modal scale*.

One Major Scale = Seven Modes

Remember that every major scale has a relative minor scale? Or how the C Major pentatonic scale and the A minor pentatonic scale have the same notes?

Modes work on the same principle. Every major scale is actually seven different modal scales. You just have to start your scale on a different note of the major scale, like the example on the next page.

Take this C Major scale and play it as shown, each time using a different note of the scale as your starting point. Listen closely to the different mood of each new mode. Some of them, like the Lydian or Aeolian, aren't all that striking while others are positively exotic.

Modes, like scales, usually go by two names, the first of which is a note name (the root of that mode) and the second is a descriptive name. These descriptive names tell you where in the major scale the root note would normally be:

Ionian (root note is identical to root note of major scale)

Dorian (root note is second note of major scale)

Phrygian (root note is third note of major scale)

Lydian (root note is fourth note of major scale)

Mixolydian (root note is fifth note of major scale)

Aeolian (root note is sixth note of major scale)

Locrian (root note is seventh note of major scale)

The seven modes of C Major.

Modes confuse the daylights out of most people, and that's understandable. They have these strange Greek names that make you wish for the simpler days of major scale or minor pentatonic scale.

But if you remember that they are just major scales, and you remember that the first part of any scale name is its root note, you'll be fine. In the last example, for instance, each mode was taken from the C Major scale, so the first mode, Ionian, was just the C Major scale because it started with C as its root note. The second mode, Dorian, would be the D Dorian scale because D would be its root note.

Here are all the modes again, but this time they are all written out with C as the root note:

Seven modes with C as root note.

Tonal Centers and Targets

When you solo over a chord progression, you need to decide on the key or tonal center of a particular progression. As you've just seen (and heard) in this chapter's second solo practice progression, key and tonal center aren't necessarily one and the same. The second practice progression was in the key of C, but its tonal center was D minor.

Go back now to this chapter's first practice progression, the one that goes C, Dm, F, and back to C. You've soloed over this progression twice now, first with the C Major pentatonic scale and then using the full C Major scale. Try it again, this time playing the F Major scale. Since C is still the tonal center, you're technically using the C Mixolydian mode. But you might prefer thinking of it as just the F Major scale with different targets.

Each time you learn about a new mode or scale to use for soloing purposes, you should take a good look at the chord progression involved. You often find some telltale signs that you can use in future decisions about scale selection.

Songs with progressions containing the ♭VII chord are usually good candidates for the Mixolydian mode. Songs with minor I, or root, chords but Major IV chords will almost always sound great with solos played in the Dorian mode.

"Dorian Rock"

Speaking of which, here is a full practice song for you to solo with. You should find that the A Dorian scale (same notes of the G Major) works well.

Track 86

The best way to learn about different modes and scales is to use them and to listen to what you can do with each one. Solo over "Dorian Rock" any number of times using different scales, such as the A minor pentatonic or even the G or D Major pentatonic scales, just to hear the differences each scale brings to a solo.

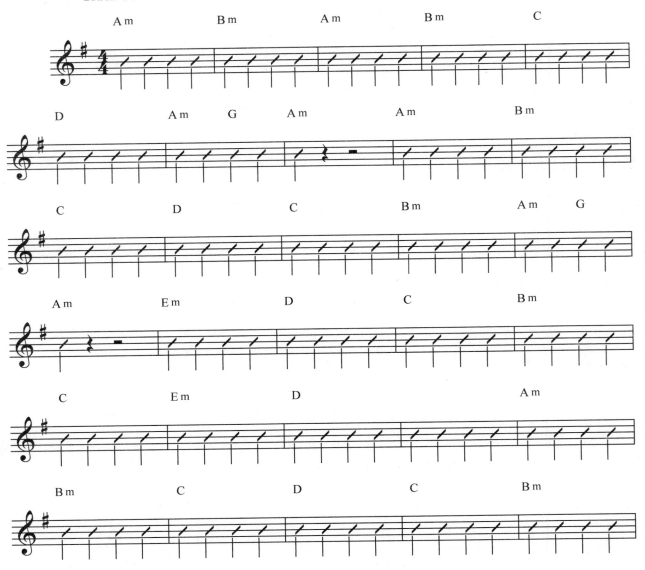

"Dorian Rock"

Remember, too, that you don't have to use a single scale throughout a song. Try one scale for one line of "Dorian Rock" and a different scale for another. You could use a third scale for the third line or go back to your first scale.

Minor Incidents

Life would be pretty boring if all songs were in major keys. Fortunately there are lots of songs in minor keys as well as many rock songs whose tonal centers are "ambiguous" at best.

Songs in minor keys can pose interesting problems because there are three different minor scales, not just one like the major scale. To make matters even more interesting, each one has its own individual harmonic flavor, meaning that you come up with different possible diatonic chords for each of the three minor scales.

Natural Minor Scale

You've already encountered the natural minor scale earlier in this book. And you've also just learned in this chapter that the Aeolian mode is another name for the natural minor scale.

Here is a generic minor scale fretboard pattern:

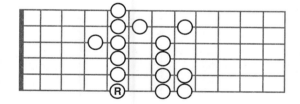

The natural minor scale.

And here are the diatonic chords made when you go through the same steps used in Chapter 14. Even though it's not technically correct, I'm using capital Roman numerals for each scale degree:

Scale Position	Diatonic chord
I	Minor
II	Diminished
III	Major
IV	Minor

continues

continued

Scale Position	Diatonic chord
V	Minor
VI	Major
VII	Major

A very common rock progression using the natural minor scale is i–VII–VI–VII, and so on. "All Along the Watchtower," Blue Oyster Cult's "(Don't Fear) The Reaper," and "Gimme Shelter" by the Rolling Stones all use this progression.

Harmonic Minor Scale

The harmonic minor scale is one of the most interesting scales to hear as well as to play. It shares the first six notes of the natural minor scale but its seventh note is like the seventh of the major scale, being just one half step lower than the root. Play it and listen for yourself:

Notes of the A harmonic minor scale.

Here is the fretboard pattern for the harmonic minor scale:

Fretboard map of the A harmonic minor scale.

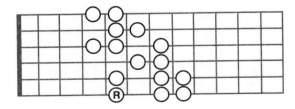

And here are the diatonic chords for this scale:

Scale Position	Diatonic chord
I	Minor
II	Diminished
III	Augmented
IV	Minor
V	Major
VI	Major
VII	Diminished

The dramatic characteristic of the harmonic minor is the step-and-a-half interval between its sixth and seventh notes. It gives the scale a very exotic sound that most Western listeners associate with Arabic music.

Melodic Minor Scale

The melodic minor also has a unique trait in that it's different depending on which direction you're playing it. Going up, it's the same as the major scale only that it has a minor third instead of a major third. The sixth and seventh positions are the same as those in the major scale.

Descending melodic minor scales are played exactly the same as the natural minor scale:

Notes of the A melodic minor scale.

And here is just the ascending pattern laid out as a generic fretboard map:

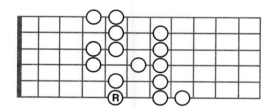

Fretboard map of the A melodic minor scale.

Here are the diatonic chords made using only the notes of the ascending melodic minor scale:

Scale Position	Diatonic chord
I	Minor
II	Minor
III	Augmented
IV	Major
V	Major
VI	Diminished
VII	Diminished

Of the three minor scales, you probably use the melodic minor the least, but it's still good to have it at your fingertips should the need arise.

Keys, Chord Progressions, and Styles

When deciding on a scale to use for soloing, the key or tonal center of a song is always the first clue, but you also want to pay close attention to the chord progression as a whole. Many songs contain brief modulations (temporary shifts in the tonal center), and spotting a modulation may give you a reason to momentarily change your choice of scale.

For example, say a song starts off with a measure each of A, E, A, and D and then the second line has a measure each of A, D, B, and E. The B chord signals the modulation to E, so if you've gone with the A Major or A Major pentatonic to start with, you could shift to E Major or E Major pentatonic for the measure of B and E and then get back to A.

The overall style or feel of a song is important, too. Blues, blues-rock, or any song that feels it could do with some blues-styled sounds means going with the "minor pentatonic over the major key" or the blues scale should sound okay. Minor pentatonic scales are also good with both old-style rockers and dark power-chord driven metal.

If a song is more of a melodic ballad, then the major pentatonic or a full major scale will probably do the trick, especially if there are a lot of IV chords.

Segmenting Solos

As much as you might want to have a single scale to use for soloing, circumstances (and chord progressions) might dictate otherwise. Sometimes you might need to "group" chords in a progression together. For instance, suppose you came across the following chord progression:

F   E   Am   Gm   C   F   E7   Am

Am would probably be the tonal center of this progression (especially given the E and E7 chords), but the tonal center also spends some time in F where F, Gm, Am, and C are the I, ii, iii, and V chords.

One way to break this up would be to use the A harmonic minor to start and then switch over to A Phrygian (the F Major scale with A as the root note) and then back to A harmonic minor to close it all out.

Also be sure to note how long each chord is used in a progression. Some chords are simply "passing," meaning that you'll go through them in a beat or less and that means you can often take them out of the equation when it comes to soloing.

On the other hand, a passing chord may be highlighted in a progression. If this is the case, then you're probably going to want to emphasize it as part of your solo as well.

Personal Choices

How you think a solo sounds is a big factor in determining which scale or scales to use for soloing. Some people are just habitual pentatonic players, partially because the pentatonic scale is relatively hassle-free, but also partially because they really like the sound of it.

Others may find themselves hooked on one or more of the modes. Getting one or two extra notes can fill out a solo quite nicely, particularly if those notes are vital components of a chord in the progression they're soloing over.

But remember that you can have no idea of the choices unless you take the time to experiment and play around with different scales and modes. And of course, listening to other musicians (whether guitarists or not) also opens your ears to the possibilities other modes and scales have to offer you as a soloist.

Hopefully you also now understand that there almost always will be more than one choice when it comes to using a scale as a soloing aid in a song. While trial and error certainly are a part of your rock guitar education, there are usually also helpful guidelines in the song itself, such as the chord progression or the song's musical style, to assist you with your choice.

And the coolest thing about choices is that you can always change your mind and try something else.

"Minor Madness"

"Minor Madness" takes its chord progression from "House of the Rising Sun" and, as you will hear, offers you a lot of options in terms of scale selection.

You can use the E minor pentatonic throughout this song, or switch between the E natural, E melodic, and E harmonic minors. It's a bit of a challenge and you're bound to hit some sour notes your first few times through. Don't worry, though, because that's how everyone learns.

Track 87

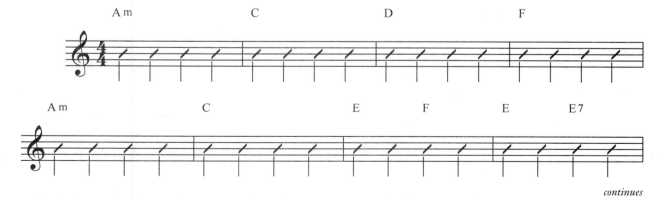

continues

continued

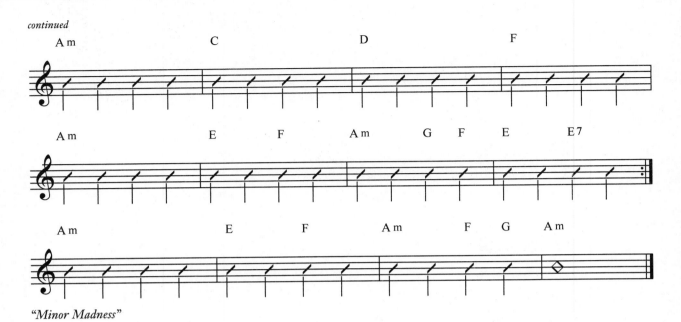

"Minor Madness"

The Least You Need to Know

◆ Target notes within scales can make solos more musical.

◆ Each major scale can be arranged into one of seven modes.

◆ There are three different minor scales.

◆ The chord progression of a song usually provides the best clue as to which scale (or scales) to use for soloing.

◆ Sometimes it's best to use more than one scale for a solo.

Chapter 17

Playing Your Fill

In This Chapter

- ◆ Finding fills
- ◆ Making a collection of riffs for yourself
- ◆ Turning a single fill into many
- ◆ Putting fills together for a solo
- ◆ Using "call and response"

I think Keith Richards is credited with saying that you don't walk into a music store and ask to see a "rhythm guitar." Or a "lead guitar" for that matter! You get a guitar and then it's up to you to do something with it. People love labels but often let those labels, like lead and rhythm guitar, dictate choices for them.

Good guitarists simply play. Rhythm guitarists can use single note lines to create rocking riffs that drive the rhythm of a song. Lead guitarists can use full and partial chords to create a solo that works well for a song, such as John Fogerty did on the first half of the solo in "Proud Mary."

For many players, sometimes the best part of a song isn't the guitar solo, it's the tasty little fills that a guitarist uses to punctuate the lyrical phrases. They can be a short melody of a few notes, almost like a phrase within a phrase, or they can be a rapid-fire outpouring of sixteenth note triplets, cascading down like a waterfall. They can shadow the singer's lines or even be a harmony part like a second vocalist.

Leading the Rhythm

Rock guitarists are always busy. There's always something to do and that doesn't usually mean just playing chords. Think about the guitar parts in the chorus of "Hotel California," the short *fills* that the guitar (guitars, actually) play between the singing. Both rhythm and lead guitar players have a hand in playing these memorable little hooks that pop up throughout most rock songs.

def·i·ni·tion

A **fill** fills space, usually the space created by a short break (or a long, held note) in the singing, such as at the end of a line or phrase of lyrics. While many guitarists use the terms *riff* and *fill* interchangeably, riffs are usually played exactly the same throughout a song while fills can be different each time.

Fills provide much more interest to a rhythm part than just playing chords. For groups with two or more guitarists, they provide a way for each musician to contribute to the overall rhythm and groove of a song. The interplay between chords, arpeggios, partial chords, and fills almost guarantees something interesting to listen to.

In bands with a single guitarist, fills create both breathing space and a break from the monotony of droning power chords. Even with distortion, fills can add a light, almost airy quality to a heavy, pounding rhythm.

Filling Spaces

Playing fills doesn't require all that much. You need some musical space, but that won't be hard to find, as most songs come ready-made for adding fills. Most chord progressions and almost all lyric lines have natural resting points. While the singer's taking a bit of a breath, you can toss in a few notes to catch the listener's ear.

If you're playing chords as part of the rhythm, you'll also want to be aware of what possibilities are available for the chord you're on as well as those for the chord you're moving to. That sounds more complicated than it really is. Remember learning about the Dsus4 and Dsus2 chords back in Chapter 7, or about other suspended chords in Chapter 13? Most guitarists think about suspended chords as ways to "just fool around" with a chord when sitting on it for some time.

"Just fooling around" with chords is often a great way to find a possible fill. Take each of the chords you know (start with the open-position ones) and tinker around with them. First take a finger away from the chord and listen to how you might use the note of an open string. Hammer your finger back into place. Fills can be made from something as simple as this.

Make a note of which fingers are free when you play a chord and also pay attention to which notes those fingers can reach while you still hold all or most of the chord in place. For example, when you play an open-position D chord, you should be able to hammer onto the fourth fret of the G string or the D string with your pinky and still play the whole D chord with your other fingers.

**Track 88
(0:00)**

Here is a rhythm fill, using a typical four chord progression, based on the "just fooling around" principle:

Hear How

Many songs have signature riffs and fills based around open-position chords. "Norwegian Wood" by the Beatles, the Pixies's "Here Comes Your Man," and Neil Young's "Ohio" all have riffs built around the open-position D chord.

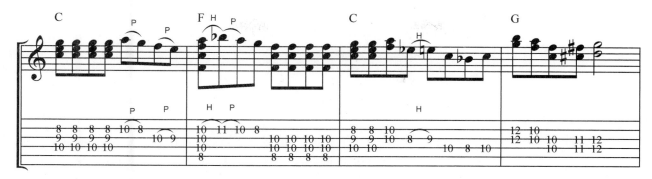

Fills based on chord shapes.

The chords here are just your normal A- and E-shaped barre chords (from Chapter 9). Playing them as partial chords and *not* using a full barre allows you to have some other fingers free to create the fill. You can hear how this is much more interesting than just strumming a chord.

Appropriate Attire

Scales, like chord shapes, are great starting places for ideas to create fills. You want to be careful, though, and choose your scale wisely. If you're playing a crunching, fast moving bluesy rock song, then pulling some notes out of the minor pentatonic is a good move. A pretty pop song–like fill will make your band mates wonder if you're even listening to the music at all.

Track 88
(0:20)

Fills based on scales.

You can overdo it with fills, though, making the music so busy that there's way too much for a listener to try to sort through. Try to use fills in an appropriate style for each song. If a fill doesn't really add anything, then why play one?

Building a Fill/Riff Repertoire

Hear How

The two rhythm fills of AC/DC's "Back in Black" are scale-based. The first one comes straight from the open-position E minor pentatonic while the second one uses a little bit of the chromatic scale, moving up from G♯ to B through half steps.

It's a great idea to put together your own "library," a collection of fills and riffs that you have learned and that you can play in any key, anywhere on the fretboard, with ease. Being able to pull out a cool riff that fits a song is a talent that many guitarists envy, but it's not all that hard to do. It starts with learning fills from songs you know (or ones you've heard and liked) and then discovering how to mold these short musical phrases to fit the songs you play.

Because fills are usually short, they are ideal musical bits to learn. Almost all songs have one or two fills, so you have a lot to pick and choose from.

As you work on getting a fill down, it's important to analyze it a bit. If it comes from a particular chord or scale, try moving it up and down on the fretboard so that you can play it in other keys:

Moving fills along the neck.

Also look for ways to combine fills into longer stretches of music. If you splice together a number of fills that work well with one chord or a particular chord progression, you've pretty much got a short solo ready to go, should you ever need to improvise one on the spot.

Copying the Masters

Whenever you go into a museum or an art gallery, you often see art students with sketch pads, making copies of paintings or drawings. Read an interview with most rock guitarists and there will be some mention of his learning to play by trying to copy the leads of his favorite guitarists.

Learning by imitation is a time-honored tradition because it works. But you also have to keep your head about it or you could be setting yourself up for no end of frustration. Unless you can devote countless hours each day to practicing (and I'm assuming you can't), you're not going to sound exactly like your guitar hero anytime soon.

Even if you had the time and even if you had the exact same equipment as, say, Jimmy Page, you don't have his fingers or his personality. Your imitation can only be so good, and you have to be happy with that and then work toward incorporating what you learn into a style of your own.

Taking Note of Notes

As before, you want to do an analysis of each fill or riff you learn. This doesn't have to be a big deal, but you do want to be able to play a fill in different keys. That means you have to know what key it's in to begin with. Or at the very least know on what chord or scale the riff is based.

Track 89

For example, here is a fill in the style of Mark Knopfler:

Mark Knopfler-styled fill.

This first fill is based on the A minor–shaped Em barre chord, and if you keep that shape you learned back in Chapter 9 in mind, you should find this easy to play. For the beginning of the phrase, use your middle finger to slide from the seventh to ninth frets of the D string. Your ring finger gets the note at the ninth fret of the G string and your index finger plays the eighth fret of the B.

You need to shift your fingers for the second measure, using your index finger on the seventh fret of the high E, your middle finger on the eighth fret of the B, and your ring finger on the ninth fret of the G. This frees up your pinky to get the notes at the tenth frets of both the B and high E strings. Your index finger is responsible for the notes at the seventh fret of the B and G strings.

Now suppose you're playing a song in the key of B minor and you want to use this fill. For a lower sound, start out with a slide from the second to the fourth fret of the D string. For a higher pitch, slide from the fourteenth to the sixteenth frets of the D string and proceed from there.

The Silly Putty Principle

Music is elastic. Notes can be stretched out or made very short. A guitarist can bend (or unbend) one note, transforming it into a different note. You should think of fills and riffs as little pictures that you can copy with silly putty—copy and then stretch or shape them to your desire.

All music is a collection of notes. A song is a specific melody played over a specific harmony or chord progression. So why does a song sound different when played by two different musicians? And how many guitarists play their songs the same exact way time after time?

Every time you play, your music will be slightly different. You may accent a note differently or not play a chord as cleanly as you'd like or possibly miss a string on an arpeggio. This is good, because it means you're not playing like a machine!

When it comes to fills, you can put this "every time is unique" philosophy to work for you by deliberately going out of your way to make the musical aspects of a fill, the component phrases or the timing of the notes, for example, different from how you originally learned it.

Cut and Paste

**Track 90
(0:00)**

To put these ideas into practice, start with a basic fill or riff that you like. Here's a fairly easy one based on the first position minor pentatonic scale shape:

Sample fill for practice.

This fill is made up of two short phrases, each one measure long. Try taking the two phrases and reversing them.

This "cut-and-paste" approach to fills won't always work. But simply testing the many ways you can piece a fill or riff together is good practice for putting together solos. By exploration and experimentation, you'll find more and more ways to connect your short fills. This is a great way to string together short musical ideas and turn them into a full solo.

Track 90
(0:10)

Sample fill, reversed.

Playing with Time

Altering the timing of the notes in a fill is another easy way to explore the art of soloing. Here is a variation of the fill you've just been working on.

Simply by changing the rhythmic value of the notes, you give yourself a wide range of possible new fills and riffs.

Track 90
(0:20)

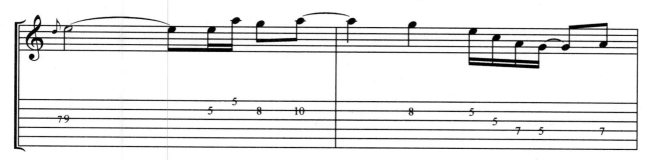

Sample fill with changes in timing of notes.

Call and Response

Another way to develop fills is by using the *call and response* approach. This is essentially a conversation between the guitar and the vocalist (or another instrument) and has long been a trademark of blues and rock playing.

Like all conversations, call and response involves listening and taking turns. First the vocalist sings a line. This is the call. In the pause between lines, the guitarist plays the response, a short fill often based on the melody line just sung.

You can use call and response as a way to accompany yourself. Guitarists from Chuck Berry to Jimi Hendrix to Mark Knopfler to Stevie Ray Vaughn have employed this technique. Playing in a band, call and response requires a good rapport of both listening and nonverbal communication between the guitarist and the singer or second instrumentalist.

Trading Spaces

A variation of call and response called *trading fours* is sometimes used in multiple instrument soloing or jamming. Originally a jazz technique, trading fours involves two or more musicians taking turns at a solo, each turn getting a preset length of musical time.

Hear How
In "The End," the next-to-last song on the Beatles's album *Abbey Road*, you hear a trading fours solo with guitar work from John Lennon, George Harrison, and Paul McCartney. It's a great snapshot of how each of the three approached rock guitar. John was more melodic, Paul a little harder-edged, and George a good combination of the two.

Usually, these turns are relatively short, perhaps a measure or two in length, so all the work you're doing on fills is great practice for this technique.

Listen to the Music

Both call and response and trading fours are terrific ways to put your fill/riff catalogue to good use, but it's easy to get lazy and fall into playing just the fills you especially like or the ones you play best.

How many people do you know whose idea of "conversation" is simply to wait until there is a pause and then start talking about themselves? That's not much of a conversation, is it?

When working with other musicians, you want to really listen to the vocalist or other guitarist or instrumentalist that you're working with. Try to pick up on ideas that he or she uses musically. You will find both these techniques provide you with an excellent chance to learn new riffs and fills, as well as to improve your sense of timing and phrasing and to hone your listening skills.

"Commuter Train Crazy"

Track 91

"Commuter Train Crazy" is a practice song that uses a trading fours format to help you work on the various topics discussed in this chapter. It starts with a basic rhythm riff of four measures, which is written out for you in both notation and tablature:

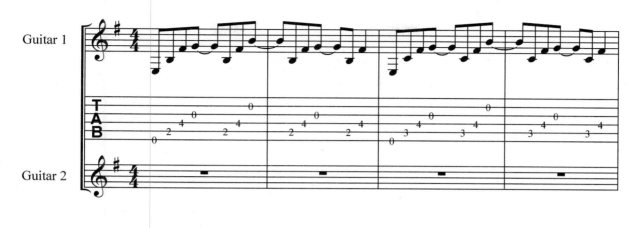

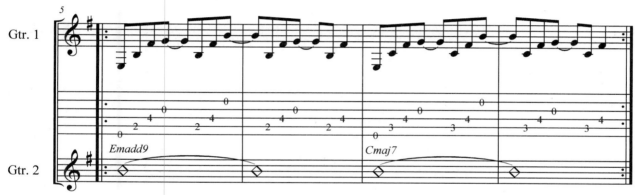

"Commuter Train Crazy"

A simple rhythm guitar part is added, just using the two chords Em and C, and then a lead guitar part comes in and plays a short, very simple lead of four measures. Then it's your turn! You and the guitarist on the CD get to trade off every four measures until the song fades out at the end.

Given the song is in the key of E minor, you might want to use either the E minor pentatonic scale or even the full E natural minor scale (making use of the minor scales you learned back in Chapter 15), but you should also take time to experiment and to work in some of the mood that the guitarist on the CD creates.

And remember that the guitarist on the CD is working at a huge disadvantage, because he doesn't get to listen to your ideas or to get musical cues from you!

Making Your Own Style

You can copy fills, riffs, and solos from other artists pretty much your whole life. Almost every guitarist starts out that way. It's in the process of your learning and collecting where you begin to develop your own personal music style.

Everyone learns things differently and at different speeds. You, for instance, may have had no trouble putting scales together while bending strings took a little (or a lot) more time to feel comfortable with.

And everybody has his or her own sweet spots. Speed may be your calling because you find your fingers can fly over the fretboard at will. Or perhaps you've a gift for quirky but catchy phrasing.

You have to remember that you actually started out not even knowing how to play a simple power chord. With each new technique you get into your fingers, with each new idea that pops into your head, you will constantly continue to evolve as a guitarist. Some of the challenges you have today will be things you can do without thinking tomorrow.

You also have to remember that of all the guitarists in the world, no one plays exactly the way you do. Don't think that you're not good enough to solo. Concentrate instead on improving what you can and refining what you can already do well.

In the end you want to play to your strengths while contributing positively to the music. As you learn more techniques and style and as you refine your finesse, speed, and musicality, you'll be able to add more of *you* to a song. That's what the world is waiting to hear.

The Least You Need to Know

- ◆ Fills are short musical phrases that spice up a song.
- ◆ Fills are usually based either on scales or chord shapes.
- ◆ Learning fills from songs and other guitarists is a fast way to build up material for soloing.
- ◆ Play around with the phrases and timing of fills you've learned to create new ones for yourself.
- ◆ Call and response and trading fours are interactive solos and require your listening skills.

Part  5

The Quest for Tone

Throughout this book, the focus has been on developing your sense of touch. Two guitarists can play the same notes with the same timing on the same guitar with the same amplifier (same settings) and effects and sound totally different. Each guitarist's personal, unique touch gives him or her a personal, unique tone.

But even while you are working on your technique and style, you need to take other external factors into account when creating your tone. In this part, you learn how scale length, strings, pickups, amplifiers, effects, and even the tuning of your guitar can make huge differences in the tone you achieve.

Chapter 18

You, Your Gear, and the Great Quest

In This Chapter

♦ Where tone comes from

♦ How scale length affects your playing

♦ Choices of pickups

♦ Differences in amplifiers

♦ Using guitar effects

Imagine if you will that you are at an Eric Clapton concert. Not only are you at the concert, but somehow, you managed to get front row center tickets. Now imagine that he's been watching you watch him playing all night and, because he's in a pretty good mood (it's been a great show), he walks over to the edge of the stage, looks directly at you and asks "Would you like to play my guitar?"

You say yes (of course!), because in your imagination you might have courage to do so. He gets you up onstage and hands you his guitar. So not only do you have Eric Clapton's guitar in your hands, it's also hooked up to his amplifier and his various effects, each one set precisely the way he wants them to be when he plays live. So you play a few notes. The question is, how much will you sound like Eric Clapton?

Now suppose that you also came to the concert with your own guitar and gear (and it's up to your imagination to figure out how you got all that stuff into the front row!) and you let Eric Clapton play your guitar through your amp and effects. Would his playing sound like yours?

You could use any other guitarist in this scenario but the answer to the question would not change. Even playing on your gear, Eric Clapton is going to sound like Eric Clapton. And you're going to sound like you no matter whose equipment you use. And it also wouldn't matter in the least if somehow you managed to put in just as many hours, days, weeks, or years practicing and playing as your guitar idol has.

As logical as this is, it doesn't stop guitarists from obsessing about tone, almost to the point of buying the same exact gear (right down to the picks and strings) that their guitar idols play. In some ways, it's like the cliché "the grass is always greener on the other side."

This isn't to say that tone isn't important. Quite the contrary! Tone is an integral part of playing because it is as much a part of musical expression as the notes themselves. But ultimately each guitarist's tone is unique because each guitarist is unique.

Tone Starts with the Fingers

Any song is just a collection of notes, whether those notes are an individual melody line (or solo or riff) or chords being strummed. But if you take a dozen guitarists and have each one play the opening riff of "Smoke on the Water," each playing the very same guitar through the same amp with the same settings, you would get 12 different versions of this riff.

One might have an aggressive pick attack while another picks with his or her thumb and fingers. One's slide technique might be heavy, creating a bit of fret noise while another's fingers might dance lightly over the frets.

Other people might have the same gear you have, but no one else has your fingers. The method of creating notes by fretting the neck of the guitar, the basic picking stroke, all the general mechanics of each guitar technique are used by just about every player. And each one does it differently enough to produce a unique tone.

This is why, from the very start of this book, you have been working on developing your own sense of touch. It's why you've been listening to each note and each chord you play. To express yourself in your music, you have to make sure what you're playing is what you mean to play and what you want to play—not only in terms of notes, but also in terms of tone.

When you're first learning a technique, you're going to be more worried about fretting notes correctly and picking the right strings. Remember what it was like to play your first power chord? Now you can probably play them at will, all up and down the fretboard. But are they as clean as you'd like them to be? Are the notes round and full or are they chopped and slightly out of tune because you've gotten lax with your fingering? Do they sound the way you want them to sound?

As you continue to practice and play, it's important that you keep listening and evaluating. Once you are comfortable with a new chord or riff or even a new technique, then concentrate on your sound. The adjustments you make, even the smallest ones, are going to become part of your personal style.

Hear How

Almost all your guitar heroes learned to play by listening to and copying riffs, chords, and solos from their favorite guitarists. You hear the influence of old blues guitarists such as Robert Johnson and B. B. King in Eric Clapton's playing, and you catch a lot of Jimi Hendrix's stylings in the guitar work of Stevie Ray Vaughn.

It's also important that you keep listening to other people's music. Hearing a new rhythm, a different type of musical phrasing, whether played on a guitar or any other instrument, seeing another guitarist use an unfamiliar technique—you want to absorb all this and more. The more ideas you have to work with, the more you can express musically.

Copying another guitarist note for note is an excellent way to learn. Go into any museum and you'll see art students doing the same thing, imitating the masters with their sketchpads. But remember that you do this for the techniques and the knowledge. Your musical expression of this knowledge, even in a note for note copy, is going to be covered in your own fingerprints, your own style. So learn all you can about tone and use it as you want to.

Body Language

Your own playing may be a huge part of your tone and style, but there are external factors as well. Your guitar also shapes your tone considerably. The type of guitar you play gives your tone a starting point.

Most electric guitars are "solid body" guitars. That doesn't mean they are made from a single piece of solid wood. Usually two or three pieces, made from the same type of wood, are glued together to form a single body block. Many guitars are made of alder or ash, and you can find guitars made of maple, mahogany, and other types of wood, as well.

There are also hollow body and semihollow body electric guitars. You don't find them used quite as often in rock music because they tend to feedback at high volumes and don't offer as much sustain as solid body guitars. But a number of guitarists favor that tone and use them for rock music. And there are also "solid body guitars" that are "chambered," having small, hollow chambers to reduce their weight or to alter their tone.

Even though solid body guitars come in all shapes and styles, most are variations on four early guitar designs that have become "classic"—the Telecaster and Stratocaster by Fender and Gibson's Les Paul and SG guitars. They are almost like the major scale is to music; all other guitars are usually described in terms of their similarities and differences to these four models.

Scale Length and Strings

A lot of the process of making notes takes place on the neck of the guitar, so how comfortable a neck feels in your hands is important as it can dictate how well you place your fingers on the fretboard. The back of the neck can come in different styles, sizes, and shapes. They can be relatively flat, slightly rounded, or almost in a *V* shape.

More important, though, is the neck's *scale length*, which is the distance from the bridge of the guitar down the fretboard to the nut. Generally, guitars come with either 25½" or 24¾" scale lengths. The longer length is typically called the

"Fender scale length" because most Fender guitars have it; the shorter one goes by the "Gibson scale length" for the same reason.

Short scale guitars have less string tension than long scale because the strings are being stretched over a shorter distance. Less string tension leads to easier playing when it comes to techniques like vibrato and string bending. Some players like to wrestle notes out of their guitars and prefer the longer scale necks, thinking the higher string tension also gives the strings a more biting tone.

The material and gauge of the strings also comes into play. You read a bit about this way back in Chapter 1. As a rule, lighter strings are easier to bend while heavier strings, which require increased tension, offer more sustain. But it's possible for guitarists to "mix and match" in creative ways. Someone who likes to play on a long scale neck and who wants the sustain of heavier strings can lower the tuning of their guitar (which you read more about in the following chapter), giving the strings less overall tension and allowing the player easy bends and vibrato.

Pickup Games

On the other end of your guitar, tone is generated by your right hand (with or without a pick) striking the strings and by your pickups, specifically the type of pickups and their placement or configuration on the body. Traditionally, pickups come in two styles and, again, each is generally associated with the four basic guitar styles: single coil pickups, such as those you find on the Fender Telecaster (which usually has two) and Stratocaster (usually three); and humbuckers, which look like two single coils glued together side by side, are found on the Les Paul and SG of Gibson.

Single coil pickups, despite generating less output, tend to give more high-end attack than humbuckers. Their clarity can really cut through the wall of sound a full band produces, making them a favorite for studio work. However, they can be noisy, especially when played around fluorescent lighting. Humbuckers are smoother and produce a fuller sound with a big midrange punch that makes them a favorite for live performance.

Then there are stacked pickups, which are humbuckers made of two single coils placed one atop the other, giving both the single coil clarity and the midrange fullness of the humbucker. You can also find humbucker pickups that turn themselves into single coils with the flip of a switch or the press of a knob. The tonal range of pickups varies from manufacturer to manufacturer. Many guitarists enjoy tinkering with their tone by swapping out a guitar's original pickups with new, old, or vintage pickups they've bought separately. Similarly, others try out different necks. If you're handy with tools, you might find yourself becoming a Doctor Frankenstein with your guitars!

Your Partner the Amp

You and your guitar are still only part of the "tone team." Your amplifier has more than a bit to contribute! Just as you've taken the time to develop a sense of touch with your guitar, you want to explore and examine the many tonal possibilities your amp has to offer you.

And to do that, it helps to understand a little about how your amplifier works. You may think of your amplifier as a single entity, but it has two separate sections, the preamp and the power amp. The guitar signal, sent from your pickups down through the cable to the amplifier, goes first into the preamp, which boosts the signal voltage significantly and sends it over to the power amp. The power amp then magnifies the input from the preamp by increasing the current driving capability, converting the signal into a form that will drive your speakers. This is a very watered-down explanation, but being aware of the two stages of amplification makes dealing with your amp a lot more logical.

Usually an amp has two channels, or signal paths. The first is called "clean," and here the preamp signal goes directly to the power amp. You control the output of the power amp with a volume control. The second channel, often labeled as "gain" or "drive," provides another section of amplification (gain) between the preamp and the power amp. This allows two things: The preamp can drive the gain amplifier input into the crunch zone (one type of sound), and/or the gain amplifier can further help the preamp drive the power amp into saturation—usually a "creamier" distortion.

In addition to preamp and power amp controls, your amp usually has "tone controls," (also called a "tone stack") labeled "bass," "midrange" (or "middle"), and "treble" (or "high"). Increasing the bass knob, for instance, boosts the low frequencies of the sound spectrum.

It's important to understand that each individual tone control affects the entire range of your guitar's sound. Boosting bass and midrange can thicken the tone or timbre of many of the notes in the guitar's range—even on the high E, as these will boost the fundamental relative to the note's harmonics. So the harmonics (highs) are not cut, but rather masked by the stronger bass and/or midrange.

Getting Better

Becoming familiar with your tone controls through experimentation can help you find tones for specific use. If you're playing rhythm guitar and want a full, warm sound, turning up the midrange should give you a lot of what you're looking for. Chopping out the midrange (also called "scooping") gives you more emphasis on the highs and lows, which you often hear from metal bands.

Tubes and Transitors

The earliest guitar amplifiers, like most electronic equipment, were powered by vacuum tubes. As solid state technology became more efficient and affordable, guitar amps followed suit. But even though solid state amplifiers are usually cheaper and require less care and maintenance than tube amps (and they are certainly lighter to carry!), they definitely have a different sound. Even non-musicians will describe the tone from a tube amp as being "warmer" when compared to a solid state model.

And technology keeps bringing both new ideas as well as tweaking old ones. You can get "hybrid amps" that use both tubes (in the preamp stage) and solid state (in the power amp). And constant advances in digital technology have led to "modeling amplifiers," which allow you to sound a lot (but not perfectly) like you're playing through almost any amplifier from rock 'n' roll history.

Added or Adding Effects

In addition to tone controls, some amps also have additional effects such as reverb, chorus, and tremolo. Reverb (shortened from reverberation) gives your guitar a slight echo, simulating the way the sound bounces around when playing in different settings from a small room to a large auditorium. You read more about chorus and tremolo in a moment. Newer digital amps offer an even wider range of effects, much like those of individual effects boxes or multi-effects units.

Many newer amps also offer you the option of plugging in effects between the preamp and power amp stages, which many guitarists find to be the optimal place to add effects. You will usually find two jacks in the back of the amplifier marked "effects loop." The "send" or "out" jack sends the preamp signal out to the effect (or group of effects) and the "return" or "in" jack passes the altered signal on to the power amp.

Effective Sounds

Creating and then amplifying the electric guitar gave birth to warm distortion and sustain, totally changing the tonal characteristics of the acoustic guitar. Making the guitar electric also created the opportunity to change that tone even further by use of effects, various devices that altered the guitar's signal in both subtle and dramatic ways. Effects can be introduced between the guitar's output jack and the amplifier, or, as mentioned earlier, through the "effects loop" panel of your amplifier, assuming it has one.

Typically, effects are bought individually. They are often called "pedals" but are more likely to be small boxes with an "on/off" switch that the guitarist activates with his foot. They also usually have two or three knobs that set the range and depth of the particular effect. These individual effects are then linked by cables in whichever order the guitarist desires.

You can also purchase multi-effects units that have several different types of effects all sharing a single housing. Multi-effects units often have pre-programmed settings and will usually also offer the option of re-editing the existing settings or creating, saving, and storing your own.

Dynamic Control and Filters

Some effects might not be at all that flashy, but when put together they give you a tremendous amount of control over the sound of your guitar.

Note Worthy

Effects pedals usually run off nine-volt batteries, although some offer the option of an AC power supply. Be sure to have plenty of spare batteries in your gig bag whenever you're playing out. You can also find electrical adapters capable of powering several effects pedals at once.

Volume pedals enable you to control the volume of your guitar signal by stepping on a floor pedal (pressing down increases the volume and rocking it back upright decreases it), which is very handy when playing solos or rhythm parts that have big changes in dynamics. You can also imitate the swelling of violins and other stringed instruments by rocking the pedal after you've hit a single note or chord.

Tremolo, on the other hand, is a very rapid change in volume, so much so that people often mistake it for vibrato (which you already know is a rapid change in pitch). Tremolo effects give your guitar a wavering effect that you often hear in surf rock songs.

Compressors first squeeze your signal, leveling out the differences between the loudest parts and the quietest parts to make it smoother, and then boost the whole thing before sending it on. This effect often gives the guitar more clean sustain as the compressed signal takes longer to fade out.

Equalizers, or EQ for short, act in much the same way as your amplifier's tone controls, but give you more specific ranges of your guitar's output to balance. They allow you to punch up or scoop out more of the midrange, for instance, or to filter out just the highest end of the higher frequencies of the signal.

Wah-wah pedals are filters that boost the level of a relatively narrow range of frequencies. Changing the position of the foot pedal from up to down moves the filter's frequency range from low to high frequencies imparting the characteristic vocal "Wa-a-a-aH" sound to the guitar's tone. Wahs are great for guitar leads but are also very cool for rhythm work.

Distortion and Overdrive

Guitarists tend to use "overdrive" and "distortion" interchangeably, much to the chagrin of engineers the world over. In fact, you often find effects pedals called "overdrive/distortion." An overdrive pedal boosts the guitar's signal enough to drive the input of the amplifier harder. All the change in sound occurs in the amp's preamp, as that larger signal will drive the input to the amp a bit too hard ("overdriving" it), causing first a thickening of the tone and eventually—as the guitarist plays harder—some crunch. It's not smooth or harsh, but sort of loose in nature, and very touch sensitive.

Distortion has taken on a particular connotation in the world of electric guitar. It refers to a self-contained "box" that creates a higher gain that's harsher and more dynamically compressed—"distorted," if you will. And while you might think that all distortion sounds the same, there are all sorts of subtle, rich nuances. This is one reason many guitarists use multiple distortion boxes or go with a single box that offers numerous types of distortion settings.

A Chorus Line

A chorus effect takes your original signal, splits it, and delays it for a dozen milliseconds or so. When the delayed signal is then mixed back with the original, it sounds like you're part of a chorus of guitars. The delay is also varied a bit over time, creating a shimmering effect. It's a great effect to help thicken your sound without using distortion, particularly if you're the only guitarist in your band.

Delays and echoes are essentially the same effect. A very short delay time, say 120 milliseconds or so, gives you the "slapback" effect of a very short echo. This effect is still used by rockabilly guitarists to emulate the sound of early rock 'n' roll records. Longer delay times are used for leads, such as Mark Knopfler's closing solo on "Romeo and Juliet."

Phase shifters (also called *phasers*) **and flangers** work in the same basic manner, but add some more effects to the mix. A phaser mixes in an oscillating filtered signal, giving the guitar a smooth whooshing sound as you play. Flangers add a shorter whoosh, like the sound of a reel-to-reel tape machine that's been held up momentarily and then let go, like the sound is trying to catch up with itself. While flangers can sound a lot like phasers, flangers have a more metallic bite to them.

Sampler

Track 92

Track 92 on the CD gives you an "audio sampler" of some of the commonly used guitar effects. To make the differences a little more obvious, the following short riff, containing both chords and single notes, is played for each of the effects examples:

First, the riff is played cleanly, just the guitar and amplifier. Then it is played again through a distortion box. Following that, you will hear the riff played with a chorus effect, then through a flanger, and then with some delay added. Finally, it is played with a wah-wah pedal.

For the purposes of this example, the effects were set to best demonstrate their sounds. Depending on the specific manufacturer and model of an effects box, one can tweak the settings in order to exaggerate the effect even further or to subtly integrate it into the guitar's sound.

Building a Chain

You can use an effect, or several effects, to create a new tone for your guitar. Changing the order of the effects also creates different tones. Generally, a guitarist starts off with a compressor or another effect to boost the signal through the chain, but there are numerous ways to mix and match your effects boxes.

Some guitarists use "pedal boards," which is basically a board to which the effects are attached, often by pieces of Velcro. This allows them to change the order of the effects as they see fit, even from one song to the next. If you're handy with tools, you can probably build one for yourself.

Evolutionary Theory

Regardless of what type of guitar you own, what pickups and scale length it has, what type and gauge of strings you play, or what kind of amplifier and effects you use, you have to be more concerned about being able to *play* before you start obsessing about tone. It's a mistake to think that your guitar hero set out to create his or her unique sound. More often than not, he probably used whatever equipment he could afford or could get his hands on and the tone came out of both the equipment and the practicing and playing he did.

It's also important to realize that your tone, like your playing, is an ongoing process. You are constantly evolving as a rock guitar player, adding new skills and techniques on a daily basis. Consequently, your tone is going to develop and mature.

But you also need to remember that even if you have the greatest tone in the universe, it won't mean a thing if you can't play cleanly, if you can't smoothly change from one chord to the next, or if you can't keep rhythm well. Let your own personal tone grow and become part of you instead of chasing after someone else's.

The Least You Need to Know

- Tone is a combination of your playing abilities and the instrument and gear you play.

- Both the guitar's scale length and pickups contribute to its overall tonal qualities.

- You can change the pickups and many other parts of your guitar.

- Tube amplifiers sound warmer than solid state. You can buy amps that use both technologies.

- Adding effects to your signal chain gives you more ways to change its tone.

Chapter 19

Alternate Tuning

In This Chapter

- ◆ Discovering alternate tunings
- ◆ Getting heavy with lowered tunings
- ◆ Using Drop D for speedy power chords
- ◆ Getting the Rolling Stones's sound with Open G tuning
- ◆ Using alternate tuning to explore new sounds

Part of the wonder of the guitar, not to mention music in general, is exploring all the different ways you can come up with cool riffs, chord voicings, and tones of your instrument. Making time to simply "noodle" and experiment should always be part of your regular routine.

For instance, suppose you're trying to play along with a Rolling Stones's song, like "Honky Tonk Woman" or "Start Me Up." Or maybe "Breathe Into Me" by RED. You might have gotten the chords from a book or an online source but, try as you might, you can't get your guitar to sound like those in the recordings.

There's a rather simple, but exciting, explanation for this. The guitar parts in these particular songs are not tuned to standard tuning. Instead of the familiar sound of standard tuning, which you know from low to high as EADGBE, these guitars have their strings tuned to different notes.

Simply tuning your guitar differently, creating what's known as an alternate tuning, is one way to begin exploring the different voicings of chords and arpeggios. It's also one of the easiest ways of changing your tone, especially because it doesn't involve physically changing your guitar or pickups, tweaking the settings of your amplifier, or using any kind of external effects.

Plus, exploring these new tunings helps you solidify your working knowledge of music theory. Alternate tuning is a terrific way to both learn more and to reinforce what you already know.

Nothing Standard

As long as there has been a "standard tuning," there have been alternate tunings, tunings that involve at least one different note than those in standard tuning. If you accidentally tune your B string up to C, for example, you have created an alternate tuning. Some alternate tunings differ very slightly from standard, with only one or two strings being changed. Others involve changing the notes of every string.

Usually people classify tunings as three types: standard, open, and alternate. Standard, which you already know, tunes the guitar strings, from low to high, to the notes EADGBE. It's important to note that most tunings will be written out in this same manner, from the note of the lowest (thickest) string to the note of the highest.

Lowered Tuning

Technically, though, you can add a fourth category, lowered tuning, to this list. In a lowered tuning, the intervals between the strings stay the same, even though the notes of each string have changed.

In standard tuning, each string except the G and B string are tuned to the interval of a perfect fourth (which you should remember from Chapter 12). A is a perfect fourth higher than E, and D is a perfect fourth higher than A. The G and B string are tuned to a major third, as B is two whole steps higher than G. The high E string is a perfect fourth higher than B.

In lowered tuning, all the notes of the strings are changed, but the intervals between all the strings remain the same. For instance, if you lowered each string by one half step in tone, you'd have E♭ standard and the notes, from low to high, would be as follows:

Standard tuning:	E	A	D	G	B	E
E♭ standard:	E♭	A♭	D♭	G♭	B♭	E♭

Getting a lowered tuning on your guitar is very easy if you have a chromatic tuner. You simply match your tuner with the new notes you want your strings to be tuned to, although you will probably have to remember that D♯ and E♭ are the same notes in case your tuner indicates only sharps.

Relative tuning also works, but you have to do a little reverse engineering. With your guitar in standard tuning, play the note at the fourth fret of the low E (sixth) string. This is A♭, or G♯ if you prefer. Lower the pitch of the A string until it matches the sound of the A♭. When you're finished, go back and this time play the fifth fret of the low E string. That will still be A, and it will sound sharp when matched to the newly tuned fifth string. Lower the pitch of the sixth string until the note at the fifth fret matches the fifth string. Now both strings will be a half-step lower and you can move on to your other strings, tuning them as you normally would when tuning to yourself.

Getting Heavy

Lowered tunings are frequently used in metal music, but you also find them in other rock genres, not to mention other musical styles as well. People often describe the resonating lower tones as "heavy," and some groups have their guitars tuned to D standard, D♭ standard (same as C♯ standard), and even as low as C standard. When using a tuner, remember that C♭ is the same note as B and that E♯ is the same note as F.

Standard tuning:	E	A	D	G	B	E
E♭ standard:	E♭	A♭	D♭	G♭	B♭	E♭
D standard:	D	G	C	F	A	D
D♭ standard:	D♭	G♭	C♭	F♭	A♭	D♭
C standard:	C	F	B♭	E♭	G	C

Hear How

Many of Stevie Ray Vaughn's and Jimi Hendrix's songs were recorded in lowered tunings, usually E♭ standard. Van Halen, Alice in Chains, and Smashing Pumpkins also used E♭ standard. Today you can find many bands whose guitars still play in E♭ standard, such as Green Day and Weezer.

The obvious advantage to lower tunings is that you don't have to learn new fingerings of chords. But you do have to remember that an open-position E chord will now be a totally different chord, such as E♭ or D or whatever note you have tuned the lowest string to. The following example is an E—A—D progression, first in E standard tuning and then in each of our four lowered tunings:

Track 93

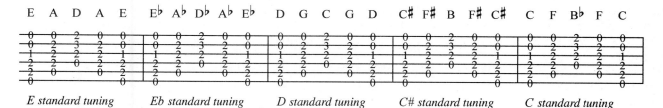

| E standard tuning | Eb standard tuning | D standard tuning | C# standard tuning | C standard tuning |

How the notes change in lowered tunings.

Alternatives to Lowered Tunings

While you can hear how heavy the guitar sounds with each successive lowered tuning, you can probably also hear that the strings sound floppier. That makes perfect sense, because you have to loosen the tension of all the strings in order to play these tunings. When you get as low as D♭ standard or C standard, all the strings are very loose and you can end up losing tonal definition. Using a heavier gauge of string can help somewhat, but the lower you tune, the more likely you are to run into this problem.

Some guitarists circumvent floppiness by playing a seven-string guitar, which has an additional low string, usually tuned to B. It also has a slightly longer neck to accommodate the low tone of the extra string. Similarly, there are also baritone guitars, which only use six strings but have longer necks and use heavier gauges of strings so that you can tune down the thickest string as low as B or A (the same A as the third string of the open bass guitar, which is an octave lower than the normal fifth string of a regular guitar). Again, because the rest of the strings are tuned to the same intervals as standard, you can use the same chord shapes you know, but they will be different chords.

There is one other major reason for using a slightly lowered tuning, such as E♭ standard, and that concerns bending. When the strings are looser, they become easier to bend. Many guitarists play in E♭ standard and use heavy gauge strings, giving their sound more sustain and allowing them to perform fairly impressive string bends.

Dropping the D

Rather than retuning all your strings, one of the more common alternate tunings involves changing only one. In Drop D tuning you lower the sixth string one whole step, from E to D. From low to high, your strings will be like this:

| Standard tuning: | E | A | D | G | B | E |
| Drop D tuning: | D | A | D | G | B | E |

It is amazing the difference that changing one string can make. Try playing an open-position D or Dm chord. Remember that you can now strum across all six strings, since D is the root note of any D chord. That full, strong sound makes Drop D a favorite alternate tuning of many guitarists, not only in rock but in folk and other genres as well.

Because you have changed the note of the sixth string, any chord that uses this string has to be altered. For instance, the open-position G and Em chords are now fingered like this:

The D, G, and Em chords in Drop D tuning.

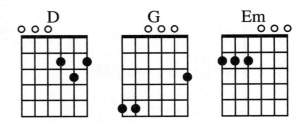

Big and Easy Power Chords

The biggest reason rock guitarists use Drop D is because this tuning allows them to play quick, one-fingered power chords. In Drop D, the three lowest strings are D, A, and D, which you no doubt remember from Chapter 5 as being D5 or the D power chord. So any Root 6 power chord, in Drop D tuning, is as easy as getting one finger (or even a large thumb) across the three low strings on the same fret, like the following:

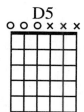
D5
o o o x x x

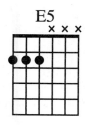
E5
x x x

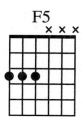
F5
x x x

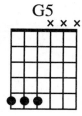
G5
x x x

Various Root 6 power chords in Drop D tuning.

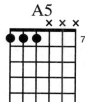
A5
x x x
7

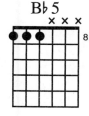
B♭5
x x x
8

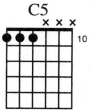
C5
x x x
10

Combining Drop D and Lowered Tunings

Many rock groups, including Fall Out Boy and Three Days Grace, combine the heavy sound of lowered tuning with the power-chord ease of Drop D. First, they retune their guitars to a lowered standard tuning, and then they drop the lowest string an additional step, resulting in tunings such as "Drop D♭" (which is more often called "Drop C♯" in computer tablature) and "Drop C."

Standard tuning:	E	A	D	G	B	E
Drop D tuning:	D	A	D	G	B	E
Drop D♭ tuning:	D♭	A♭	D♭	G♭	B♭	E♭
Drop C tuning:	C	A	D	G	B	E

Note Worthy
When it comes to alternate tuning, names can get very confusing. While most people accept "Drop C" tuning as meaning D standard tuning with the lowest string tuned down to C, others will insist that Drop C is regular standard tuning with *only* the low E (sixth) string tuned down two full steps to C.

"Drop D Rock"

To help you get a little feel for playing in Drop D tuning, here is a "practice song" custom-made for the occasion:

Track 94

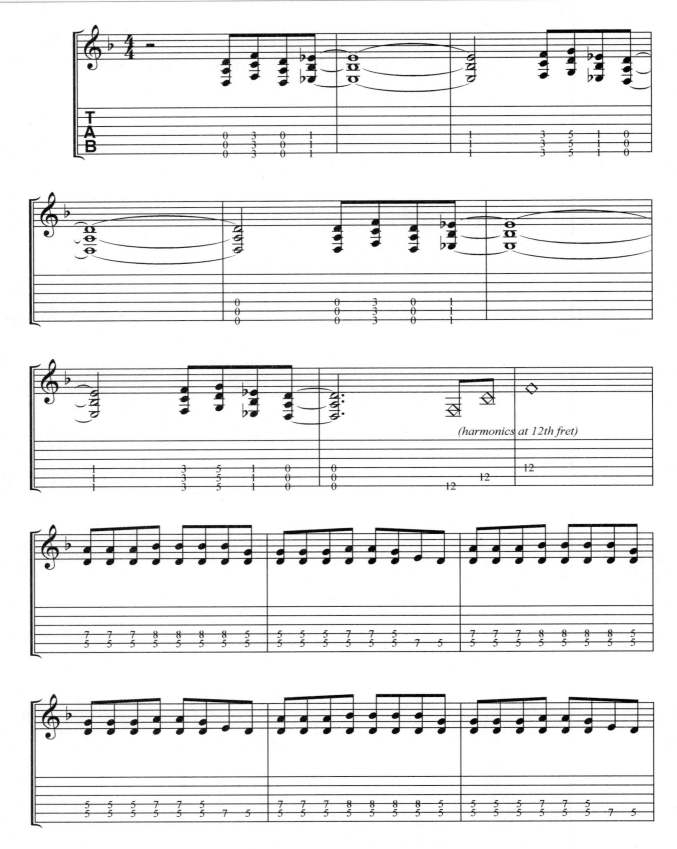

(harmonics at 12th fret)

"Drop D Rock"

Open Tuning

An open tuning is one where playing all six open strings of your retuned guitar results in a readily recognized major or minor chord. Just as Drop D gives you one-finger power chords, an open tuning gives you not only power chords, but full six-string chords by simply barring a finger across all six strings on the same fret. Open G, Open D, Open A, and Open E are the most common open tunings, but there are many other possibilities.

Open G

Because three of your guitar strings—the B, G, and D—are already part of the G Major chord, tuning to Open G involves only three steps. First, tune *both* E strings, high and low, down one full step to D. Then retune the A (fifth) string down one full step to G. And there you go!

Standard tuning:	E	A	D	G	B	E
Open G tuning:	D	G	D	G	B	D

When you strum all six strings in Open G tuning, you get a G Major chord. Some people prefer to strum just from the fifth string down (Keith Richards of the Rolling Stones actually removes the sixth string from his Open G-tuned guitars!) in order to have the root note (G) in the bass.

Barring across all six strings, at any fret, gives you a major chord. At the second fret is A Major. B Major is at the fourth fret, C Major the fifth, and so on:

The G, A, B, C, D, and E chords in Open G tuning.

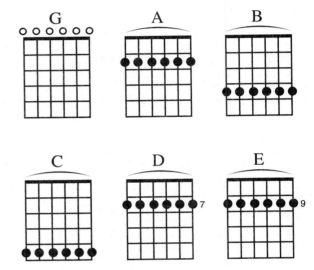

The "Rolling Stones" Sound

Track 95

The driving, crunching rock shuffle that defines the Rolling Stones's sound comes directly from Keith Richards's use of Open G tuning. Using any major chord, either open or barred, he then adds the Am7 chord shape to it and creates musical magic:

The Am7 shape with Open G tuning.

Open D

In Open D tuning, your guitar sounds a D chord when all six strings are played open. Getting to Open D from standard takes a few more steps than Open G does, but you start out the same way, and that's lowering both E strings down one full step to D. You then want to lower the B string down a full step to A. Finally, retune the G string one half step lower to F♯.

Standard tuning:	E	A	D	G	B	E
Open D tuning:	D	A	D	F♯	A	D

Getting Better _____

Drawing out fretboard maps is one of the smartest things you can do to help yourself navigate in open and alternate tunings. Make several copies, one just to show the notes and others to plot out chord positions.

As with all open tunings, you can make any major chord you'd like by barring all six strings at the appropriate fret. Because the root notes of major chords in Open D are easily found on the sixth string, you know that barring at the fifth fret will give you a G Major and that A Major is at the seventh fret.

Having the D notes on both the first and sixth strings can also help you create some interesting droning chord voicings. Here are a few examples of the many possible chords to be found in Open D:

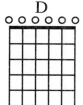 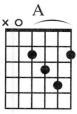 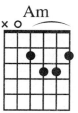 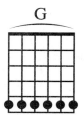

Various chords in Open D tuning.

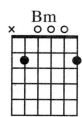 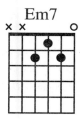 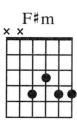 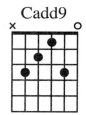

Now you can probably see how all that time reading about chord construction back in Chapter 13 can pay off. Knowing what notes make up a chord makes it a lot easier to find them in open and alternate tunings.

Open A, Open E, and Capos

If you've explored and learned a few things in Open G and Open D tuning, working in Open A and Open E will be easy, as the intervals between the strings are the same. In Open A tuning, all the strings are one step higher than those of Open G. Likewise, the strings in Open E tuning are all one step higher than they are in Open D.

A lot of guitarists don't like tuning their strings up all that much. So instead they might tune down to Open G or Open D and then use a *capo*, placing it on the guitar's second fret to raise the pitch up to Open A or Open E.

Having a capo is also handy if you play a lot with lowered tunings but still want to play with other guitarists in standard tuning. Suppose you normally

def•i•ni•tion _____

A **capo** is a small clamp-like device that you attach to the neck of the guitar. Essentially, it barres all six strings at whichever fret you choose, raising the pitch of every string one half step for each fret up from the nut. If you put a capo on the fourth fret, for example, you have raised the guitar two full steps (four half steps) higher in tone.

keep your guitar in E♭ standard tuning. Instead of retuning each string up a half step to play with another guitarist in standard tuning, you can place a capo at the first fret and then you'll be in standard because you've raised the pitch of all your strings up a half step.

Even More Open Tunings

When you think about it, you can come up with all sorts of open tunings for your guitar. If you lower the F♯ string of Open D a half step, making it an F, you've got Open D minor tuning.

With some open tunings, though, you want to think a little bit. If you decide to create an Open C tuning, for instance, your first inclination might be to leave the sixth string alone, but using that low E note could really muddy up your chords. It's always a good idea to use a root note as your lowest note whenever possible. If that's not an option, then go for the fifth of the chord.

Also, try to use only one string as the third of the chord. It will give you more than enough definition of "major" or "minor."

Where you decide to put the third of the chord will also change the overall tone and character of your tuning. Look at these two Open C tunings, for example:

Standard tuning:	E	A	D	G	B	E
Open C tuning:	C	G	C	G	C	E
Open C variation:	C	G	C	E	G	C

In standard tuning, the E note (the third of the C Major chord) is on the highest string. It will ring out and draw a lot of attention to itself, sounding a lot like a regular open-position C chord, in fact.

In the "Open C variation," the E note is buried in the midrange of the guitar's strings. The sound will be more subtle, like an open-position E Major chord.

And you can certainly make more variations of these by tuning some strings to the same note. For instance, Soundgarden uses a CGCGGE variation of Open C tuning, keeping the third string tuned to the original pitch of G and also lowering the B string to that same pitch.

"Open G Rock"

Track 96

Before taking a look at some other alternate tunings, here is a "practice song" in Open G tuning.

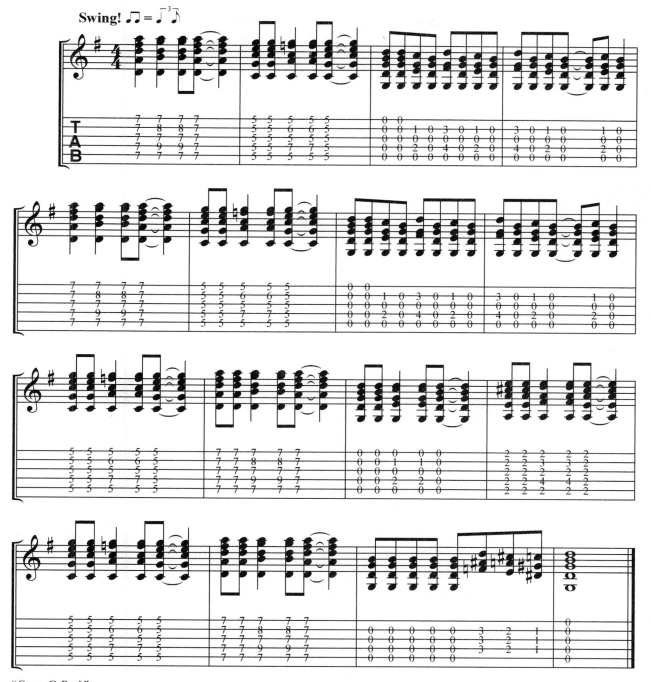

"Open G Rock"

A Universe of Alternate Tunings

In addition to lowered tunings, drop tunings, and open tunings, there are *alternate tunings*, which are any tunings other than standard that don't fit the other three categories. As mentioned earlier, an alternate tuning can be as simple as changing one string—lowering the G string to F#—for instance, or it could involve changing the tuning of each string, as in lowered tunings.

Hear How

There are some decidedly wild alternate tunings used in music. Alt rocker Ani DiFranco has been said to have employed more than 30 different tunings (so far) over the course of her career!

Alternate tunings aren't given formal names. Usually they are designated by writing out the new tuning of each string from low to high. Occasionally this results in a name one can pronounce (such as "DADGAD" tuning), but not often enough that you should worry about it.

Double Drop D

One exception to this is "Double Drop D," in which both E strings are tuned down a full step to D. This is a favorite of both Neil Young (used in the songs "Cinnamon Girl," "No More," and many others) and Lindsey Buckingham (Fleetwood Mac's "The Chain").

Standard tuning:	E	A	D	G	B	E
Double Drop D tuning:	D	A	D	G	B	D

If you look at this tuning you'll see you've not only got the easy three-string power chords of Drop D in the bass strings, you also have an Open G chord in the four high strings.

Almost Limitless Possibilities

Bands and guitarists of all types use alternate tunings to explore the different sounds their guitars are capable of. When you listen to Led Zeppelin's "Bron-Yr-Aur" (CACGCE) or "Kashmir" (DADGAD), or "Pattern Recognition" by Sonic Youth (CGDCGD), or "St. Anger" by Metallica (CGCFAG), you can understand that these songs wouldn't even begin to sound like they do if the guitars were in standard tuning.

Alternate tuning is an almost endless source of potential new tones for you and your guitar playing and, unlike some of the options explored in the previous three chapters, you don't have to purchase any new or additional equipment to make it happen!

The Least You Need to Know

◆ Alternate tunings involve changing the pitch of the strings, any one string or up to all six, from standard tuning.

◆ Lowered tunings create heavier sounds. They also make bending strings easier.

◆ Drop D and similar tunings allow you to play one-fingered power chords on the lowest three strings.

◆ Open tunings sound like major or minor chords when you strum all six strings open.

◆ Many guitarists use alternate tunings to create unique sounding songs.

Slip Sliding Away

In This Chapter

◆ Choosing a slide

◆ Learning proper slide position

◆ Dealing with string muting

◆ Playing single notes and chords

◆ Playing slide in standard and open tunings

Sometimes exploring for new ideas and sounds leads one straight back into the past. This is certainly the case with *slide* guitar, or bottleneck guitar as it is often called. The use of a piece of metal or glass instead of one's fingers to fret a note produces an unmistakable tone that can mimic a human voice or even that of a bird.

Like many techniques of rock guitar, slide playing seems deceptively simple at first, and this can lead many a beginner to frustration. But with a little bit of preparation and some concerted practice, you can easily add slide guitar playing to your ever-growing repertoire of skills.

In some ways, slide guitar is a test of all your skills and finesse up to this point. You will need to know open-position chords and chord shapes and soloing scales up and down the neck. You'll also need to combine a light touch, fretting accuracy, and good string muting skills. In return, you'll be adding a wide range of sounds and tones to your rock guitar repertoire.

A Little History

The idea of changing the notes of a stringed instrument by means of a "slide" has been around for a long, long time. Numerous single-stringed African instruments are played by plucking the string and using a piece of bone or another smooth, hard substance, to "fret" a note. In India, the Vichitra Veena was played much like an ancient ancestor of the lap steel guitar. It sat on the floor and the performer would pluck the strings with one hand and use a smooth stone or a piece of glass on its fretless neck to create notes.

The use of a slide on a "modern" guitar has been noted since the early 1900s. Famous Bluesman W. C. Handy's autobiography *Father of the Blues* (Da Capo Press, Inc., 1991) contains an often quoted passage of his hearing a guitarist in a railway station who used the blade of a knife as a slide. It's very interesting to note that in his writing he mentions that this slide technique was already "popularized by the Hawaiian guitarists who used steel bars."

The Hawaiian influence on the early blues guitarists was important in that the islanders used the low strings to produce a bass/rhythm accompaniment while the slide sang out a melody on the high strings. This full-bodied sound was a huge gift to the solo performing blues singer as it allowed his or her guitar to do the work of a full band.

The early blues guitarists like Robert Johnson and Son House influenced the early electric blues guitarists such as Muddy Waters, Elmore James, and Hound Dog Taylor. And they, in turn, were the idols of Eric Clapton, Ry Cooder, Lowell George, and other slide guitarists of the sixties and seventies. Today the scorching slide guitar sound is heard from Ben Harper, Warren Haynes, Derek Trucks, and many others.

More Choices

You need two things to play slide guitar—and you've already got the guitar! So now you need to choose a slide. Like strings, picks, pickups, and so many other things about the guitar, slides come in many, many varieties and each has different tonal qualities to offer.

def•i•ni•tion

A **slide** is a hollowed tube, usually made of metal (steel, chrome, or brass) or glass. It is slipped over a finger of the fretting hand and used to play the notes on the neck of the guitar.

Note Worthy

In an ideal world, you'd have a second guitar devoted especially for playing slide. But if you think about it, a guitar that might be considered problematic because of high action is ideal for playing slide. A cheap electric guitar found at a garage sale might be exactly what you're looking for! Now if you only had a guitar for each alternate tuning you use …

First you want to know some important overall techniques. To play slide well, you have to have a light touch. In slide guitar, the slide gently sits on the strings—you don't press it onto the fretboard. In fact, the frets of your guitar become nothing but note markers.

This means that the low action (the height of the strings from the frets) most rock guitarists prefer for their electric guitars can be problematic. You're bound to bang into the frets quite a bit if you're heavy handed with a slide. You'll also create a lot of string noise if you aren't careful moving around on the neck.

Heavy Metal or Smooth Glass?

Slides are made of all sorts of material, but most are either metal (usually steel, chrome, or brass) or glass. There are also ceramic and porcelain slides and even some made from the same composite glass material as Pyrex. Generally, metal slides will be a bit raspier, especially on the low strings, while glass slides sound smooth.

The weight of a slide is also an important factor. Heavier slides produce a fuller sound and more sustain than lighter ones, but lighter ones are easier to maneuver up and down the fretboard.

You also want to consider how long a slide you need. Acoustic blues guitarists, who often tend to barre across all six strings, use long slides that comfortably cover all six strings. Rockers who play single-note leads tend to go for shorter slides, sometimes small enough to cover just two or three strings.

If you take to slide playing, your first slide is very likely to be just that, your *first* one. You probably will find that some of the initial choices you made in choosing one will be amended as you learn more about the nuances of this technique.

Note Worthy
Heavier gauged strings usually translate to better sustain when playing slide. This doesn't mean you can't play with medium or light gauges, but your notes may sound a little thin or tinny.

Still More Choices

One thing that might help you decide on a slide, or simply drive you crazy because it's still another choice, is figuring out which finger will wear it. Ultimately, this has to be a matter of comfort, which also means that you may end up changing your decision several times.

Part of the decision involves what else you may decide to do with your hands. Using the pinky, as Lowell George or Hound Dog Taylor did, frees up three fingers for chord or riff work. Warren Hayes wears a slide on his ring finger, as did Duane Allman, changing from slide to single note solos, sometimes in the middle of a song. Bonnie Raitt and Jeff Beck favor the middle finger for slide play.

Whichever finger you initially, or ultimately, decide upon, you want a slide that slides easily onto your fingers without you worrying about it flying off mid-solo.

Your right hand also gets choices. Many slide players feel using their fingers to pick the strings (instead of using a pick) gives them better control over their dynamics and string muting. But others prefer the biting sound that the pick gives the strings.

Successful Sliding

Besides some of the obvious differences, you have to make one big adjustment in your thinking when playing slide. Up to this point when you've fretted a note, you've placed your finger between the wire frets on the neck. Now you want to place the slide directly over the wire fret to produce the correct sound, the same sort of position you used to create natural harmonics back in Chapter 10. The contact point of the slide on the string determines the note instead of the string being in contact with the wire fret because of the pressure of your finger on the fretboard.

In other words, you want to have as light a touch as possible. Slide pressure on the strings is a compromise between creating good, consistent contact between the slide and string without inadvertently pushing the string onto a fret, creating an undesirable rattling. The less pressure you place on the strings with the slide, the less noise you'll make as you slide up and down the neck. The frets are actually the last thing you even want to think about. Your slide stays above the wire frets, so essentially you're playing a fretless guitar! You only need them as guide markers to tell you where the notes are on the neck of your guitar.

You want to keep the slide as parallel to the frets as possible, as shown in the following illustration.

Holding the slide.

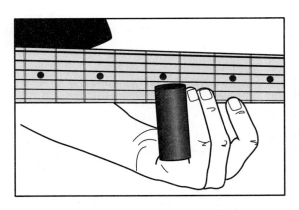

Holding the slide on the finger, again as shown, means that your pinky and middle fingers can assist in keeping it exactly where you want it to be on the neck of your guitar.

Being in a straight line keeps you in tune when you play more than one string at once.

You also want to keep a light touch on the strings with any free fingers of your fretting hand that sit between the slide and the nut of the guitar. This helps you cut down on unwanted string noise as you slide from one note to the next. And with your free fingers resting lightly on the strings, you can easily mute a note by simply lifting the slide.

Whether you decide to pluck the strings with your fingers or to use a pick, any free fingers of your right hand need to be devoted to string muting. Stay close with the heel of your palm so that it, too, can help with muting duties.

All this concern with extraneous string noise initially seems awkward and possibly even tedious, but with a bit of practice, you eventually find yourself muting with both hands without even thinking about it.

Getting Better

Good posture and hand position are essential to slide playing. If you're having trouble lining your slide up parallel to the frets, check your posture first. Make certain your fretting hand and arm are loose and relaxed and have free movement all along the neck of your guitar.

Putting Your Guitar Knowledge to Good Use

Just as you have throughout the course of this book, you want to start simply so you can understand the mechanics involved in slide playing and so you can develop a sense of finesse. Begin with single notes, first playing them with a slide and then playing one note and sliding to another, as in this example:

Track 97
(0:00)

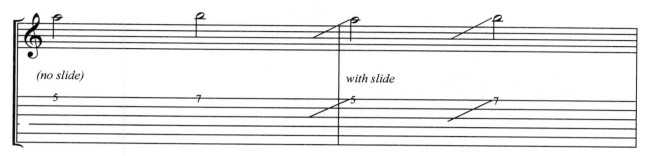

Single note slide playing.

As you work on sliding from one note to another, experiment with *when* you slide. You don't have to strike the string each time you change notes. You can be as quick as a grace note, but you can also take two, three, even four beats or more to move from one place on the neck to the other. That's a bit of artistic expression that you've not had a chance to try before, so play around and listen to what you can do.

Vibrato also plays a big part in sliding, but you now want to apply classical-style vibrato, moving the slide back and forth *along* the strings in the same direction they run along the neck. The quicker the vibrato movement, the more intensity you get. The wider the range of movement around your target note, the wider the tonal range of the vibrato will be. Good vibrato technique helps you "cover up" when you don't hit a note spot-on with the slide and gives you the chance to gracefully get the correct pitch.

Track 97
(0:15)

After practicing single notes, move up to double stops:

Double stop slide playing.

Majors

If you're going to play chords with the slide, then you need to remember a bit about barre chords from Chapter 9, particularly the Root 5 A-shape:

A Major–shaped chords.

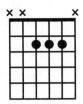

Track 97
(0:30)

The three notes of this chord all lie on the same fret on adjacent strings (the B, G, and D), which makes it ideal for slide playing. Try out this next example and see how easy playing chords can be:

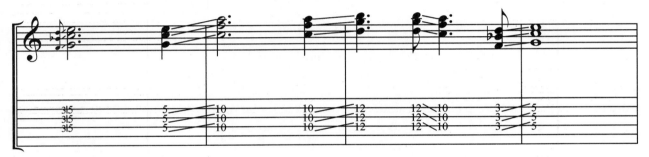

Playing major chords with the slide.

Minors and Minor Sevenths

For minor chords you want to go with the E-shape, which means shifting the slide up to the high E, B, and G strings:

E minor–shaped chords.

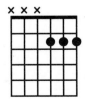

Minor seventh chords, which use the notes of the first four strings across the same fret, allow you easy access to both major and minor chords. For instance, if you lay your slide across the fifth fret and play the notes on the high E, B, and G strings, you would have an Am chord. Playing just the B, G, and D strings gives you C Major. Playing all four would produce an Am7 chord.

Some Sample Slide Riffs

You can build a repertoire of slide guitar riffs the same way you put together lead guitar riffs in Chapter 17. In fact, you can tweak many rock riffs and fills so that you can play them with a slide.

Here are some very simple, basic riffs to get you started:

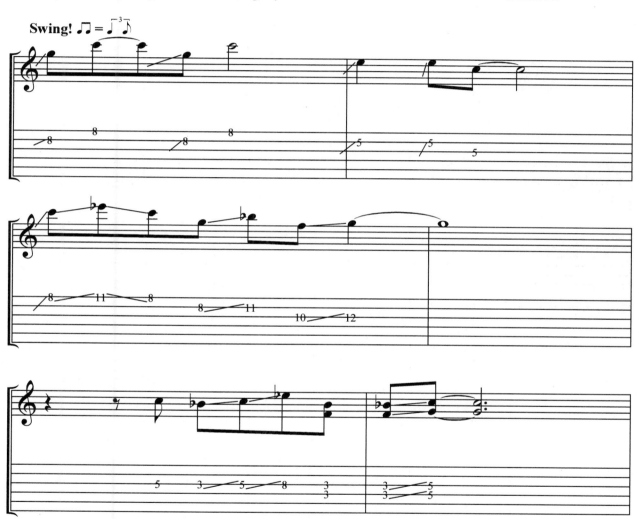

E minor–shaped chords.

Remember that you should take the time to learn a riff so that you can play it in any key by moving it to the appropriate place on the fretboard. To play the very first riff, which, as written, goes nicely over an E Major chord, in the key of A, you'd want the first note either at the fifth or the seventeenth fret and then follow along in the same pattern.

Hear How

You can listen to many great rock slide players for inspiration: Ry Cooder, George Harrison, Sonny Landreth, Billy Gibbons (of ZZ Top), as well as Eric Clapton, Duane Allman, Derek Trucks, Bonnie Raitt, and the incredible Warren Haynes. Many acoustic slide players can turn in astounding rock performances as well. You should definitely check out Rory Block and David Bromberg!

And again, just as you did in Chapter 17, you can also play around with the timing of these riffs, making them more your own musical expression and less like examples from a book!

Sliding in the Open

Many slide players prefer to play in open tunings, especially Open G and Open E because these two tunings contain many notes similar to standard tuning:

Standard tuning:	E	A	D	G	B	E
Open G tuning:	D	G	D	G	B	D
Open E variation:	E	B	E	G♯	B	E

In open tunings you can play your slide across all six strings anywhere on the fretboard and have a major chord. This makes playing rhythm very easy, provided the song in question only uses major chords!

The obvious disadvantage to open tunings is that you have no way to make a minor chord with a slide. But you can effectively deal with this by putting your chord knowledge to good use. In Chapter 15, you learned that every major key has a relative minor. Em, for example, is the relative minor of G Major.

Let's put this knowledge to use. Suppose you are playing in Open E tuning. Playing the open strings creates an E Major chord, which has the notes E, G♯, and B. Playing all the strings across the third fret gives you G Major, the notes being G, B, and D. The notes of Em are E, G, and B and the notes of Em7 are E, G, B, and D. Playing parts of the G chord, then, gives the impression that you could be playing Em.

Slide players have been doing this for ages. Even though your guitar is tuned to an open major chord, keeping in mind the minor pentatonic scale (the root, minor third, fourth, fifth, and flat seventh) helps you create very cool slide riffs in open tuning.

Better yet, these locations will be the same regardless of which open tuning you use. The minor third, for instance, will always be found three frets higher than the root, while the flat seventh is located either ten frets higher or two frets lower.

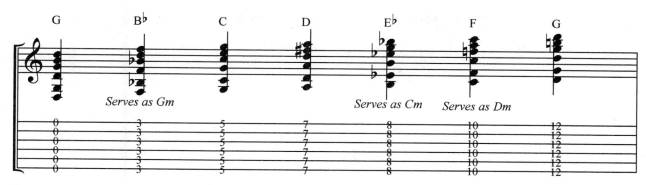

Where to find minors.

You can see that open tuning actually takes away a lot of the mystery of where to find the notes you want, especially for blues and blues-oriented rock. If you're in open tuning for the key of the song you're playing (in Open G for a song in G, for instance), then your best soloing notes are going to be at the open strings, the third fret, the fifth fret, the seventh fret, and the tenth fret. At the twelfth fret it all starts over again (twelfth, fifteenth, seventeenth, and so on).

"Slide Song"

To help you practice slide technique, not to mention put some of the riffs you've learned to practical use, here is a practice song for you. It uses notes not played with a slide in order to give you a chance to work with your free fingers as well:

Track 99

continues

"Slide Song"

This is deliberately slow so you can play around with both vibrato and the speed of sliding from one place on the neck to another. Don't feel you have to copy the recording exactly. It's actually better if you come up with your own interpretation. After all, you're the slide guitarist now!

The Least You Need to Know

◆ Slide guitar is very expressive and has a distinct sound.

◆ Slides come in many different sizes and are made from different materials. Most guitarists use either metal or glass slides.

◆ You can play single notes, double stops, and even chords with a slide.

◆ Many guitarists play slide in open tunings.

Afterword

This is, hopefully, the start of a lifelong adventure for you. Nothing compares to the rush of creating your own music.

Even if you've gone through every exercise in this book, you've barely gotten your feet wet when it comes to playing rock guitar. But you should have a good grasp of the basic ideas and techniques, such as power chords and hammer-ons, bends, slides, arpeggios, and broken chords. And by now you probably know enough about chords, rhythm, and strumming to be able to sit in with a band—or even to start one of your own—or jam with friends. Or you can simply sit and play guitar for your own enjoyment.

But all of this is just the beginning. As much as you might want a magic short-cut that instantaneously makes you a rock guitar god, the only way that you'll get better at playing your guitar is by playing and practicing your guitar. It's really that simple.

Far and away, the best possible way to learn is to play with other people. And you can do this once you know just a few basic chords, even just power chords if you're playing some styles of rock music.

You might think that you're not good enough to play along with others, and it might be hard at first. But you'll be giving yourself firsthand experience. You'll immediately grasp why it's so important to know your basic chords, or at least power chords. You'll understand why rhythm is much more than "down and up" strokes, and that listening is one of the most important skills you can develop as a musician. And playing with others shows you that no one ever plays without mistakes. You have to learn to play through them and to laugh about them later. Perhaps most importantly, playing with others gives you a *reason* to practice.

Every rock guitarist, every musician you meet, has something—a new chord, a cool fill, an easier fingering for a bit of a solo—to teach you if you are open to learning. Most musicians are very open and friendly when it comes to help-ing others learn about music and about the guitar. Music, to them, is not about being better than anyone else. They simply want to be a better player than they were yesterday.

The coolest thing about playing music is that you never stop learning. Even if you could spend 10, 12, 14 hours a day each day of the rest of your life, you'd still find more to learn, new musical styles and interests to study and to incor-porate into your own playing.

Every song, every piece of music—whether it's rock or blues, country or pop or R&B, even jazz and classical—has something to teach you. Every new thing you learn, whether it's a new chord or a classic rock solo, finds its way into your unique style.

At its heart, rock music is all about bringing people and musical styles together. That's why it is always growing and changing and expanding, becoming more powerful with each new musical genre it adopts as part of its own.

We began this book with a discussion of power, the power of music and the power of the rock guitarist in particular. Throughout this book you have made the first of many steps toward giving yourself a powerful musical voice, one capable of knocking down barriers, of carrying hearts away in a joyful dance, of uniting people from all over the world with a whisper.

Use your power well and wisely.

Play well. Play often.

Appendix A

Glossary

accent   Applying extra stress to a note, usually by striking it harder with the pick.

accidental   A sharp sign, flat sign, or natural sign.

anticipation   Arriving at your target note or chord before the beat, usually coming in a half a beat earlier.

arpeggio   A chord played one note at a time, usually in ascending or descending order.

articulation   How a note is played—crisply, long, short, slurred, and so on.

augmented chord   One of the four basic chord types, made up of the root, major third, and augmented fifth degrees of the major scale.

bar   Also called a "measure"; a distinct measurement of beats, which is dictated by the time signature; the end of a bar is indicated by a vertical line running through the staff or bass guitar tablature lines.

chord   Three or more different notes played together at the same time.

chord progression   A sequence of chords played in a song or in a phrase of a song.

chromatic notes   Notes taken from outside of a given major scale; *see* "diatonic."

chromatic scale   A scale made up of all 12 possible notes, each one a half step from the other.

circle of fifths   A pattern that can be used to study the relationship of keys to one another; also an excellent tool for practicing scales, riffs, or phrases in all keys.

common time   The symbol *C* used as a time signature; another name for "4/4" time.

diatonic   The notes used in a given major scale or the chords derived from the triads of that scale.

diminished chord   One of the four basic chord types, made up of the root, minor third, and diminished fifth degrees of the major scale.

dotted note   A dot added to a note in order to give it more length; a dotted half note is three beats long; a dotted quarter note is one and a half beats long, and so on.

dynamics   Changes in volume or tempo while playing.

eighth note   A note of a half a beat's duration.

eighth note rest   A rest of a half a beat's duration.

fill   A short musical phrase that fills a space in the music. Similar to riffs except that riffs are usually repeated note by note while fills usually are different each time.

flat   An accidental sign indicating lowering a note a half step.

fret   Metal wire on the neck of the guitar; also the act of placing one's finger on the neck of the guitar.

grace note   A note played and then quickly changed to another note within the shortest time possible.

half note   A note of two beats' duration.

half rest   A rest of two beats' duration.

half step   The difference, between two notes, of one fret of the bass guitar.

hammer-on   A left-hand slurring technique, in which a second note is sounded by the addition of a finger.

harmonics   Clear bell-like tones that can be created by lightly touching a string at various node points on the fingerboard while picking.

harmony   Two or more notes played simultaneously.

interval   The distance, in terms of steps and half steps, of one note from another.

key   The tonal center of a piece of music.

key signature   The number of flats or sharps (if any) used in a song, which indicates the key the song is in.

major chord   One of the four basic chord types, made up of the root, major third, and perfect fifth degrees of the major scale.

major scale   The basic building block of music theory, the major scale begins on any note and uses the following sequence:

> root   whole step   whole step   half step   whole step   whole step
> whole step   half step (the root again, one octave higher than first played)

measure   Also called a "bar"; a distinct measurement of beats, which is dictated by the time signature; the end of a measure is indicated by a vertical line running through the staff or bass guitar tablature lines.

metronome   A device used to audibly count out the tempo of music. Some metronomes use flashing lights to visually count out the tempo.

minor chord   One of the four basic chord types, made up of the root, minor third, and perfect fifth degrees of the major scale.

modes   A scale created by taking a major scale and beginning on a note other than the root and going through the steps of the scale until reaching the starting note again. There are seven modes: Ionian, Dorian, Phrygian, Lydian, Mixolydian, Aeolian, and Locrian.

music notation   A system for reading music using a staff and notes placed upon it; the location of the note on the staff determines its name, and the type of note indicates its duration.

natural sign   An accidental sign indicating to play a note with neither flats nor sharps.

note   A musical tone of a specific pitch.

octave   An interval of eight named notes from the root note; always bearing the same name as the root note.

pick   Also called "plectrum," a hard flat piece of material (usually plastic) used to strike the strings instead of a finger of the strumming hand.

pickups   A device for converting a guitar's acoustic string vibrations into electric signals. A pickup is most often comprised of at least one magnet and one coil, both placed in close proximity to the guitar's strings.

pull-off   A left-hand slurring technique in which a second note is sounded by the removal of a finger.

quarter note   A note of one beat's duration.

quarter rest   A rest of one beat's duration.

riff   A short musical phrase, often repeated during the course of a song.

root note   The note named by a chord; *C* is the root note of a C Major chord.

sharp   An accidental sign indicating raising a note a half step.

shuffle   A rhythm using the first and third of a set of triplets, commonly used in blues, jazz, and swing styles.

sixteenth note   A note of one quarter of a beat's duration.

sixteenth rest   A rest of one quarter of a beat's duration.

slide   A left-hand slurring technique involving sliding a finger from one fret to another. Also a glass, ceramic, or metal tubular device placed over one of the left hand fingers and used to lightly touch the strings thereby "fretting" notes on a guitar in lieu of normal fretting.

slur   Using a left-hand technique to articulate a note or series of notes.

staff   A set of five lines, used in music notation to indicate note names.

standard tuning How the strings of a guitar are usually tuned; from low to high: E, A, D, G, B, and E.

step The difference, between two notes, of two frets on the neck of the guitar.

tablature A system of reading music involving six horizontal lines (indicating the strings of the guitar) and numbers (indicating which frets to play in order to sound the notes).

tempo The speed of a song, usually indicated in BPM (beats per minute).

tie A line connecting two notes of the same pitch, adding the time value of the second note to the first; a whole note tied to a half note will last for six beats.

time signature Usually indicated by a fraction at the start of a piece of music, the time signature tells you how many beats each measure receives (the upper number of the fraction) and which type of note is designated as a single beat (the lower number).

transposing Changing the notes (and chords) of a song from one key to another.

tremolo A rapid quivering change of volume; used as a guitar effect.

trill A left-hand technique involving a rapid change from one note to the next higher (or lower) note.

triplet A note of a third of a beat's duration.

turnaround A quick chord progression at the end of a song to prepare the listener for a second verse; usually ends on the V chord.

twelve-bar blues A standard blues song format involving specific chord changes over the course of 12 measures.

vibrato A left-hand technique which adds a variable quavering of pitch to a note; usually used with notes of longer duration.

vibrato bar Also called "whammy bar"; a small metal rod attached to the guitar's bridge that, when pressed or pulled, changes the pitch of all six strings at once.

wah-wah pedal A guitar effect that imparts a dynamic, vocal-like "wah" tone to an electric guitar's sound.

whole note A note of four beats' duration.

whole note rest A rest of four beats' duration.

For Further Study

Besides all the hundreds upon hundreds of books, videos, CD, and DVD tutorials available to rock guitarists, there are also hundreds (if not thousands) of rock guitar tutorial websites on the Internet. Anyone who is serious about learning rock guitar has no end of sources, and you owe it to yourself to make use of as much tutorial material you can find!

And remember, despite this wealth of knowledge, one of the best methods of learning is through the one-on-one personal instruction that a guitar teacher can give you. There are many, many teachers out there. Take the time to choose one who is right for you. Before deciding on a teacher, have an in-depth talk with him or her about your goals and what you want to learn. Do your best to make sure your teacher is a good fit for you.

Don't fall into the trap of using a single learning source because no one source can possibly teach you everything there is to know. And use *all* your brain! Videos, especially those on the Internet, can seem ideal but you're likely to learn more from a few written pages than from watching someone else play a song.

The Complete Idiot's Guide to Playing Rock Guitar is meant to be a primer, a book that gets you started playing (even if you've never touched a guitar before) and introduces you to the basic techniques and principles of rock guitar. When you're comfortable with these basics, you might want to read *Total Rock Guitar: A Complete Guide to Playing Rock Guitar* by Troy Stetina. Troy also has some wonderful books on speed playing and metal guitar, by the way.

For more on music theory, you can't do better than these two books:

Miller, Michael. *The Complete Idiot's Guide to Music Theory.*

Serb, Tom. *Music Theory for Guitarists*, (Milwaukee, Hal Leonard), 2005.

When it comes to soloing, Michael Miller has also written a terrific book to help beginners get started:

Miller, Michael. *The Complete Idiot's Guide to Solos and Improvisation.*

And there are thousands of note-by-note transcription books that detail songs of all genres throughout rock history. Learning solos note by note is a good way to improve your personal soloing skills. Pick an artist you like and see what you can find.

If you're interested in exploring more in the area of slide guitar, try:

Hamburger, David. *Electric Slide Guitar*, (Milwaukee, Hal Leonard), 1996.

Appendix C

Track Guide to *The Complete Idiot's Guide to Playing Rock Guitar* CD

Chapter 2

Chapter 3

Chapter 4

Track 14: Vibrato

Track 15: "Good Vibrations"

Track 16: Tracking Targets

Track 17: "Straight Time" Bends and "Grace Note" Bends

Track 18: Full-Step Bend

Track 19: Half-Step Bend

Track 20: Quarter-Tone Bend

Track 21: Bend and Release

Track 22: Unison Bends

Track 23: "Bending Matter"

Chapter 5

Track 24: Changing Em into E Major

Track 25: Em7 and E7

Track 26: Am and A Major

Track 27: A7 and Am7

Track 28: E and A Power Chords

Track 29: Power Chord Stretching Exercise

Track 30: Power Chord Changing Exercise

Track 31: Octave Changing Exercise

Track 32: "Power Point"

Chapter 6

Track 33: Strumming Em and A7

Track 34: Varying the Pattern

Track 35: Combining Quarter Notes and Eighth Notes

Track 36: Mixing Strums

Track 37: Skipping the Third Beat

Track 38: Rhythm Practice Exercise

Track 39: Strumming Triplets

Track 40: Swing Eighths

Track 41: "Woke Up This Evening"

Track 42: Alternate Picking Exercises

Track 43: "Shuffle Rock"

Chapter 7

Track 44: G to C Walking Bass Line

Track 45: "Open Chord Rock"

Track 46: Twelve-Bar Blues Patterns

Track 47: "7 to 9 Blues"

Chapter 8

Track 48: Rhythm with Partial Chords

Track 49: Hammer-On Exercise

Track 50: Multiple Hammer-Ons

Track 51: Pull-Off Exercise

Track 52: Multiple Pull-Offs

Track 53: Combining Hammer-Ons and Pull-Offs

Track 54: Trills

Track 55: Slides

Track 56: Nonspecific Slides

Track 57: Adding Slurs to a Rhythm Part

Track 58: More Slurs in Action

Track 59: "Velvet Noir"

Chapter 9

Track 60: Practicing Barre Chords

Track 61: Half Barre Riff

Track 62: Sliding Barre Riff

Track 63: Left-Hand Muting

Track 64: "Chunky Barre Rock"

Chapter 10

Track 65: Strumming Notes of Different Timing Values

Track 66: Practice Rhythm Patterns

Track 67: Practice Rhythms with Sixteenth Rests

Track 68: Low E String Palm Muting

Track 69: Combining Palm Muting and Strumming

Track 70: Anticipation

Track 71: Natural Harmonics

Track 72: Pinch Harmonics

Track 73: "Metal Mettle"

Chapter 11

Track 74: Accents

Track 75: Rhythms with Sixteenth Notes

Track 76: Sixteenth Note Triplets

Track 77: Quarter Note Triplets

Track 78: Single Note Funky Riff (0:00)
Funky Riff with String Muting (0:16)
Funky Riff with Pinch Harmonics (0:32)
Complete Funky Riff (0:48)

Chapter 13

Track 79: "Jazzing It Up"

Chapter 15

Track 80: C Major Pentatonic Scale (0:00)
Combining Positions of the A Minor
Pentatonic Scale (0:12)

Track 81: "Minimal Rock"

Track 82: Combining Major and Minor
Pentatonic Scales

Track 83: "Bucketful of Blues"

Chapter 16

Track 84: C Major Progression

Track 85: D Minor Progression

Track 86: "Dorian Rock"

Track 87: "Minor Madness"

Chapter 17

Track 88: Chord-Based Fills (0:00)
Scale-Based Fills (0:20)

Track 89: Mark Knopfler–Style Fill

Track 90: Sample Fill (0:00)
Sample Fill Reversed (0:10)
Sample Fill with Timing Changes (0:20)

Track 91: "Commuter Train Crazy"

Chapter 18

Track 92: Effects Examples

Chapter 19

Track 93: Lowered Tunings

Track 94: "Drop D Rock"

Track 95: The Am7 Shape with Open G Tuning

Track 96: "Open G Rock"

Chapter 20

Track 97: Single Note Slide (0:00)
Double Stop Slide (0:15)
Playing Major Chords with
the Slide (0:30)

Track 98: Slide Riffs

Track 99: "Slide Song"

Index

sixteenth notes, 132
triplets, 83
upstrokes, 77-78
vibrato, 50
classical, 51
defined, 51
"Good Vibrato-ations"
exercise, 53
notation, 52
rock, 51
tension, 196
third position, 192
thirds, 166-167
thirteenth chords, 172
three-string power chords, 68-69
thumb over barre chords, 126
ties, 41-42
anticipation, 137
compared to slurs, 107
timbre, 48
time signatures, 34
timing
bends, 56-57
fills, 219
tonal centers, 178
tone
amplifiers
channels, 229
effects, 230
hybrid, 230
modeling, 230
stages of amplification, 229
tone controls, 229
tubes, 229
copying, 227
effects, 230
chorus, 231
compressors, 231
delays and echoes, 232
distortion, 231
equalizers, 231
examples, 232
flangers, 232
multi-effects units, 230
ordering, 233
overdrive, 231
pedals, 230
phase shifters, 232
tremolo, 231
volume pedals, 231
wah-wah pedals, 231
evolution, 233

fingering, 226
fundamental, 48
guitar influences
pickups, 228
scale length, 227-228
shapes/styles, 227
harmonics, 48
artificial, 138-139
defined, 48
minor scale, 208-209
natural, 138
pinch, 149
listening, 227
major versus minor chords, 62
timbre, 48
touch, 49
trading fours approach to fills, 220
treble, 229
treble clefs, 32
tremolo effects, 231
triads, 166-167
trills, 110
triplets, 83
quarter note, 147
sixteenth note, 146-147
strumming, 83
tritons, 162
truss rods, 8
tuners, 8, 15, 18-19
tuning
alternate, 236, 245-246
Double Drop D, 246
Drop D, 238-239
example songs, 246
lowered tuning, 237-238
open. *See* open tuning
lowered, 236
advantages, 237
alternatives, 237-238
Drop D tuning combination,
239
heavy tones, 237
machines, 8
open, 241
A, 243
capos, 243
D, 242-243
E, 243
G, 241-244
options, 244
slides, 254-255
song examples, 244

relative, 19, 236
standard, 18-19
types, 236
tunks, 62-63
twelve-bar blues, 85
"Two String Rock," 25-26, 36
two strings at a time play, 25-26
two-string power chords, 66

U–V

unbending notes, 218
unison bends, 59
upstrokes, 77-78

"Velvet Noir" practice song, 115
vibrato, 50
bars, 9, 141
classical, 51
defined, 51
"Good Vibrato-ations" exercise,
53
notation, 52
rock, 51
sliding, 251
voicings, 173-174
volume pedals, 231

W–X–Y–Z

wah-wah pedals, 231
walking bass line exercise, 95
whole notes, 76
writing
scales, 156
rhythm, 146

*X*s, 29